ZEW Economic Studies

Publication Series of the Centre for
European Economic Research (ZEW),
Mannheim, Germany

ZEW Economic Studies

Vol. 1: O. Hohmeyer, K. Rennings (Eds.)
Man-Made Climate Change
Economic Aspects and Policy Options
1999. VIII, 401 pp. ISBN 3-7908-1146-7

Vol. 2: Th. Büttner
Agglomeration, Growth, and Adjustment
A Theoretical and Empirical Study
of Regional Labor Markets in Germany
1999. XI, 206 pp. ISBN 3-7908-1160-2

Vol. 3: P. Capros et al.
Climate Technology Strategies 1
Controlling Greenhouse Gases.
Policy and Technology Options
1999. XVIII, 365 pp. ISBN 3-7908-1229-3

Vol. 4: P. Capros et al.
Climate Technology Strategies 2
The Macro-Economic Cost and Benefit
of Reducing Greenhouse Gas Emissions
in the European Union
1999. XIII, 224 pp. ISBN 3-7908-1230-7

Vol. 5: P. A. Puhani
Evaluating Active Labour Market Policies
Empirical Evidence for Poland During Transition
1999. XVI, 239 pp. ISBN 3-7908-1234-X

Vol. 6: B. Fitzenberger
Wages and Employment Across Skill Groups
An Analysis for West Germany
1999, XII, 251 pp. ISBN 3-7908-1235-8

K. Rennings · O. Hohmeyer · R.L. Ottinger
(Editors)

Social Costs and Sustainable Mobility

Strategies and Experiences in Europe and the United States

With 40 Figures
and 39 Tables

Physica-Verlag
A Springer-Verlag Company

ZEW
Zentrum für Europäische
Wirtschaftsforschung GmbH
Centre for European
Economic Research

Series Editor
Prof. Dr. Wolfgang Franz

Editors
Dr. Klaus Rennings
Centre for European Economic Research (ZEW)
L7,1
68161 Mannheim
Germany

Prof. Dr. Olav Hohmeyer
Professor for Economics, Energy, Environment
University of Flensburg
Kanzleistraße 91–93
24943 Flensburg
Germany

Prof. Richard L. Ottinger
Pace University
School of Law
Center for Environmental Legal Studies
78 North Broadway
White Plains
NY 10603
USA

ISBN 3-7908-1260-9 Physica-Verlag Heidelberg New York

Cataloging-in-Publication Data applied for
Die Deutsche Bibliothek – CIP-Einheitsaufnahme
Zentrum für Europäische Wirtschaftsforschung ⟨Mannheim⟩: ZEW economic studies / Zentrum für Europäische Wirtschaftsforschung. – Heidelberg; New York: Physica-Verl.
[Neue Schriftenreihe]
Social costs and sustainable mobility: strategies and experiences in Europe and the United States /ed.: Klaus Rennings ... – Heidelberg: Physica-Verl., 2000
(ZEW economic studies; Vol. 7)
ISBN 3-7908-1260-9

Cover design: Erich Dichiser, ZEW, Mannheim

SPIN 10748066 88/2202-5 4 3 2 1 0 – Printed on acid-free paper

Contents

Part I: Introduction

Opening Remarks 3
by Richard Ottinger

Fair Payment for Infrastructure Use: White Paper of the European Commission 7
by Wim A.G. Blonk

External Environmental Costs of Transport - Comparison of Recent Studies 15
by Gunther Ellwanger

Part II: Valuation Studies

QUITS – Quality Indicators of Transport Systems 23
by Andrea Ricci and Sigurd Weinreich

The Impacts of the Kyoto Protocol on Full Cost Transportation in the U.S. 55
by Stephen Bernow and William Dougherty

Optimal Urban Transport Pricing and Sustainability 71
by Margaret O'Mahony, Stef Proost, and Kurt Van Dender

Part III: Pricing Strategies and Sustainable Mobility

Goal Driven Design of a Sustainable Transport System 91
by Wolfgang Schade, Werner Rothengatter, Astrid Gühnemann, and Karsten Kuchenbecker

Distance-Based Vehicle Insurance - A Practical Strategy for More Optimal Vehicle Pricing 115
by Todd Litman

Valuation of Road Pricing on Selected European Roads 135
by Lionel Clement, Yves Crozet, and Jean-Michel Gambard

Constitutional Constraints on Social-Cost Pricing 159
by Daniel Lazare

Strategic Niche Management for Sustainable Mobility.................................. 167
by René Kemp, Bernhard Truffer, and Sylvia Harms

Instruments for Attaining Urban Sustainability: The Case for
Tradable Vehicle Use Permits 189
by Haynes Carson Goddard

The TransPrice Project: Experiences with Transport Pricing in
Eight European Cities 197
by Manos Vougioukas

PART I

INTRODUCTION

Opening Remarks

Richard Ottinger

Pace University, School of Law
78 North Broadway, White Plains, NY 10603
USA

This 4th International Social Cost and Sustainability Conference is convened to discuss the important issues surrounding the subject, "Policy Instruments for Incorporating Social Costs into the Transportation Sector." The Pace University Center for Environmental Legal Studies has been privileged to host this and our past conferences, both in Germany and the United States, jointly with the Centre for European Economic Research. This is the second conference to be held in the United States and it is exciting that we are able to meet this time in New York City, one of the world's busiest and most vibrant cities, but also one of the most congested and challenged by the unceasing growth in the use of the automobile.

The World Trade Institute, recently acquired by our parent, Pace University, has graciously made it possible to hold this conference in their beautiful quarters in the World Trade Center. The World Trade Institute has a distinguished 25-year history. It offers academic programs, seminars, conferences and on-site training related to international trade and language classes to a wide variety of groups. The partnership with the World Trade Institute reflects upon Pace University's mission of preparing men and women for careers in a increasingly global economy.

Since our last conference in Ladenburg, Germany in May 1995 I have been spending most of my time as Dean of the Pace Law School, strengthening Pace's curriculum in international law and environmental law on which Pace is consistently rated one of the top law schools in the nation. Pace Law School provides a unique opportunity for individuals from the United States and abroad who wish to practice in the increasingly important field of environmental law. Strengthening the practice of environmental law needs to be a world-wide priority. Pace is participating in an IUCN program to train environmental law professors in Asia. We are also reaching out to legal scholars in Latin American countries to elaborate environmental protections into their legal systems as they integrate their economies into global markets. And we will be starting next year a master of laws (LL.M.) program for foreign attorneys in Comparative Legal Studies.

A little over a year ago we recruited a new executive director to the Pace Energy Project, Ed Smeloff from California where he served on the Board of Directors of the Sacramento Municipal Utility District, an electric utility that has been a leader in the United States in promoting energy efficiency, renewable technologies and transportation alternatives, with the largest fleet of electric vehicles in the country. Ed Smeloff is building upon the reputation that the Pace Energy Project has gained over the years through our work on environmental externalities and social costs. I'm pleased to note that Pace's seminal study, *The Environmental Costs of Electricity* is still cited often as a source on quantifying the environmental damages caused by the production of electricity. The Pace Energy Project has drawn from this study to develop what we call the Power Scorecard which is designed to inform consumers about the effects that different power technologies and resources have on the environment.

As electricity markets are deregulated in the United States it is our intent to make the Power Scorecard available to organizations and individuals who are interested in demanding environmentally cleaner electricity. We expect that this consumer tool will allow renewable energy developers to independently verify the environmental superiority of their products to facilitate markets for renewable energy supplies like photovoltaics, wind and biomass.

While minimizing the environmental damage of electricity production is important, if we are to achieve a sustainable economy in the United States we must address the transportation sector as well. Sometime last year, vehicles miles driven in the United States reached the staggering annual rate of 2.5 trillion, double the rate 25 years earlier, and almost 10,000 miles for every man, woman and child in the United States.

Driving automobiles on this scale imposes huge hidden costs through air emissions, highway congestion, death and injury through accidents, destruction of human and natural habitats and contribution to global climate change. The social costs of vehicle use in the United States are rising as larger and heavier sport utility vehicles, vans and trucks capture growing market share of the personal vehicle market. Also troubling is the increasing use of automobiles for American's personal travel. These unsettling trends can also be seen elsewhere as other nations follow the U.S. in increasing automobile use at the expense of transit and simpler forms of travel such as walking and cycling. Few measures have been adopted anywhere to account for these large hidden costs or to incorporate them into the prices of vehicles and their use.

To counter these trends it is imperative that we identify effective strategies to internalize the costs incurred in using automobiles for travel. This conference affords us the opportunity to explore and compare a number of innovative strategies. It is exciting to see the spectrum of transport researchers and reform advocates from both Europe and the United States who have come together to focus on these issues. We must focus during the next two days on how we can put our ideas into practice. We need to aggressively accelerate and expand the implementation of policies that shift and internalize social and environmental costs in industrial countries.

I would like to acknowledge the generous support that we have received to organize this conference from the German Marshal Fund of the United States and to thank Marianna Ginsberg for her encouragement of our work and for her advice that we need to take our ideas into the political arena and make them relevant for public policy. Much credit, too, goes to the organizers of this conference, Ed Smeloff of the Pace University, Klaus Rennings of the Centre for European Economic Research, Charles Komanoff of Komanoff Energy Associates, and Tom Bourgeois, consultant to the Pace Energy Project.

I'd also like to recognize the important work of my colleague, Dr. Olav Hohmeyer, from the Centre for European Economic Research which together with Pace has co-hosted these conferences on Social Costs and Sustainability. Dr. Hohmeyer did the seminal work on social costs of electricity and was an advisor to the Pace study.

Acknowledgements

I would like to acknowledge the financial support that we have received to [illegible]

[illegible]

Fair Payment for Infrastructure Use: White Paper of the European Commission

Wim A. G. Blonk

Director Transport Research, European Commission, BU31, 5176
Directorate General VII-Tranport, BU31, 4/52
Rue de la Loi, Wetstraat 200, B-1049 Bruessel
Belgium

1 Introduction

In 1992 the Commission presented its White Book on the future of the Common Transport policy; a global approach to the construction of a Community framework for sustainable mobility. Since then considerable progress has been made. However, at this moment important questions still need to be tackled and solved.

One of the outstanding problems is the great diversity of infrastructure charging systems in the European Union. For example, we have 9 different charging systems for railway infrastructure, with cost recovery ratios varying between 0% and 100%. Annual vehicle taxes on trucks can vary from 350 to over 4000 ECU[1] and only 4 Member States levy tolls on significant parts of their motorway network. Furthermore, the treatment in terms of VAT imposition and energy taxation (fuel taxes), differ widely across modes and between Member States.

This undermines the efficiency and the sustainability of the Union's transport system as it gives rise to significant distortions of competition within and between modes, and between Member States, often on the basis of the nationality of the transport provider. It also limits the incentives to reduce the environmental costs and holds back the efficient provision of transport infrastructure.

The title of this speech, and indeed of this session, is derived from the European Commission's 1995 Green Paper, Fair and Efficient Pricing in Transport. This discussion document outlined an economic approach, using pricing signals to deal with the transport sector's problems, and to achieve the general goal of sustainable mobility in the EU. It analysed the current problems of the transport sector (traffic jams and congestion, air and water pollution, noise, poor quality and lack of infrastructure and accidents), and proposed a general solution. The Green Paper called

---

1 1994 figures for Portugal and UK respectively, PETS D1, p64.

for greater co-ordination and harmonisation of charging approaches, and for the internalisation of external costs – that is, the incorporation of social costs into the transportation sector, the subject of this conference.

Consultations on this discussion paper with the various stakeholders led to some very useful seminars and conferences on transport pricing and a report on best practice and charges in freight transport, amongst other things. The Commission also appointed a High Level Advisory Group made up of senior business and academic transport experts, to provide specific advice on infrastructure charging. The report of this High Level Group was published in June this year.

I am pleased to be able to say that the Commission adopted in July a policy paper of even greater relevance to this session of the conference. The White Paper is entitled "Fair Payment for Infrastructure Use: A phased approach to a common transport infrastructure charging framework in the EU". It defines concepts and detailed policy responses, and addresses the issue of public acceptance and implementation – the very subject of this session.

In my presentation I will explain the approach taken to these issues in current Commission policy – in "Fair Payment for infrastructure Use".

2 The White Paper

The White Paper addresses the key problems of the transport sector on which a considerable amount of research has been produced since Jules Dupuit in the 19th century:

- Efficiency of the use of existing infrastructure
- Provision of efficient levels of infrastructure
- Financing of the necessary investments.

The perspective of the White Paper is at the European level. And the Commission's recommended solutions to the transport problems clearly uses an economic framework rather than more traditional regulatory command and control measures and standards or simple political decision making processes. The Commission believes the inefficiencies of the transport sector can be addressed more clearly and rationally by using economic policy instruments at the most appropriate decision-making level

- Appropriate pricing, marginal cost pricing, to achieve efficiency in use and a sustainable mobility patters

- Proper investment appraisal (cost benefit analysis) to ensure efficient provision of infrastructure
- Subsidiarity principle in financing to enable national, regional and local specificities and contexts to be taken into account.

3 Marginal Cost Pricing to Achieve Efficient Infrastructure Use

It is a well known economic proposition that, under certain market conditions, setting price equal to marginal costs optimises the allocation of resources, minimises "dead weight loss" and achieves an economically efficient result. The policy of developing marginal cost pricing rules for the use of transport infrastructure was advanced in the Green Paper, supported by the High Level Advisory Group, and the White Paper refines and elaborates on this concept and its application.

In the White Paper, the concept of marginal cost charging is defined as a means of implementing the user pays principle; shifting to more direct cost based charges for transport infrastructure use. In practical terms, to reflect marginal costs, charges should be based on the cost of infrastructure use (operating costs, infrastructure damage and congestion costs, and environmental and health costs) and vary with time of day (to reflect congestion costs), engine size or type (to reflect emission costs) and transport unit size or weight (to reflect infrastructure damage). Such an approach will improve the use made of infrastructure within a country.

4 Marginal Cost Pricing and Financing

Problems of finance and the provision of infrastructure can at times constrain charging decisions.

First, the Commission believes that the use of more direct transport charges will facilitate the collection of revenues that can be used to fund infrastructure maintenance or extension. A recent and very good example of this approach is contained in the UK's White Paper on integrated transport, "A New Deal for Transport". Allowing infrastructure managers to retain at least some fraction of the revenues they collect both provides an incentive to manage and collect charges, and can help fund investment.

Second, whilst the capital value of existing infrastructure is a sunk cost, and should not be reflected in marginal cost pricing charges, the White Paper, as recommended in the High Level Advisory Group, acknowledges that there may be cases where the proposed marginal cost charging principles do not recover sufficient revenue. It states explicitly that for some new investment projects and for some investment in transport terminals, charges based on more than social marginal costs may be necessary to raise sufficient revenues to recover all costs in full and attract private investment. For infrastructure facing direct competition, particularly terminals such as airports and ports, this is particularly important. Not only is private investment more common with such infrastructure, but the greater competition can act on its own to ensure charges lead to efficient use.

The proposal for a directive on rail charging in the European Union acknowledges that some rail infrastructure managers in the Union face government requirements for a large degree of self financing, and may need to apply some form of "two part tariff" or other pricing arrangement to raise higher revenues.

The High Level Advisory Group arrived at the conclusion that a necessary corollary for the provision of an efficient level of infrastructure is the development of sound investment appraisal techniques and the use of full social cost benefit analysis techniques.

Using such tools to get the level of investment right is important because building unnecessary infrastructure wastes resources and distorts the modal balance and use of transport. Over-investment, be it in roads, ports, or airports, can artificially lower local costs and lead to excessive use of a particular mode or specific piece of infrastructure. Efficient investment decisions are therefore as important as efficient infrastructure use.

Consistent and harmonised investment appraisal and charging measures are therefore necessary to improve the efficiency of the transport sector. Two 4th Framework Programme research projects, TRENEN (which will be presented by Prof. Proost in more detail this afternoon) and EUNET, show that citizens' welfare improves in all the cities and regions[2] examined when efficient pricing is implemented. This happens because the benefits of the reduction in congestion and pollution achieved, combined with the recycling of tax payments back to the economy, outweighs largely the "loss" resulting from the price increase of certain transport services. The price changes were found to induce positive technological improvements, urban peak time traffic volumes fell by between 19% and 33%, and external costs fell by between 13% and 35%.

2 Cities: Brussels, London, Dublin, Amsterdam, Helsinki and Naples and Regions: Belgium, Ireland, Basque region.

The studies indicate that introducing a policy of marginal social cost charging at EU level could lead to overall welfare benefits in the order of 30-80 billion ECU per year.

Other areas that the White Paper deals with include the development of greater transparency in transport accounting practices; the harmonisation of the development of technologies for implementing user charges, such as the technologies that allow road pricing; the special needs of remote and peripheral regions, who may need a more gradual approach to implementing the principles, and greater financing flexibility to attract investment; and the overall fiscal implications of the new charging regime, suggesting that some degree of fiscal neutrality is appropriate in the development of new charges.

On this last point, it is clear that only to a very limited extent, do existing transport charges and taxes such as registration fees, purchase taxes and fuel duties, reflect the costs of transport use, be it infrastructure costs, pollution or accidents. When other, more accurate and efficient charges are introduced that better reflect such costs, it is reasonable to expect that the existing charges should be reduced. We should be more interested in making our charges more efficient and so improving the competitiveness of industry than in raising ever higher revenues from the transport sector.

Such measures, particularly transparency of charges and the use that is made of revenues, are very important for creating effective measures that infrastructure users can understand, accept, and respond to. They are also important for creating incentives for infrastructure managers to favour, accept and use direct charging policy tools.

These policy issues are discussed in detail in the White Paper and specific actions are recommended within a three-phase approach:

1st Phase (1998-2000): where the Commission and all stakeholders will work on the establishment and refining of the charging approach. Key actions in this phase include:

- Providing guidance and advice on methods to estimate costs of transport, accounting practices, statistical and research needs.
- Promoting road pricing, charge differentiation, demonstration projects.
- Discussion of the proposed Directive on railway access and charging (based on marginal costs, with the option of additional charges for passenger services, and compensatory payments for uncovered external costs of competing modes).

- Discussion of the other Communications and Directives planned for the aviation sector (developing cost related airport charges, studying the effects of taxation on aviation fuel, and possibly pollution (cost) related en route flight charges).

2nd Phase (2001-2004): will be used to consolidate the consistent charging basis for road, rail, air and sea. Here, specific actions include the further development of full marginal cost pricing for all modes (including external costs), and the extension of harmonised electronic road charging.

3rd Phase (beyond 2004): the Commission hopes to complete the transition to a consistent, harmonised charging approach and update and review infrastructure charges.

5 Conclusions

Over the next ten years the Commission plans to take forward this user pays approach in every transport mode, beginning with the roads and ports sectors, and the railway sector, where the Commission has simultaneously produced a proposal for a directive on railway capacity allocation and charging. The measures outlined are examples of how transparent, direct and cost based charges can be developed and presented as both fair and efficient, lowering social, financial, and time costs of transport use, improving the operation of the single European market in transport, thence the competitiveness of European industry. As with the very title of the Commission's paper, we are presenting fairness and efficiency in transport pricing as Fair Payment for Infrastructure Use.

Finally, it is also clear that further research is needed to allow for successful implementation. The most pertinent topics are the following:

- In order to ensure greater transparency and commonality in the treatment of transport costs and revenues in the Member States, and to assist in the differentiation between transport charges and taxes there is a need for the development of transport accounts. This was also recommended by the High Level Group on Infrastructure Charging.

- Determination of steps to be taken so that the "theoretical optimum" can be reached with least harm and distortions and that the steps are acceptable to the citizens.

- Analysis of the impacts, costs and benefits and their distribution, of each of the steps to be taken towards the "optimum".

Fair Payment for Infrastructure Use is a tremendous and comprehensive approach that has not yet been implemented anywhere despite the long research tradition in this field. In addition to open questions to be further studied, there is a need for many discussions, plans and designs at different policy and decision-making levels. It is clear that this is also a learning process and thus can only be implemented in a phased way.

External Environmental Costs of Transport - Comparison of Recent Studies

Gunther Ellwanger

International Union of Railways
16, rue Jean Rey, F - 75015 Paris
France

1 Introduction

During the past decades the negative influences of the transport sector on the environment has grown. The actual development of transport and the modal split are in contradiction with sustainable mobility. On the other hand, transport has a major influence on the economy and the quality of life of the general public, therefore measures are necessary to increase the market share of environmentally friendly modes of transport.

Motorised transport is too cheap, since the consumption of natural resources is scarcely reflected in the prices. Nonetheless, considerable differences do exist between the different modes of transport: the environmentally friendly railway, with its low external costs, is under-represented on the market.

In 1992, the conference in Rio served to heighten public awareness of the need to preserve the natural basis of life and confirmed the "polluter pays" principle: "National authorities should endeavour to promote the internalisation of environmental costs and the use of economic instruments, taking into account the approach that the polluter should in principle bear the cost of pollution".

During the last 5 years several studies on external costs of transport were realised in Western Europe.

2 IWW/INFRAS - Study ('94)

The report "External Effects of Transport" completed at the end of 1994 by IWW (Karlsruhe) and Infras (Zurich) pays particularly close attention to the definitions of external effects.

The authors also investigate the "external benefits" of road transport as described in particular by Aberle, Diekmann and Willeke. However, none of these undoubtedly important benefits (for the national economy) can be considered external benefits, since they work to the direct advantage of road-users themselves or those associated with them in the market and are offset by compensatory services. It is extremely difficult to find examples of real external benefits of transport - the enjoyment that some people experience in seeing certain types of vehicle might perhaps qualify - and this leads us to conclude that, where infrastructure use is concerned, transport generates no external benefits of any significance.

The results of IWW/INFRAS put the total external costs of transport in 17 European countries (15 European Union States, plus Norway and Switzerland) in 1991 at 272 billion ECU. Overall, 92% of these costs are generated by road traffic, with rail traffic producing only 1.7%. On average, external costs represent 4.6% of the GDP.

Table 1 shows that the larger part of external costs is attributable to passenger traffic (77%), with freight traffic picking up the remaining 23. The greatest share of the external costs is generated by private cars (60%). Road freight traffic is the second biggest polluter with a share of 21%, whilst motorbikes also make a considerable contribution with around 8%. The costs generated by air traffic (passenger traffic 4.5%, freight traffic 1.5%) appear low, but should be understood as the lower limit of the "real" figures for this type of transport, since neither accidents nor the influence of emissions at high altitudes could be quantified. Compared to other modes of transport, rail and shipping are responsible for a relatively small share of the total costs.

Table 1 also makes clear that the relative significance of each of the effects varies from one mode of transport to another. For the private car, accidents are by far the highest cost factor, whilst air pollution and the costs of avoiding climatic change are at similar levels and are higher than those for noise.

For air traffic, climatic costs are far and away the largest cost factor. In any case, the external costs for air traffic are underestimated as a result of the method applied.

The external costs for freight and passenger traffic vary considerably between the different modes of transport rail, road, air and inland waterway. Table 2 shows the European average values.

For private cars, the average external costs in the 17 countries amount to 50 ECU/1000 Pkm, a figure that would correspond to an increase in today's petrol prices of some 0.8 to 0.9 ECU per litre (based on a consumption of 9.5 litres/100 km and an occupation of 1.6 persons per car). The relative external costs of bus traffic are significantly lower at 20 ECU/1000 Pkm, and the same goes for the relative costs of rail passenger traffic, which are around one-fifth of the value for private cars. The estimate for air passenger traffic is also lower than that of road traffic. However, a direct comparison of the air traffic figures with those of the other modes is not possible, since, in addition to the fact that not all effects were taken into consideration, the relative costs of air transport apply to much greater distances than the effects of road and rail traffic.

Table 1: Absolute external costs of transport in Western Europe by type of effect

	ROAD				RAIL		AIR[1)]		SHIP	TOTAL	
Effects	Cars	Busses	MC[2)]	Freight	Pass.	Freight	Pass.	Freight	Freight	Pass.	Freight
	Billions ECU/a										
Accid.	106	4.2	16.0	21	0.5	0.2	*	*	*	126	22
Noise	15	1.9	4.4	12	0.9	1.2	2.1	0.7	*	24	14
Air Pollu.	22	1.8	0.6	13	0.6	0.2	3.5	1.1	0.5	28	14
Climate	22	1.2	0.3	10	0.8	0.3	6.8	2.2	0.2	31	13
Total	164	9.1	21.0	56	2.8	1.8	12.0	4.0	0.7	209	63

1) Only for take off and landing
2) Motorcycle
* Statistics not available

Table 2: Relative external costs of transport in Western Europe

	Passenger Traffic (ECU/1,000 Pkm)				Freight Traffic (ECU/1,000 tkm)			
	Road Car	Road Bus	Rail	Air	Road	Rail	Air	Water-ways
Accid.	32.3	9.4	1.9	*	22.2	0.9	*	--
Noise	4.5	4.2	3.1	3.0	12.7	4.7	16.5	--
Air Pollu.	6.6	4.1	2.0	5.0	13.0	0.7	26.3	4.2
Climate	6.6	2.7	3.0	9.8	10.6	1.1	50.5	1.9
Total	50.1	20.4	10.0	17.8	58.4	7.3	93.2	6.1

* Statistics not available

The relative external costs for freight traffic on the roads (average for light and heavy goods) amount to 58 ECU/1000 tkm. The external costs of rail freight traffic constitute a mere 11% of those of heavy goods vehicles. The relative costs for shipping are similar to those of the railways. The highest values are produced by freight traffic by aeroplane, in spite of the fact that the figure is an underestimation of the actual external costs.

Table 2 also shows the relative significance of each effect for the different modes. The most apparent feature is the predominance of accidents for private cars and climatic costs for air traffic.

3 Comparison of Studies

In December 1995 the European Commission published the Green Paper "Fair and efficient pricing in transport". The magnitude ranking of the values of the external costs of rail versus road is 1 to 4.4 for passenger traffic and 1 to 6.3 for freight traffic.

The total amount of external environmental costs (without congestion) is estimated by EU only at about half of IWW/INFRAS values. The new ECMT (European Conference of Ministers of Transport) estimates are very close to IWW/INFRAS's (Table 3 and 4).

Table 3: Estimates of absolute external environmental costs of transport, % of GDP:

	IWW/INFRAS	EU Green paper	ECMT [1)]	ECMT '98
Air pollution	0.7	0.4	0.25-0.65	0,6
Climate change	0.7	--	0.75	0,5
Noise	0.6	0.2	0.65	0,4
Accidents	2.5	1.5	1.5-4.5	2,5
Congestion	--	2.0	2-3 [2)]	
Total	**4.6**	**4.1**	**1.7-7**	**4,0**
Total (bio ECU)	**272.4**	**250.0**		

1) ECMT/CS/SOC (95) REV1; 23rd Feb. 1996, table 35
2) already internalised

Table 4: Comparison of relative external environmental costs of transport in Western Europe (ECU/1000 Pkm or Tkm)

	ROAD		RAIL	
	Passenger	**Freight**	**Passenger**	**Freight**
IWW/INFRAS '94	50,1	58,4	10,0	7,3
ECMT '96	50 - 65	18 - 30	10 - 19	4 - 7,5
ECMT '98	49	62	12	9
EU-Greenbook '95	35,5	33,2	8,0	5,3
ZEW - QUITS*	44,3	30,6	4,9	2,8

* Frankfurt - Milan ('95)

In a comparison of the transport modes, the railways come out very well. In order to improve still further their role as an environmentally friendly means of transport, they must however continue to make a big effort to reduce their impact on the environment (especially reduce noise and energy consumption) and thereby cut their external costs.

4 Sustainable Mobility

Sustainable mobility can only become a feasible goal if environment, financial and regional planning policies make their respective contributions alongside transport policy. Transport policy should accept the following points:

1. Internalisation should begin now
2. External effects are a major distortion in the transport marketplace
3. A mix of policy instruments is necessary to ensure better decision-making aimed at sustainability
4. Relevant "benefits" are already internalised in the market

To achieve a sustainable mobility the following measures are necessary:

- improve the market position of the railways through higher levels of investment in passenger and freight traffic. The cost/benefit analyses for all infrastructure investments must take full account of all costs and benefits.
- introduce a system of charges for all modes of transport, to cover external environmental costs and depreciation. In the short term, this can be achieved by a tax on mineral oil, although in the medium term an ecologically driven tax reform is required.

- introduce a weight-related kilometre charge for road freight traffic.
- introduce charges for vehicles/aircraft to provide an incentive for reducing air pollution and noise.
- increase the environmental awareness of the general public and develop "safety and environment programmes" for transport education to bring about long-term changes of attitude in the interests of achieving environmentally compatible mobility.

5 Conclusion

Today it is possible to quantify damage to the environment and internalisation ("polluter pays" principle) can be applied. Total internalisation of the external environmental costs of transport would, firstly, do away with a certain amount of traffic altogether and, secondly, improve the position of the railways on the market, generating a certain shift of traffic to the rail mode. The internalisation of the external costs will also be an important step towards sustainable mobility and fair and efficient pricing.

Part II
Valuation Studies

QUITS[1] – Quality Indicators of Transport Systems

Andrea Ricci

Istituto di Studi per l'Informatica e i Sistemi (ISIS)
Via Flaminia, 21; 00196, Roma
Italy

Sigurd Weinreich

Zentrum für Europäische Wirtschaftsforschung (ZEW)
Centre for European Economic Research
P.O. Box 10 34 43, D-68034 Mannheim
Germany

1 Introduction: The Bottom-Up Approach

The objective of the QUITS project is to develop a methodology to improve decision-making in the transport sector by drawing attention to the ***internal and external quality*** dimensions. The investigation is based on the main assumption that the quality of a transport system depends on both internal and external variables.

QUITS is a bottom-up study. Bottom-up studies are based on micro data, specifically related to individual routes, or trips, while top-down studies calculate average values for a whole transport network at the national or regional level, and subsequently allocate the resulting costs to specific routes or trips. This applies to both internal and external costs. In particular, the impacts of an externality and with it the external costs can show enormous variations **depending on the time and place of the activity**. In the cases of air and water pollution, for instance, the same concentration of pollutants creates higher external costs in densely populated areas than in less densely populated areas. As for congestion, its severity, and hence the amount of time lost, heavily depend on the time of the day selected for travelling, i.e. in peak or off-peak periods. The bottom-up approach is therefore in principle to be recommended for accuracy reasons.

1 QUITS was partially funded by the European Commission - 4th Framework Programme - Transport RTD (Strategic).

Based on the detailed analysis of the three main factors contributing to the total cost of transport services (travel time, direct costs, externalities), a comprehensive valuation framework of the **global quality** of the transport system has been established; owing to the need of homogeneity of the units of measure, the result of such a comprehensive valuation has been expressed, as shown in Figure 1 below, as the "total cost of the travel", which is nothing but the sum of the costs of:

- travel time (or value of the travel time)
- direct costs, and
- external costs.

Starting from a high level of disaggregation of the inputs, QUITS achieves the desired output by way of successive aggregations. Consistent with its bottom-up philosophy, the methodology has been tested for a set of three specific routes, selected on the basis of the features of transnationality and intermodality (namely Lille-London, Milan-Frankfurt, Munich-Patras), for which disaggregated data are collected accordingly. Due to limited space, this paper will focus on the comparison of internal and external costs between modal alternatives for the route Frankfurt-Milan. This origin-destination relation is transnational, covers all major kinds of transport-related externalities and offers a real modal choice.

As a result, the values of the indicators produced are directly correlated with the specificities of each route, thus representing both an improvement in accuracy and a significant innovation (most previous studies, in particular in the externalities area, follow a top-down approach). Conversely, this very feature stands as a barrier to automatic generalisation, or extended application, of the QUITS method: the fact that a significant part of the data contributing to the production of the final quality indicators is not the result of a calculation but incorporates - at some stage - a direct measure specific of this or that route (or route segment, or site), makes it impossible to foresee a direct application of data from route A to the valuation of route B.

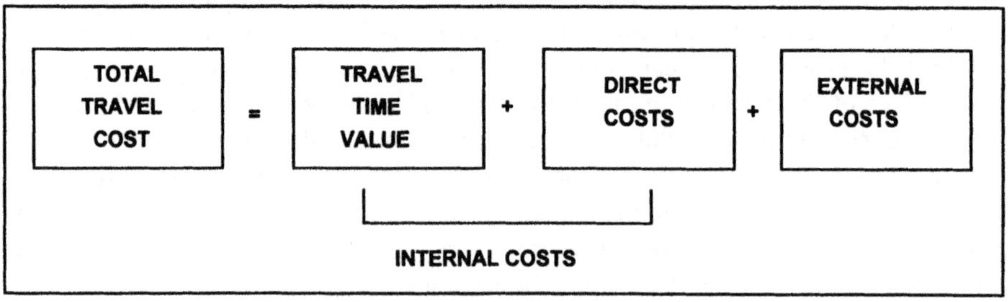

Figure 1: Global quality evaluation framework

In particular, it should be clearly stated that the result obtained through the application of the QUITS methodology to inter urban routes should not be taken as reference for evaluations in the area of urban transport. The very nature of the transport function and its organisation, the differences in the modes available, the role of time in decisions, and, above all, the differences in the shape of the environment make it impossible to extrapolate quality and/or cost values from inter-urban to urban transport systems. However, the overall approach and methodological developments carried out in QUITS, as well as the general logic behind the QUITS software could usefully serve as a starting base for a similar endeavour targeting the urban transport sector.

2 Internal Quality Valuation

Valuation of travel time plays a fundamental role in the overall QUITS exercise, in particular with respect to the quantification of congestion costs.

The total time spent for a given trip is typically split into four basic components:

Pure travel time can be considered as the so-called "in vehicle time" and is the time spent while actually using the specific mode of transport. Its amount depends, of course, on the existing infrastructure and on the technology used for the inter-urban transport.

Disposition time is defined as "the time spent while planning a trip, adjusting to the time scheduling of the transport services (before leaving origin) and waiting at destination (due to 'slack'-time allowed for uncertainty in travel time or due to the frequency of service)"; therefore it is particularly conditioned by the frequency of the transport operations.

Access/egress time represents the time required to reach the railway station or the airport from the effective departure point, usually within the city (and, naturally, to reach destination from stations or airports). For road trips on toll motorways (which is what QUITS examines), access/egress refers to the distance (and time) between the starting point and the toll booth. The duration of these trips clearly depends on the distance travelled, but also on the organisation, the technology and the infrastructure of the urban transport, therefore including urban congestion.

Wait/search time depends on the intrinsic organisation of the transport mode and is independent from the resolution of the individual passenger; an example could be the waiting time elapsing between the check-in operations and the beginning of the boarding procedures in air transport, or the time margin that travellers usually maintain in order to identify and locate the right railway-track or the check-in desk of their flight.

Table 1 presents the monetary values of time used in QUITS. They are drawn from the EVA manual (DRIVE Programme of the EU).

Table 1: Value of the travel time for business and leisure travel

Value of the travel time for business travel	
Disposition time	8,5 ECU/PERSON-HOUR
Access-egress time	17 ECU/PERSON-HOUR
Wait-search time	21,8 ECU/PERSON-HOUR
Pure travel time	17 ECU/PERSON-HOUR
Value of the travel time for leisure travel	
Disposition time	2,1 ECU/PERSON-HOUR
Access-egress time	4,3 ECU/PERSON-HOUR
Wait-search time	8,5 ECU/PERSON-HOUR
Pure travel time	5,3 ECU/PERSON-HOUR

The sequence of steps for the calculation of travel time starts with a survey of **expected** travel times for each mode (i.e. scheduled travel times for rail and air transport, expected travel time for highway). It then proceeds to consider all the issues and events which in reality determine of **actual** travel time.

Those can be roughly classified into:

- Frequencies of the scheduled departures;
- Accessibility to the different transport modes;
- Congestion and delays.

Once travel time is known, both globally and broken down into its sub-components (pure travel time, disposition time, access/egress time, wait/search time), QUITS proceeds to its monetary valuation. This is carried out through:

- the use of travel time values differentiated according to travel purpose (i.e. business or leisure) and
- a separate calculation for each of the pre-defined sub-components of travel time.

It is then possible to derive the **value of travel time**, which is in fact the first step for the calculation outlined in Figure 1 above.

The bottom-up approach also applies to the calculation of **direct costs**. Based on the same disaggregation of a given trip in its four sub-components, the QUITS methodology proceeds with the calculation of direct costs associated to each transport mode, i.e. air and rail fares, fuel and car use costs, highway tolls, the costs of the urban public transport and taxi fares.

As a result, the second component of internal costs as defined above can be derived, therefore allowing a further step in the overall valuation exercise summarised above.

3 The Valuation of Transport Externalities

A uniform methodology is applied for calculating external costs of transport for different types of impacts and transport modes. The evaluation of the external costs of road, rail and air traffic for both passenger and goods transport is based on a bottom-up approach, which means that the starting point for the analysis is the micro-level. This is standard in cost-benefit analysis. We adopted the impact pathway approach developed in the ExternE project (IER *et al,* 1997). The bottom-up approach can be applied both to support a netwide analysis and for local and route specific cost-benefit analysis. Monetary valuation is essential to get an orientation towards fair and efficient pricing.

3.1 External Costs of Transport

Externalities are changes of welfare which are caused by economic activities without being reflected in market prices (Rothengatter, 1993). With regard to the transport sector, relevant external costs are negative externalities which occur when transport consumers/producers impose higher costs on society than they bear themselves. In the enclosure of this paper, the external costs of transport include:

- air pollution,
- climate change,
- traffic noise, and
- accidents (as far as they are not internalised through insurance premiums).

Due to a lack of micro-data, infrastructure costs (as far as they are not covered by charges) and subsidies were not analysed in detail and will not be presented here.

Table 2 gives a survey of the various categories of external costs of transport activities, as described in a report of the project Pricing European Transport Systems (PETS, 1997).

Table 2: Transport externalities

<table>
<tr><th colspan="3" rowspan="2"></th><th colspan="2">Internal Costs</th><th rowspan="2">External Costs</th></tr>
<tr><th>to individuals</th><th>to the sector</th></tr>
<tr><td rowspan="10">Social Costs</td><td rowspan="6">Environ-mental costs</td><td>Fauna & flora</td><td rowspan="6">Own disbenefits (individual)</td><td rowspan="6">Own disbenefits (sector)</td><td rowspan="6">Uncovered environmental costs</td></tr>
<tr><td>Energy</td></tr>
<tr><td>Noise</td></tr>
<tr><td>Air,water,land</td></tr>
<tr><td>Landscape eff.</td></tr>
<tr><td>Vibrations</td></tr>
<tr><td colspan="2">Congestion costs</td><td>Time lost by the user (and the increase of other direct costs)</td><td>Time lost by other users (and the increase of other direct costs)</td><td>Costs provoked on others outside the transport sector</td></tr>
<tr><td colspan="2">Accidents</td><td>Own accident cost and costs covered by insurances</td><td>Costs covered by insurances</td><td>uncovered accident costs</td></tr>
<tr><td colspan="2">Infrastructure costs</td><td>Tolls, vehicle and fuel taxes</td><td>Unperfected allo-cation of costs</td><td>Uncovered infrastr. costs</td></tr>
<tr><td colspan="2">Transport expenditure</td><td>Fuel/vehicle costs or tickets and fares</td><td>unperfected allo-cation of costs</td><td>Costs covered by others</td></tr>
</table>

Sources: adapted from Button, 1993a and CEMT, 1996; cited in PETS (1997)

An ongoing debate revolves around the question whether **external benefits** have to be considered in valuation studies. Some studies tried to identify specific external benefits of transport, like regional development effects or productivity benefits (Aberle, 1995). However, a critical review of these studies shows that nearly all benefits of transport services have to be paid by the users, i.e. the benefits are **internal** and they are included in market prices.

Congestion, as a non-environmental effect, induces external costs between individuals, but not between the transport system and other systems. Hence, from the perspective of the QUITS project, congestion is part of the internal quality of the transport system, and is discussed there.

3.2 Valuation of Health Risks Due to Air Pollutants and Accidents

The valuation of mortality is often criticised from an ethical standpoint for attributing monetary values to human lives. From an ethical point of view, it is argued that monetary valuation "neglects to account for the popularly perceived 'right' not to be subjected to physical harm by other people" (Goodstein, 1994) and that people would value a certain human life infinitely high. However, such a standpoint cannot explain the real behaviour of people, because it would imply that legislation can prevent all external health effects and that people are willing to pay infinitely high amounts of money for risk reduction.

In reality, people weigh the costs and benefits of investments in seat belts, air bags, or earthquake protection carefully. This economic behaviour of people is the object of research in studies valuing risks to life and health. Values of mortality and morbidity risks are derived from individual preferences revealed by people's market behaviour or by contingent valuation surveys.

Thus, the value of statistical life (VSL) is used in economic studies as a measure of welfare losses caused by risks to life. Mathematically, the average willingness to pay (WTP) for reduced mortality risks is divided by the risk reduction being valued. For instance, the VSL is 1 million dollars if the average WTP for a risk reduction of 1 in 10,000 is $ 100. It is important to mention that the VSL is not a measure of the life of a known individual or the death of a specific individual. Rather it refers to the statistical risks before the damage occurs, i.e. it is not known which individuals will actually be damaged, but it can be ascertained to what extent damages are to be expected. The economic value of a health risk is the amount an individual is willing to pay to avoid a risk, or the amount for which the individual would be willing to accept the risks (Ewers *et al,* 1994).

In the ExternE study commissioned by the European Commission, a meta-analysis of contingent valuation and hedonic pricing studies was made. Thus, a VSL of 2.6 million ECU was recommended (Markandya, 1993). For the base year 1995, this value was updated to 3.1 million ECU (i.e. 2.6 million ECU in 1990-prices adjusted with the consumer price index to 1995-prices, IER *et al*, 1997). The VSL is a rough, average value for an average risk reduction and does not distinguish between determinants like the age at exposure, latency or future quality of life, which are important factors for the individual WTP. In the ongoing ExternE project (phase III) it was decided to introduce values of a life year lost (VLYL). The approach is based on the assumption that the VLYL is independent of people's age and life expectancy. There is little empirical evidence for this assumption in the literature, especially for acute mortality (IER *et al*, 1997). Concerning the limited empirical evidence of each approach with regard to acute mortality, values for both VSL and VLYL (and years of life lost (YOLL), respectively) were calculated in QUITS. For chronic mortality, only YOLL values will be quantified due to a lack of VSL impact data. Due to limited space, for health effects caused by air pollutants only values calculated on the basis of the YOLL concept will be presented here.

In analogy to mortality risks, morbidity risks can be estimated by using contingent valuation and hedonic pricing studies or by calculating production losses. The latter is referred to as costs of illness (COI). COI values calculate medical treatment plus lost earnings. A survey of the methods and their empirical evidence is given in Rennings (1995).

For the QUITS project the following values were used (1995 prices in ECU):

- mortality with a VSL of 3.1 million ECU,
- non-fatal accidents with the values from a recent study commissioned by the British Transport Research Laboratory (TRL) (in 1995 ECU values: 134,320 ECU for a serious, 13,210 ECU for a minor accident) and
- other morbidity effects with ExternE values (see Chapter 4.2).

As was shown by Rennings (1995), these social costs are only partially internalised through compensations paid by health insurance companies and employers′ liability insurance associations. Such compensations are mainly based on the costs of illness. For morbidity, COI covers around 30 per cent of the induced social costs. Compensation for mortality risks exists in the form of rents for surviving dependants. However, even an average rent of ECU 10,000 per year paid for a period of 25 years covers less than 10 per cent of VSL. Thus, it can be concluded that around 30 per cent of non-fatal and not more than 10 per cent of fatal health effects are internalised through payments made by health insurance companies and employers` liability insurance associations.

Although external costs of health risks depend on income and different values can be calculated for different European countries (Kageson 1993), in QUITS we preferred using an average value for the European Union.

3.3 Valuation of Global Warming

Damages due to climate change are one of the most important categories of fossil fuel emission related damages, but also among the most uncertain and controversial. The impacts of climate change due to emissions from the European transport sector are global. They will extend over many generations and a very wide range of resources and human activities. Currently, most scientists agree to the existence of a causal relationship between anthropogenic emissions of greenhouse gases and global warming.

In QUITS, the results of the global warming sub-task of the ExternE Phase III are used, which took both inter- and intragenerational equity into consideration (Table 3). For other greenhouse gases, CO_2 equivalents will be used according to Schimmel *et al* (1996) and Hauschild *et al* (1996). The CO_2-equivalents are e.g. 21 for methane, and 2 for CO.

Table 3: Recommended global warming damage estimates for use in the ExternE study

	Low	High
ECU (1995)/tC		
Conservative 95 % confidence interval	14	510
Illustrative restricted range	66	170
ECU (1995)/tCO_2		
Conservative 95 % confidence interval	3.8	139
Illustrative restricted range	18	46

Source: Eyre *et al* (1997)

3.4 Valuation of Noise Nuisance

Nearly all valuation studies on noise nuisance deal with the transport sector. Either the hedonic pricing method or the contingent valuation method are appropriate techniques for valuing welfare losses caused by noise nuisance (Pommerehne *et al*, 1992). The most common method in this field is the hedonic pricing approach. Only a few contingent valuation studies are available. Some other studies (e.g. Planco, 1990) calculate avoidance costs which are only adequate for estimating a lower bound of noise damage (Wittenbrink, 1992).

Noise emissions of transport activities affect humans mainly in two ways:

- negative physiological effects, e.g. change in heart rate, and blood pressure. 2% increase in heart attack risk (Ising *et al*, 1992).
- negative psychological effects, e.g. annoyance, disturbance of communication and recreation, insomnia, loss of (mental) productivity.

Due to the fact that over 60% of the noise nuisance is determined by psychosocial factors and not directly by the physical burden measured in Leq, the CVM seems to be the appropriate monetisation method. Furthermore, our valuation relates to 5 dB(A)-classes instead of 1 dB(A)-steps, because a change in the latter cannot be perceived and therefore not reported by the persons affected. This subjective perception of noise makes it difficult to measure marginal impacts. Another reason for the fact that even for very low traffic density the marginal costs of transport noise are very close to zero, is the rule in physics according to which the addition of sound sources is described by a logarithmic function.

Our approach is founded on the Swedish valuation study by Hansson (1985) cited in IWW/INFRAS (1995). There are two reasons for this choice. First, the figures calculated by Hansson represent a (European) mean of current assessments. Second, values for noise nuisance classes >60 db(A) are included, too (IWW/ INFRAS 1995). The applied "railway bonus" of 5 dB(A), which is prescribed in the German noise protection ordinance 16. BImSchV (BMV 1990), becomes evident in a shift of valuation classes to the right (see Table 4). The reason for the bonus is that at the same emission levels noise from trains annoys people less than noise produced by road traffic.

Table 4: Noise costs per person exposed

Leq in dB (A)	50-55	55-60	60-65	65-70	70-75	>75
Road: *ECU/a*	15.46*	61.85	247.41	618.52	1237.04	2474.08*
Rail: *ECU/a*	3.87**	15.46*	61.85	247.41	618.52	1237.04

* additionally given by IWW/INFRAS (1995)

** own estimation

Source: Hansson (1985) cited in IWW/INFRAS (1995). The original Hansson values are given in 1991 Swedish Krona.

From the bottom-up analysis we derive separate emission values for day and night, as prescribed in the above mentioned ordinance. Hence it is necessary to make a distinction in the valuation process. We therefore consider the WTP functions for silence evaluated by Weinberger *et al* (1991). The specific values for one hour of silence are about 10 % higher for the night than for the day.

To get specific values (ECU/pkm and ECU/tkm), we follow the Planco study (1991). For road traffic, the external costs for day and night are divided between passenger and goods traffic according to a 1:10 ratio. For rail traffic, the differences between passenger and freight traffic have already been taken into consideration in the formulas for the bottom-up emission calculation. In general a freight train is about three to four times louder than a passenger train (IWW/INFRAS 1995).

4 Methodological Framework for Measuring Environmental and Health Impacts of Transport Systems

4.1 Overall Approach

The method which will be used to evaluate external costs is a "bottom-up" approach for the route Frankfurt-Milan. This means that the starting point for the analysis is the micro-level. The bottom-up approach applies detailed models of emissions and impacts and offers several advantages compared to top-down approaches, which are widely used in damage assessment. Different fuels, technologies and sites with different traffic situations (speed, congestion, slope, etc.) can be addressed. This makes it possible to develop a more comprehensive, consistent accounting framework for estimating external costs of transport activities. QUITS focuses on the analysis of the external costs caused by the current traffic situation on the route, thus, main results are calculated for a given technology mix. Besides, for road and rail traffic specific values are calculated for the main technologies (petrol cars with and without catalytic converters, diesel cars, highspeed trains).

The calculation of the external costs involves four stages: emissions (burdens), dispersion (concentrations), quantification of impacts, and external costs. These steps are derived from the damage-function approach developed in the ExternE project (European Commission, 1994).

It has to be mentioned that in the external valuation methodology the emphasis is on the use of infrastructure for transport activities. The impacts of fuel production (in the case of road and air traffic), vehicle production, maintenance and disposal and the supply of infrastructure are not taken into account. This is in contrast to the ExternE methodology which takes impacts from all stages of the fuel cycle into consideration.

The methodological approach of the QUITS externality analysis is summarised in Table 5, and will be used in this paper, too. The first column lists the transport modes considered (passenger and freight transport for road and rail traffic as well as passenger air traffic) and the accompanying transport technologies. The next four columns include the four stages of the damage pathway:

The analysis starts with the exposure (number and kind of kilometres driven). Burdens (mainly emissions) in the form of air, soil and water pollutants, noise, or vibrations and possibly also accidents occur. The burdens can be quantified for one trip or for one year, i.e. the reference year 1995. For the calculation of air-borne road traffic emissions a specific model (Workbook on Emission Factors for Road Transport, short: hb-efa; Infras, 1995) is used allowing a very complex analysis of road traffic emissions on particular routes, both for passenger and freight transport. This complex computer programme allows the choice of the parameter emission type (hot and cold emission factors), vehicle category (cars, vans, trucks, busses, motorbikes and country-specific vehicle-mixes), traffic situation (type of road, speed, traffic flow) as well as the reference year and the slope of the road

Depending on the parameters chosen, the programme calculates the resulting emission factors (in g/vehicle-km) for each vehicle category (assuming a typical mix of vehicle types of the reference year) or for each vehicle type. Road emissions are calculated by taking into account the country-specific vehicle mix on each part of the route (see Table 6).

For the other transport modes, emissions are calculated for the different technologies (airplane types, train engines), taking into account the route-related vehicle flows and occupancy (load) factors, the specific energy consumption, and the accompanying emission factors. For rail traffic, the country-specific emission factors of electricity generation are used. The country-specific fuel mix of the railway electricity generation is an important factor for the railway results which differ hardly between the countries involved.

Besides the calculation of air pollutants, the first stage of the damage pathway approach includes the counting of accidents (see Chapter 4.5) and the calculation of noise emissions from rail and road traffic (see Chapter 4.4).

In the second stage, burdens are translated into concentrations. The results of this stage are emission **levels (concentrations)** relating to the modes of transport. In the case of road transport, the dispersion of airborne emissions is calculated with an integrated model which is explained in the next chapter. The dispersion of noise is quantified taking into consideration the population concerned along the road/rail track. For accidents, this stage of the analysis is not relevant.

Table 5: QUITS methodological approach of the externality analysis

Traffic modes (technologies)	**Burdens (emissions)**	**Dispersion modelling, concentrations**	**Quantification of impacts**	**Valuation of impacts (burdens)**
Road traffic a) Passengers - "car"-mix: petrol with and without cat, diesel b) Goods - Mix of vans, light and heavy trucks	Air pollutants: - CO_2 - CH_4 (CO_2-equivalent) - CO (CO_2-equivalent) - SO_2 - Nox - Particulates (PM_{10},...) - Benzol - HC - Non-methane HC - Pb - Other micro-pollutants Other pollutants: - Soil - Water Accidents Noise Others: - Vibration - Cutting-off-effects - Visual intrusion	**Emission source: linear** Integrated model: •0-200 m: ln-function from MLuS-model •200-5,000 m: empirical exp.-function •>5,000 m: EcoSense Results: Concentration changes: SO_2, NOx, PM, nitrates,sulphates, acid deposit.	Human health: - Mortality - Morbidity Environmental: - Materials: *maintenance façade of buildings* - Crops: *Yield losses* - Forests: *timber losses* Climate: - Global warming Non-environm: - Infrastructure - Subsidies	Direct valuation methods: - Contingent valuat. method (CVM) - Market simulation Indirect valuation methods: - Hedonic price analysis (HPA) - Wage risk analysis (WRA) - Travel cost approach - Production losses - Avoidance costs - Costs of illness (COI)
Rail traffic a) Passengers - Conventional - High-speed b) Goods - Only electric. powered trains		**Emission source: point** Model used: •EcoSense Results: Concentration changes: SO_2, NOx, PM, nitrates, sulphates, acid deposit.		
Air traffic a) Passengers - Diff. airplanes		**Emission source: linear** •Rough calculation with EcoSense		

Source: Weinreich *et al* (1998)

Table 6: Country-specific vehicle mix (cars and trucks), share in %

Cars	D	CH	I	Trucks	D	CH	I
Petrol with cat.	66.2	73.3	16.1	**70's and 80's**	72.7	84.0	75.0
Petrol (no cat.)	12.7	19.9	68.4	**EURO1**	22.7	16.0	25.0*
Diesel	21.0	6.8	11.3	**EURO2**	4.6	0.0	
Other	0.0	0.0	4.3				

* On the assumption, that all built in the nineties trucks correspond to the EURO1 norm
Sources: Infras, 1995 (D, CH); A.C.I. (1996); estimates made by ISI

The third stage is the **quantification of impacts**, which are divided into human health, environmental, climate, and non-environmental effects. These impacts have to be identified and – if possible – quantified by exposure-response functions (E-R funktions). The impacts on human health (mortality and morbidity) can be caused by both accidents and pollutants. The environmental and climate impacts are caused by emissions or concentrations.

The fourth stage includes the **valuation of the impacts**, or in some cases directly of the burdens. The valuation methods listed in the column are based on willingness to pay analyses. The results of this evaluation process are expressed in monetary units, i.e. external costs.

When applying the impact pathway methodology a decision has to be made as to which impacts should be included and next as to which emissions should be taken into account in the assessment of the impacts chosen. Methane (CH_4), carbon monoxide (CO), and carbon dioxide (CO_2) are known to contribute to the greenhouse effect. Therefore, they are included in the analysis of climate change costs according to their global warming potential.

Sulphur dioxide (SO_2), oxides of nitrogen (NO_X), carbon monoxide (CO), and particulate matters (PM) are responsible for impacts on human health, crops, forests, and materials, both directly and as secondary pollutants formed in the atmosphere. A weakness of this analysis is that the assessment of transport requires a distinction between different size fractions of particulate matter, PM_{10} and $PM_{2.5}$, which is not the case in the model. This differentiation would be important due to the very fine nature of transport particulate emissions.

Ozone, as a major photochemical oxidant, results from atmospheric chemical reactions between hydrocarbons and oxides of nitrogen in the presence of sunlight. At present, no regional model of ozone formation and transport is applicable to the European situation. There are some simplified approaches to the assessment of ozone effects (Rabl and Eyre 1997, and Hurley and Donan 1997, cited in IER et al 1997). They provide damage factors of 1,500 ECU/t NO_2, 930 ECU/t

NMVOC, and 130 ECU/t CH_4. However, these results are not included in our analysis.

Other air pollutants which are quantified in the emission model are not included in the further calculation of external costs due to limited availability of reliable exposure-response functions. Some substances have been identified as potential initiators of cancer. But "carcinogens, which were expected to play an important role due to their high specific toxicity, proved to be of much lower importance compared to the particles" (IER et al 1997).

4.2 An Integrated Model for the External Cost Analysis of Inter-urban Road Traffic

An integrated model will be presented for the calculation of road emissions, the dispersion of these emissions, the quantification of impacts by applying exposure-response functions and the valuation of the impacts. The use of the integrated model is limited to roads along which there are no or only a few buildings. This applies to nearly all segments of the route Frankfurt - Milan, as this inter-urban connection consists of a motorway running through the three countries concerned. It has to be mentioned that the results should not be transferred to the analysis of urban transport systems without making major modifications to the model. At least the dispersion in street canyons has to be included.

The integrated model consists of three models linked together. The model "Workbook on Emission Factors for Road Transport" analyses the emissions on roads/motorways as shown in the previous chapter. The bottom-up calculated emissions are the basis for the two dispersion models "MLuS" and "EcoSense" to calculate the external costs of inter-urban road transport. While MLuS only aims at analysing the concentration change due to emissions from road traffic on a very local scale (up to 200 metres around the road), EcoSense covers the dispersion of emissions over much greater distances up to several thousand kilometres.

EcoSense was developed as an integrated computer system for the assessment of environmental impacts and external costs resulting from electricity generation systems (IER 1997). Based on the impact pathway approach, the model provides relevant environmental and population data and two air transport models (local: up to 100 km distance, regional: focus on the chemical formation of secondary pollutants) required for an integrated impact assessment of airborne pollutants. MLuS is a static regression model based on concentration measurements which were made at different distances of up to 200 metres from the edge of the road along three German motorways (Forschungsgesellschaft für Straßen- und Verkehrswesen, 1996). In order to link the two dispersion models it is necessary to extend the MLuS scale to a range of 0 to 5,000 m. The dispersion function of the air pollutants included in the MLuS model is used and extrapolated to 5,000 m.

The two dispersion models are linked to form an integrated model by relating the concentrations and impacts to geographical sectors. The whole route Frankfurt - Milan is divided into route segments each about 10 km in length. A 10x10 km square is related to each route segment the road runs through. For each square around the road the dispersion of the emissions is calculated using the extended MLuS model. The 10x10 km square is placed in such a manner that on each side of the motorway there is an area about 5 km wide. We apply the extended MLuS model for calculating the concentration change up to 5 km on both sides of the motorway. The valuation of the external costs of road traffic relating to the inner 10x10 km square has to be made step by step following the impact pathway. Therefore, the recipients of the impacts have to be identified and located, and the exposure-response-functions used in the EcoSense model have to be applied for the quantification of the impacts. In the last step, we will value the impacts in a way that is similar to the valuation method in the EcoSense model applied.

The local EcoSense model yields results for a grid of 100x100 km made up of 100 squares 10x10 km in size. The point source of air pollutants (normally the power plant) is located at the centre of square "44" which lies in the middle of the whole grid. As road traffic is a linear source of emissions, we calculate the dispersion within square "44" by using MLuS as explained above. The assumption is made that any concentration beyond the inner 10x10 km square is analysed as a point source emission. Thus, we apply the local EcoSense model beyond this inner square for the calculation of the concentration change due to air pollutants emitted while driving through square "44". The values relating to the concentration change in the inner square must be subtracted from the result of the local EcoSense model run to avoid counting square "44" double. The whole procedure is repeated for each route segment. The methodology of linking the two dispersion models is illustrated in Figure 2. EcoSense calculates a concentration change value for a representative point in each square. To be consistent, also for square "44" one representative value is calculated by using the results from MLuS. It has to be mentioned that concentration changes in the direct neighbourhood of square "44" calculated by the local EcoSense model lie within the range of the figures of the extended MLuS model at a distance of 5,000 m.

In a next step the route segments of each country involved in the route are aggregated to national route sections. The amount of emissions produced by driving through these route sections is the input data for the regional EcoSense model to calculate the dispersion, environmental and health impacts as well as the resulting external costs. Technically, the emissions are directly fed into the database system of the regional EcoSense model, which is divided into 100 x 100 km squares for the whole of Europe. Existing background concentrations have to be taken into account.

At present, we assume for all sites (all countries) on our route the same meteorological data as an input for the local EcoSense model (in the regional model the climate data is included), because the collection of this hourly data is extremely difficult. The data for population, buildings, agricultural areas and forests around the motorway are calculated by using district data in Germany, canton data in Switzerland, and regional data in Italy.

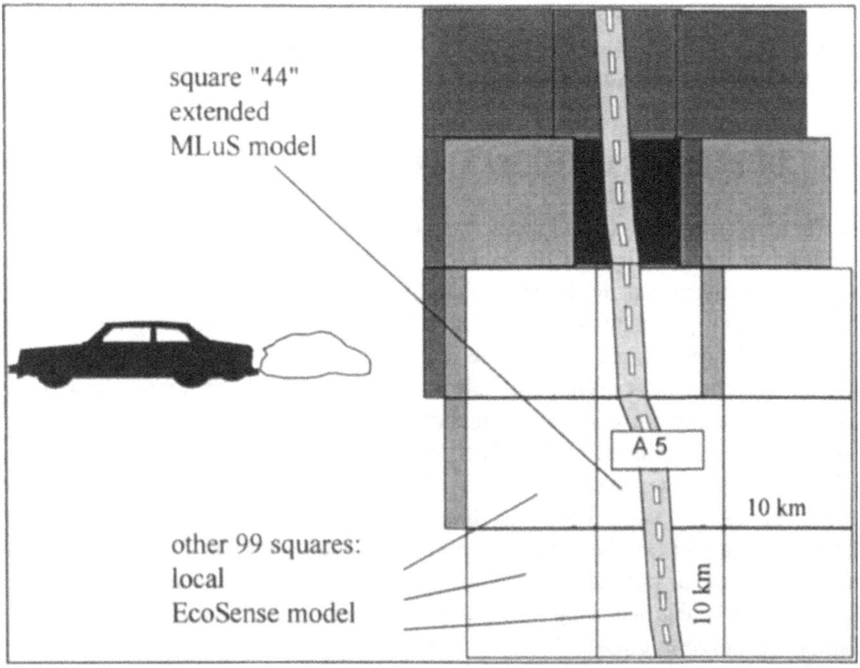

Figure 2: Methodology of linking the two dispersion models

For the quantification of health impacts E-R functions are applied for acute mortality, respiratory hospital admissions, cerebrovascular hospital admissions, cardiovascular hospital admissions, emergency room visits (ERVs), restricted activity days, acute effects in asthmatics, respiratory symptoms in the general population, chronic mortality, and chronic morbidity.[2] Crops, forests and material are chosen

2 Exposure-response functions are linear functions between concentration changes and human health impacts. The exposure response slope refers to Western Europe and has units of cases/(yr-person-µg/m3), except for mortality which is expressed as percentage increase per µg/m3. Monetary values for the main health impacts are (in ECU 1995): acute mortality: 116250, chronic mortality: 84330, respiratory hospital admissions, cerebrovascular hospital admissions, cardiovascular hospital admissions: 7870, ERVs: 223, restricted activity days: 75, cough and wheeze in asthmatics: 7.5, bronchodilator usage: 37, and chronic bronchitis: 105000.

as priority environmental impacts. In selecting the E-R functions we followed the recommendation of the ExternE project group (IER *et al*, 1997). The applied E-R functions are all included in the current EcoSense model 2.0 and listed in the final report of QUITS (ISIS *et al* 1998). A comprehensive overview of the applicability and reliability of E-R functions is given in the reports of the ExternE project (European Commission 1994) and, especially for transport purposes, in the report by IER *et al* (1997). The latter gives a survey of the epidemiological literature with the resulting E-R functions and includes levels of uncertainty.

4.3 Dispersion and Impact Modelling for Rail and Air Traffic

As far as possible the same burden categories, impact groups and E-R functions are used in the calculations for each transport mode. Concerning air traffic, no appropriate dispersion model is available which includes the specific conditions for emitting air pollutants high up (above 1,000 m). Thus, neglecting the emitting character of line sources, we assume that all the air pollutants are emitted at the two airports: half in Frankfurt and half in Milan. This crude approach allows us to use EcoSense for the dispersion, impact assessment and calculation of external costs as a rough estimate of the effects of air traffic air pollutants. Local impacts of starting air planes are neglected in the QUITS project for air pollutants and noise (see next chapter) due to limited resources. Thus, only the regional EcoSense model is applied. The environmental and health effects may be overestimated (not all air pollutants come down to the ground), but it can be argued, too, that the high global warming potential of high-level emissions leads to an underestimation of these impacts (Schumann, 1996).

Electrified rail traffic only produces air emissions from power plants as a point source. The dispersion of emissions from rail traffic is treated in the same way as in the energy sector. The regional EcoSense model is applied with an assumed location for the emission source, due to very limited information about the locations of the railway electricity plants. We argue that since obviously the power to run a locomotive on a South German route will not come from North Germany, an artificial point in the middle of the national route section is assumed. Thus again, the calculation of local impacts does not seem to be appropriate. Applying the regional impact quantification to airborne emissions from all transport modes ensures the comparability of the results.

4.4 Noise

Noise is unwanted sound or sounds of a duration, intensity, or other quality that causes physiological or psychological harm to humans (Marvin, 1993). Because of the complexity of noise, objective burdens are difficult to evaluate. The perception of sound as noise differs from person to person, from moment to moment.

Only about 40% of the noise nuisance reaction can be described directly by means of the equivalent sound level (Leq). If psycho-social factors are also meant to be taken into account, the CVM is appropriate. For the 5 dB(A)-classes from 50 dB(A) to >75 dB(A) (see the valuation Chapter 3.4), the number of people exposed along each of the specific route segments has to be calculated using an Excel-based computer model (for detailed description see Geßner/Weinreich 1998).

For road emissions daytime and nightime noise emission levels per hour (L) in dB(A) are calculated for each route segment following the German traffic noise protection ordinance 16.BImSchV 1990 (BMV, 1990).

$$L = Leq\ (metre)\ (DTV/h\ ;\ \%\ of\ trucks) + Dv + Dsurf + Dslop + Dwall \qquad (1)$$

$$Leq\ (25) = 37.3 + 10\ lg\ (DTV/h\ (1+0.082*p))\ dB(A) \qquad (2)$$

The basis of the calculation is the equivalent sound level (Leq) measured at a distance of 25m from the emission source. It provides an average burden value per hour for day and night. The Leq (25) is a function of the Average Daily Traffic per hour (DTV/h) and the percentage of trucks (p). The following route-specific information is taken into account in the form of adders to the standardised Leq (25):

- Speed, traffic situation (Dv)
- Road surface (Dsurf)
- Slope of the segment (Dslop)
- Noise reduction facilities (screens, walls, etc.) (Dwall).

The dispersion formula given in the German ordinance provides dB(A) values which reduce the emission level L by the amount of Ddist.

$$Ddist = 15.8 - 10 * lg\ (d) - 0.0142\ (d)0.9,\ d = distance\ in\ metre \qquad (3)$$

Free dispersion is assumed. One exception: tunnels reduce noise emissions to the level of zero. For Switzerland we have bottom-up data including information about the location of road tunnels. For the other countries involved in our route no tunnels are assumed.

The influence of the geographical and meteorological situation is not included, because no data is available. In Switzerland in particular an underestimation of external noise costs may be the consequence, because in valleys noise nuisance is partly four times higher than average.

Building up a matrix for various distances, we get a range of 10m strips along the route which are polluted with certain noise levels and can be clustered in the appropiate decibel-classes. The metres exposed of each dB(A)-class are multiplied by the segment-related persons per metre value, which was derived from population density (pers/km²) data. Again, data for population around the motorway are calculated by using district data in Germany, canton data in Switzerland, and regional data in Italy.

Concerning rail traffic the main assumption made is that passenger trains run only in the daytime (06.00 to 22.00), freight trains only at night (22.00 to 06.00). According to 16. BImSchVO §3 Anlage 2 (BMV, 1990) we calculate for each train technology and route segment a noise emission level per hour (L) in dB(A).

$$L = Leq\ (trains/h\ ;\ \%\ of\ disc\text{-}braked\ waggons) + Dvl + Dwall\ (+\ Dtrack) \qquad (4)$$

$$Leq\ (25) = 51+10*lg\ (n*(5-0.04*p))\ dB(A) \qquad (5)$$

The basis of the calculation is the equivalent sound level (Leq), which provides an average burden value per hour for day and night at a distance of 25m from the middle of the track. The Leq is a function of the number of trains/h (n) and the percentage of disc-braked waggons (p) (of the total train). Route-specific information can be taken into account in the form of adder to the standardised Leq (25):

- speed and length of the train (Dvl)
- noise reduction facilities (screens, walls, etc.) (Dwall)
- track surface (Dtrack) (no data available).

Regarding these route-specific characteristics, we get an emission level for each segment divided by class of train. Following the German ordinance, we add these up the technology-specific sound levels to a total emission level for each segment:

$$Ltotal=10\ lg\ (100.1*L1 + 100.1*L2 + 100.1*L3 + 100.1*L4), \qquad (6)$$

where L1 is the highest (e.g. the ICE) and L4 the lowest sound level.

We assume for road and rail transport that roads and railway tracks run exactly parallel. Hence the above mentioned characteristics of dispersion also apply to rail traffic.

In this paper aircraft noise cannot be taken into account due to problems with the specification of the duration and the location of the sound around the airports concerned. Besides, the method for measuring aircraft noise takes peak sound levels into account and differs from the road/rail method (continuous noise sources).

4.5 Accidents

From the literature on economics, we know that the accident costs which are relevant for the pricing of infrastructure use can be defined as the difference between marginal social and marginal private accident costs, which is called marginal external accident costs. Due to our empirical bottom-up approach the calculation starts by counting the number of accidents on our route in 1995 for each mode divided according to passenger and goods transport. These accidents are valued with the recommended monetary values minus the part which is covered by insurance.

Formally we can express the total external accident costs (AC) for each transport mode as follows:

$$AC = \sum_{j=1}^{2} \sum_{n=1}^{3} v^{n} * (1 - c^{n}) * A_{j}^{n} \tag{7}$$

Index ***j*** represents the distinction between passenger and goods transport (for road traffic: car accidents or truck accidents). Index ***n*** indicates the severity of the accident. We differentiate between fatalities, serious and minor injuries from accidents. Variable ***A*** represents the number of persons (for each severity class) involved in the accidents. ***v*** represents the recommended monetary values for each severity class, while ***c*** indicates the percentage by which the valuation function is reduced due to the already internalised accident costs borne by the health insurance companies and employers' liability insurance associations.

This approach is independent of the traffic volume (vehicle km travelled), thus, marginal costs in dependence of the traffic flow cannot be calculated. However, Jansson indicates that for inter-urban traffic the accident rate is more or less independent of the traffic flow (PETS, 1997). In other cases, if no real data is available, a risk approach has to be applied including the probabilities that accidents of every severity occur (for an example see Mayeres *et al*,1996).

With regard to road traffic a difficulty arises when we try to distinguish between accidents related to cars and trucks. From the German Statistical Office (1995) we know the number of one-vehicle and two (or more)-vehicle accidents. It is the latter ones that are critical. The assumption was made that all accidents involving trucks are subsumed under the category "truck accidents" even if cars are also involved.

On our route there were no train or plane crashes causing fatalities or injured persons in 1995. Thus, for these transport modes the external accident costs are zero. One could argue that in this case a risk approach seems to be appropriate.

However, due to the lack of probability data for each transport mode on our route, the application of a risk-based method would not be serious.

5 Results for the Route Frankfurt-Milan

5.1 Internal Quality

The monetary valuation of internal costs carried out for the three routes considered in QUITS cannot be expressed as a single set of final figures, owing to the approach followed, which performs calculations of travel time value and other costs according to the desired time of arrival at destination and to the expected length of stay in the destination city. Clearly this approach yields numerical outputs differing from one set of assumptions to the other. The results are therefore expressed in ad hoc graphical forms (examples are presented below) allowing to compare the effect of different travel decisions, both in terms of modal choice and in terms of time choice.

Sample results are presented in Figure 3.

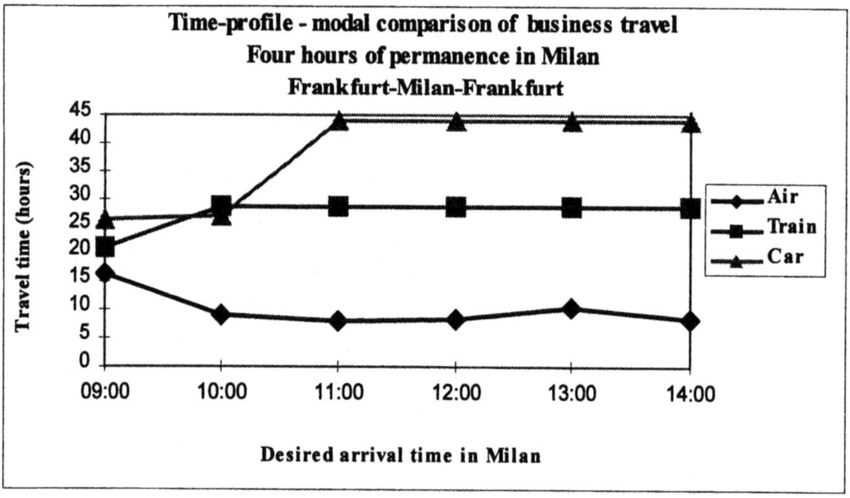

Figure 3: Frankfurt-Milan-Frankfurt business travel: comparison of travel time

On the other hand, it is deemed crucial, in view of the decision support objectives of this research, to analyse the performances of transport systems in strict correlation with the users' expectations. To this end, **targeted arrival time** is clearly a meaningful representation of users expectations (at least in terms of time related quality). In fact, as far as business travel is concerned, return trips should also be considered, therefore introducing the notion of **earliest possible departure** as a more accurate representation of time related users' expectations on their way back.

Once monetised, Figure 3 translates into Figure 4.

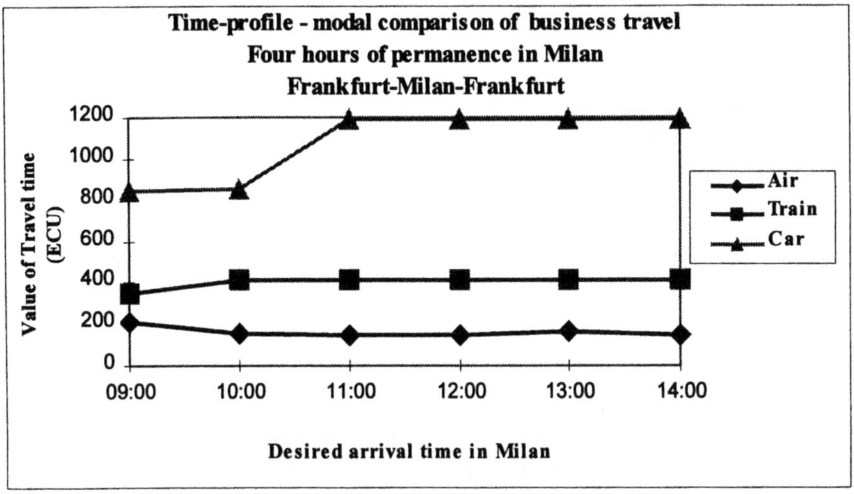

Figure 4: Frankfurt-Milan-Frankfurt business travel: comparison of travel time value

Direct costs are then calculated as shown in Figure 5.

Finally, total internal costs (travel time costs plus direct costs) are derived as shown in Figure 6.

For modal comparison purposes, performance ratios can be calculated, allowing to visualise the relative quality of modal alternatives.

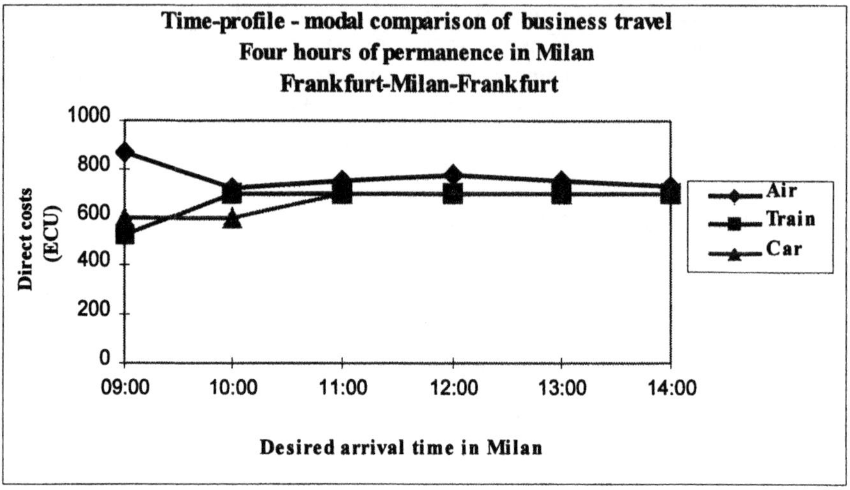

Figure 5: Frankfurt-Milan-Frankfurt business travel: comparison of direct costs

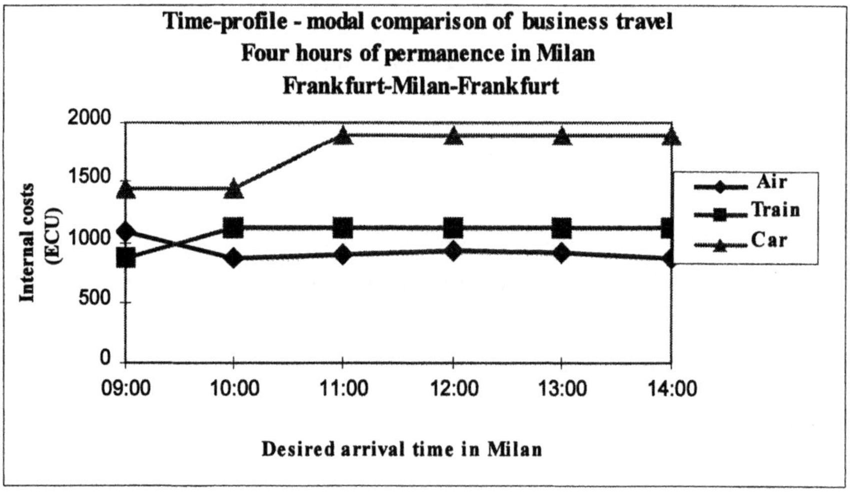

Figure 6: Frankfurt-Milan-Frankfurt business travel: comparison of internal costs

5.2 External Quality

Due to limited space, not all the specific calculation steps and results of the external cost analysis can be presented in this paper. Therefore, we will concentrate on results which allow a modal comparison for passenger and goods transport. In the QUITS final report the results from each step of the process of identification, quantification and valuation of external effects are documented separately to make the assumptions transparent and to provide all relevant information for decision-makers (see ISIS *et al,* 1998).

Concerning road traffic, our route has a length of 634.8 km including the motorway A5 from Frankfurt to Basel (310.1 km), the A2 from Basel to Como (282.7 km) crossing the St. Gotthard pass, and the A8/9 from Como to Milan (42 km). An average occupancy factor for the whole route for long-distance traffic is assumed which is usually higher than the average factor including short and long distances. For cars, an average occupancy factor of 1.81 passengers per vehicle is assumed, the corresponding figure for trucks is 8.77 tons per vehicle.

Concerning rail traffic, the input data for the calculation of emissions and external costs was gathered from the responsible railway companies, for the route Frankfurt-Milan primarily from the German railway company. Four passenger train technologies are included, highspeed (ICE for Germany and partly for Switzerland, and one Cisalpino/day from Zurich to Milan), Intercity/Eurocity (IC/EC), Interregio, D- (express), and night-trains (IR/D/N), and local trains. 183.8 passengers per train is the average occupancy of all four train technologies. For goods transport only one full load train technology (1,600 tons train) powered by electricity is analysed to represent this very inhomogeneous transport mode. The total route is 715 km long and is made up of 343 km in Germany (D), 326 km in Switzerland (CH), and 46 km in Italy (I).

With regard to air traffic, the average length of the flight is 535 km. Seven types of airplanes (B737, MD80, AVRA, A322, A300, A310, and A321) cover more than 98 % of all flights so that the calculations are limited to these types. In 1995 the average number of passengers per airplane was 84.3.

Concerning the emissions and external costs of one trip, only passenger-related or ton-related figures are comparable, i.e. ECU/passenger or ECU/ton and ECU/passenger-km or ECU/ton-km. Table 7 presents the emissions per trip from different transport modes.

Table 7: Comparison of the emissions per trip from different transport modes, direction Frankfurt-Milan (one way), passengers and goods in 1995

Passengers	g/passenger-km			Goods	g/ton-km	
	road	Rail	air		road	rail
CO_2	105.78	33.11	181.25	CO_2	73.24	13.335
CO	2.59	0.01	0.39	CO	0.23	0.004
HC	0.15	0.00	0.06	HC	0.11	0.001
NO_x	0.69	0.04	0.60	NO_x	0.72	0.017
SO_2	0.015	0.06	0.03	SO_2	0.04	0.023

The external costs due to air pollutants, global warming, noise, and accidents will be compared in Table 8 for passenger traffic and in Table 9 for goods transport summarising the results for each transport mode.

Table 8: Specific external costs of passenger road, rail and air traffic per trip, direction Frankfurt - Milan, 1995

	Air pollutants	Global warming	Noise	Accident	Total external costs
	ECU/1000 pkm				
ROAD-PASSENGER					
Frankfurt - Basel (D)	14.77	5.11	4.37	13.16	**37.41**
Basel – Como (CH)	12.98	5.17	1.82	31.63	**51.60**
Como - Milan (I)	34.25	5.60	7.35	27.48	**74.68**
Frankfurt - Milan	**15.63**	**5.16**	**3.83**	**19.64**	**44.26**
RAIL-PASSENGER					
Frankfurt - Basel (D)	2.95	2.82	2.79	0	**8.56**
Basel – Como (CH)	0.18	0.09	0.52	0	**0.79**
Como - Milan (I)	4.62	2.81	0.31	0	**7.74**
Frankfurt - Milan	**1.71**	**1.54**	**1.62**	**0**	**4.87**
AIR-PASSENGER					
Frankfurt - Milan	**9.60**	**8.55**	**3.76***	**0**	**21.91**

For air pollutants, the figures given are calculated with the YOLL concept. For global warming, the results are based on the high value of 170 ECU/ton of carbon. The asterisk (*) indicates a value from IWW/Infras (1995) for Germany, as noise from air traffic is not quantified in the QUITS project.

Table 9: Specific external costs of road and rail freight traffic per trip, direction Frankfurt - Milan, 1995

	Air pollutants	Global warming	Noise	Accident	Total external costs
	ECU/1000 tkm				
ROAD-GOODS					
Frankfurt - Basel (D)	14.26	3.23	8.79	2.44	**28.72**
Basel – Como (CH)	18.81	3.84	3.98	5.03	**31.66**
Como - Milan (I)	19.28	3.78	15.55	8.87	**47.48**
Frankfurt - Milan	**15.74**	**3.42**	**7.96**	**3.50**	**30.62**
RAIL-GOODS					
Frankfurt - Basel (D)	0.90	0.86	1.97	0	**3.73**
Basel – Como (CH)	0.06	0.03	0.53	0	**0.62**
Como - Milan (I)	1.80	1.09	1.20	0	**4.09**
Frankfurt - Milan	**0.68**	**0.62**	**1.50**	**0**	**2.80**

For air pollutants the figures given are calculated with the YOLL concept. For global warming, the results are based on the high value of 170 ECU/ton of carbon.

Regarding the Swiss route sections, the difference between road and rail traffic is enormous, because the electricity for the railway system is mostly generated without fossil fuels, which has a strong impact on both air pollutants externalities and global warming.

For noise the differences between the national route sections seem to be too high; this can be explained by the limited population data available and the exclusion of valley effects. The inclusion of tunnel segments is another reason for the low Swiss noise results.

The comparison of the specific external costs also indicates that the results are route-specific. The Italian figures in particular, which refer to a very short route section 46 km in length, cannot be seen as averages for the whole country.

Concerning the external environmental and health costs due to air pollutants, the results for cars are aggregated figures that take into account the vehicle-mix of each country involved. An approximation based on the specific emission factors is made for all major car technologies. These figures are presented in Table 10.

Table 10: Specific external environmental and health costs due to air pollutants from different car technologies per trip, direction Frankfurt-Milan, 1995,

ROAD-PASSENGER	Germany	Switzerland	Italy	Total FM
		ECU / 1000 pkm		
Petrol with catalytic converter	9.1	6.2	8.6	**8.1**
Petrol conventional	47.4	35.6	42.7	**42.5**
Diesel	13.0	20.2	23.8	**14.6**

6 Conclusions

Finally, we are able to draw the following conclusions from the externality analysis:

- The application of the integrated model for the calculation of road-specific external costs is a first step towards the complex analysis of the dispersion of air pollutants, the identification and quantification of impacts, as well as the valuation of these impacts.
- Concerning the comparison of transport modes, external costs of passenger road traffic are about 9 times as high as those from rail traffic and about twice as high as those from air traffic. Even if we exclude accident costs which dominate the external costs of car traffic, road traffic results for the whole route are about 5 times as high as those from rail traffic. For goods transport, it can be concluded that the external costs of road traffic are about 11 times as high as those from rail traffic.
- For the valuation of external costs of global warming, new estimates were used which were derived from the current ExternE study of the European Commission. The global warming damages estimated in this study are significantly higher than calculations in earlier studies. However, they are lower than estimates derived from an avoidance cost approach, which was used in some recent top-down studies (e.g. IWW/Infras 1995).
- For noise impacts it can be concluded that there are great differences between the national route sections due to different population densities along the route. Besides, the inclusion of tunnel segments (noise dispersion is set to 0) is a reason for the low Swiss noise results.
- The bottom-up approach for the route-specific external cost analysis produces plausible results. In comparison to top-down approaches the results are about twice as high for passenger road transport with regard to external environmental and health costs due to air pollutants. 99.2 % of the external costs of

road traffic are due to health damages caused by air pollutants, only 0.8 % are caused by impacts on crops, forests and material. This can be explained by the high mortality impacts of air pollutants in the current EcoSense version.

- With regard to impacts of air pollutants, some sensitivity analyses were made. This is particularly important in order to show the sensitivity of results to the use of alternative concepts for valuing health risks (YOLL vs. VSL approach). It can be concluded that the total external costs as well as the specific ones double when the VSL concept is applied.

References

Aberle, G. (1995): Zum ökonomischen Nutzen des Autoverkehrs, in Mobilität um jeden Preis, 382. FGU-Seminar, 6.11.1995, 61-68.

A.C.I. (Automobile Club d'Italia) (1996): Analisi dell'Anzianita dei veicoli corcolanti in Italia negli anni 1980-1995. Roma.

Azar, C. et al (1996): Discounting and Distributional Considertions in the Context of Global Warming. In: Ecological Economics 19 (1996), 169-184.

BMV (1990): Bundesimmissionsschutzgesetz - Verkehrslärmschutzverordnung (16. BimSchV). Bonn.

Cline, William R. (1991): The Economics of Global Warming. Institute for International Economics. Washington.

European Commission, DG XII (Ed.) (1994): Externalities of Fuel Cycles - ExternE Project. Summary Report. Bruxelles.

Ewers, H.-J. et al (1994): Economics of nuclear risks - a German study. In: Hohmeyer, Olav, Richard L. Ottinger (Eds.): Social costs of energy - present status and future trends. Berlin, Heidelberg, New York, 150-166.

Eyre, N. et al (1997): Global Warming Damages. Final report of the ExternE Global Warming sub-task, November 1997, EU Contract JOS3-CT95-0002.

Fankhauser, S. et al (1995): The Social Costs of Climate Change: The IPCC Second Assessment Report and Beyond. Instituut voor Milieuvraagstukken (IVM), Frije Universiteit Amsterdam. Discussion paper W - 95/34.

Forschungsgesellschaft für Straßen- und Verkehrswesen (1996): Merkblatt über Luftverunreinigungen an Straßen. MLuS-92 (revised version 1996). Köln.

German Statististical Office (1995): Fachserie 8, Reihe 2, Wiesbaden.

Geßner, Christian; Weinreich, Sigurd (1998): Externe Kosten des Straßen- und Schienenverkehrslärms am Beispiel der Strecke Frankfurt - Basel. ZEW-Dokumentation Nr. 98-08, Mannheim 1998.

Goodstein, E. B. (1994): In defense of health-based standards. In: Ecological Economics, 10/1994, 189-195.

Hauschild, M. et al (1996): Drivhuseffekten som vurderingkriterie ved miljovurdering af produkter. Institut for Produktudvikling. Technical University of Denmark.

IER (1997): EcoSense Version 1.02 - User Guide, unpublished paper, Stuttgart.

IER et al (1997): External Costs of Transport in ExternE, final report. Stuttgart.

Infras (1995): Handbuch für Emissionsfaktoren des Strassenverkehrs. HB-EFA, Version 1.1, Bern.

IPCC Working Group III (1995): Summary for Policymakers: Economic and Social Dimensions of Climate Change. IPCC Secretariat, Geneva.

Ising, H. et al (1992): Zur Wirkung von Lärm auf den Menschen. In: Psychomed 4, 274-278.

ISIS et al (1998): QUITS – Quality Indicators for Transport Systems, Final Report for Publication in European Commission: Transport Research, Fourth Framework Programme, Strategic Transport, Rome.

IWW/INFRAS (1995): Externe Effekte des Verkehrs. Studie im Auftrag des internationalen Eisenbahnverbandes (UIC). Paris.

Kageson, Per (1993): Getting the Prices Right - A European Scheme for Making Transport Pay ist True Costs, Transport Federation for Transport and Environment, T&E 93/6.

Markandya, A. (1993): Valuation of life and accidents in fuel cycle studies. Metroeconomica

Marvin (1993): Noise as an Air Pollutant. In: Living Within the System of Nature. Third edition, Englewood Cliffs, New Jersey, 438-448.

Mayeres, I. et al (1996): The Marginal External Costs of Urban Transport. In: Transport Research, Vol. 1, No. 2, 111- 130.

Nordhaus, W. D. (1991): To Slow or not to Slow? The Economics of the Greenhouse Effect. In: The Economic Journal, Vol. 101, 920-937.

PETS - Pricing European Transport Systems (1997): Review of Current Situation, deliverable D1, authors: Viegas, J., Fernandes, C., interim report to the DG VII.

Planco Consulting GmbH (1990): Externe Kosten des Verkehrs; Gutachten im Auftrag der Deutschen Bundesbahn, Essen.

Pommerehne, W. et al (1992): Ansätze zur Erfassung der Präferenzen für öffentliche Güter - Ein Überblick. In: Jahrbuch für Sozialwissenschaft 43, 171-210.

Rabl, A. (1994): Discounting and intergenerational costs: why 0 may be the appropriate effective rate, in: Ecological Economics 17 (1996), 137-145.

Rennings, K. (1995): Economic Valuation of Fuel Cycle Externalities. In: ExternE - CEC/US Study an the External Costs of Fuel Cycles. Implementation of the

Accounting Framework in Germany. Final Report, CEC, DG XII. Institute for Energy Economics and the Rational Use of Energy, University of Stuttgart.

Rothengatter, W. (1993): Externalities of Transport, in European Transport Economics, 81-129.

Schimmel, D, et al (1996): Radiative Forcing of Climate Change. In: Climate Change 1995 - The Science of Climate Change. Contribution of WGI to the Second Assessment Report of the Intergovernmental Panel on Climate Change. Cambridge University Press.

Schumann, U. (1996): Globale Auswirkungen der Emissionen auf Ozon und Klima, Seminar Nr. 19606 "Luftreinhaltung im Flugverkehr", 19. März 1996, Weßling.

Tol, R. S. J. (1996a): The Damage Costs of Climate Change: Towards a Dynamic Representation. In. Ecological Economics 19 (1996), 67-90.

Tol, R. S. J. (1996b): The Damage Costs of Climate Change: Towards an Assessment Model, And a new Set of Estimates. Draft Paper, Instituut voor Milieuvraagstukken (IVM), Frije Universiteit Amsterdam.

Wittenbrink, P. (1992): Wirkungen einer Internalisierung negativer externer Effekte des Straßengüterverkehrs auf die Güterverkehrsnachfrage. Universität Münster, Heft 127, Göttingen.

Weinreich et al (1998): External Costs of Road, Rail and Air Transport - a Bottom-Up Approach. ZEW-Discussion Paper No. 98-06, Mannheim.

[illegible]

The Impacts of the Kyoto Protocol on Full Cost Transportation in the U.S.

Stephen Bernow and William Dougherty

Tellus Institute
11 Arlington Street
Boston, MA 02116-3411
USA

1 Introduction

The Kyoto Protocol is an important step taken under the United Nations Framework Convention on Climate Change to avert the buildup of anthropogenic greenhouse gases in the atmosphere to dangerous levels. Emissions of carbon dioxide from transportation activities are a major source of such greenhouse gases, about one-third in the U.S. and potentially very large globally as developing country economies grow. The use of full social costing of transportation is attractive as a part of U.S. policy to meet, or indeed surpass, its emission reduction obligations under the Kyoto Protocol. For example, full cost transportation could be reflected instrumentally in a comprehensive ecological tax reform across the entire economy. In this approach transportation and other energy prices would embody taxes that reflect imputed costs of carbon emissions as well as environmental, health and other external costs, while existing taxes (e.g., on business, labor or households) would be reduced.[1] This would have the pragmatic advantage of linking climate protection to other health and environmental co-benefits.

In this paper we address some foundational issues raised by the rhetorical and policy linkage of climate, transportation and social costing, lest its pragmatic allure pull us into an unnecessary and problematic intellectual corner. Then we will describe the energy and emissions characteristics of the U.S. transportation system projected over the next decade. We will then turn to an example of social costing

---

1 Ecological tax reform could be broadened to ecological tax/fiscal reform, wherein the pollution taxes are not be exactly offset by tax reductions. This goes beyond sending better price signals; it is important to ensure that the tax system continues to serve its societal purposes, and that the pricing is complemented by enabling and ameliorative policies. The taxes and tax offsets could thus be accompanied by some targeted spending to complement and augment the price signals (e.g., infrastructure, subsidies and R&D for pollution reduction technologies), to ensure distributive equity, and to support transitions for workers, industries and communities.

of transportation, as one consideration in the design of climate policies and measures for the sector. Finally, we will present an evaluation of a set of transportation policies for the U.S., as part of a national climate policy package to achieve carbon reductions to Kyoto levels and below, along with co-benefits.

Carbon emissions from transportation reflect the carbon content of the fuels used, the energy-efficiencies of the carriers and technologies, the vehicle miles traveled, the modes employed and their load factors, and the underlying activities reflected in person-miles traveled and ton-miles hauled. Figure 1 provides a schematic of that chain for. Policies and measures that affect any of these links in the transport chain could reduce carbon emissions, each with different kinds and degrees of pollution reduction and other social benefits. At the two ends of this chain, respectively, are two complex interacting systems - carbon emissions, which have far-reaching climate, ecological and socio-historical implications, and transportation activities, which derive from deep-rooted physical, spatial and socio-historical conditions.

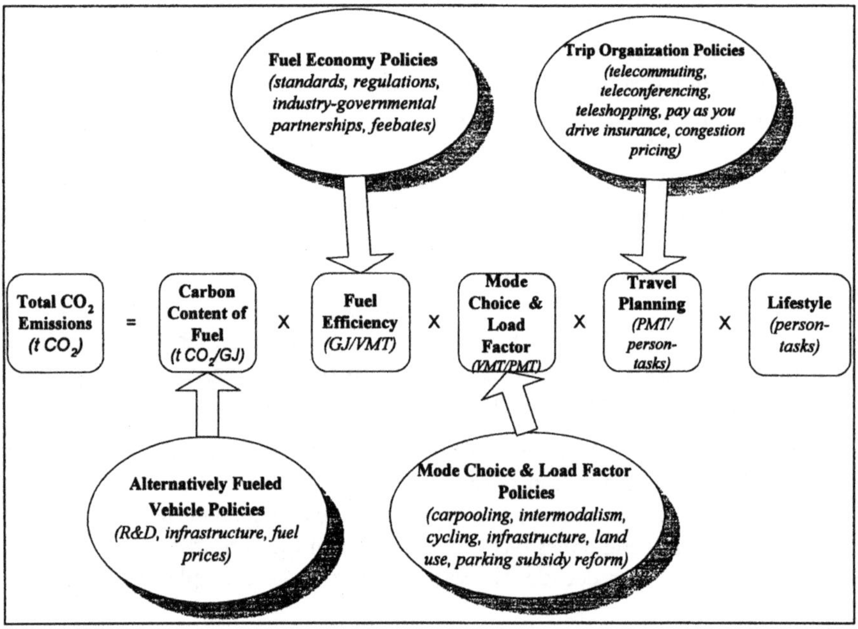

Figure 1: Policies and measures that affect carbon emissions from transport

The challenge of climate protection and the nature of transportation each teach us that the enterprise of social costing based on the neoclassical economic paradigm is limited, even if *prima facie* compelling and useful. By looking at these "extremes" within a spectrum of phenomena, some of which more readily fall into the framework of consumer preferences upon which the notion of externalities rests, the limits of the welfare economics program of getting the right prices and setting prices right, are most starkly illuminated. To be sure, some impacts, which are ephemeral, isolated and individually experienced, with little physical or social complexity, could arguably be represented in terms of consumer preferences, how individuals might wish to spend their household budgets. But both our climate and transportation are systems so complex, so deeply implicated in the fabric, organization and values of our social systems, that consumer preferences and the marginalist economic theory in which they are involved, do not stand up as the sole legitimate basis for rational policy in these areas. In addressing these issues we act as citizens not merely as consumers.

The transportation of people and materials, and its physical, spatial and cultural support systems, permeates our individual, economic and civic lives. A wide variety of transport modes, technologies, fuels, infrastructures and manufacturing activities are involved in providing mobility and access for work, leisure, household and communal activities, for the movement of freight and delivery of services, and for executing public functions. Automobiles and their use have cultural meaning in our society, and individuals derive satisfactions from them beyond mobility itself. Transportation-related sectors comprise a large and important component of our economy, while transportation itself, and the systems that support it, contributes to economic output.

At the same time, transportation causes many problems for the environment, public health and amenity, and the economy. At the local and regional levels are congestion and pollution, primarily around highly urbanized areas, and impingement on natural habitats. Global impacts arise from the large and fast-growing emissions of greenhouse gases from transportation, and the geopolitical consequences of growing consumption accompanied by limited and heterogeneously distributed resources. Social and communal problems include the loss of public space, inequitable access, accidents and crime, which are associated with the massive use of private vehicles and the infrastructure and land-use that they often require. Given the interdependent nature of these multiple impacts, strategies aimed at realizing co-benefits are both desirable and attainable.

2 Climate: Complexity and Policy

In a business-as-usual scenario, cumulative global carbon emissions over next century would be about 1500 billion tons (GtC), with annual emissions reaching 20 GtC/yr and accelerating upward (IPCC, 1995; 1996). Under such a scenario, atmospheric concentrations would rise to more than 550 parts per million (ppm), about double pre-industrial levels, and the world could expect a global average warming of 1.4 to 2.9 ° C, with higher regional and temporal extremes. Sea level would rise about 19 to 86 cm by 2100, endangering island and coastal communities and economies. More frequent, severe weather events would exacerbate these effects and would reach other areas. The full range, magnitude, timing and spatial distribution of the consequences of this degree of change can not be precisely predicted. However, it is likely that this extent of climate change would adversely affect built environments, natural habitats, agricultural systems, human health, and socio-political systems.

If atmospheric greenhouse gas concentrations were to stabilize at 450 ppm[2] by the end of the next century, current best estimates indicate that global average temperature would increase by 0.7° to 1.4° C, accompanied by a sea-level rise of 10 to 65 cm. This rate of temperature rise exceeds natural variability, but would likely allow many – though not all – ecosystems to adapt. It can thus be tentatively taken as an upper limit on the tolerable rate of climate change. Stabilizing at 450 ppm would require that cumulative greenhouse gas emissions be limited to about 600-800 GtC between now and the end of the 21st century, by which time the annual emissions will need to have diminished to less than 3 GtC per year, declining thereafter.

The 450 ppm stabilization trajectory, while a dramatic deviation from business-as-usual, is not without considerable risks. Not only would it commit the world to a non-trivial degree of climate change, it could subject the global climate system to a radical shock due to nonlinear mechanisms that are incompletely accounted for in existing climate models. Evidence gleaned from the prehistoric record indicates that the climate system as vulnerable to rapid shifts with dramatic ecological impacts (Schneider, 1998).

Relatively small human-induced changes could thus be amplified by positive feedbacks that operate within larger systems beyond human control. Several irreversible or positive feedback mechanisms could render climate change unexpectedly severe, such as the collapse of polar ice shelves, the large-scale realignment of ocean currents, the weakening of carbon-absorbing forest and ocean ecosystems, and the release of methane from arctic ecosystems or deep-ocean sediments. Similarly, ecological, economic, social and political systems might also respond to such levels of climate change with unforeseen and extreme changes. Therefore, a precautionary approach advisable because there are three levels of uncertainty involved in predicting the behavior of these complex systems, statistical, epistemological and material; uncertainty in measurement and modeling them, uncertainty in our understanding of them, and uncertainty inherent in their chaotic behavior.

---

2 This concentration refers to the sum of all greenhouse gases, expressed in terms of CO_2.

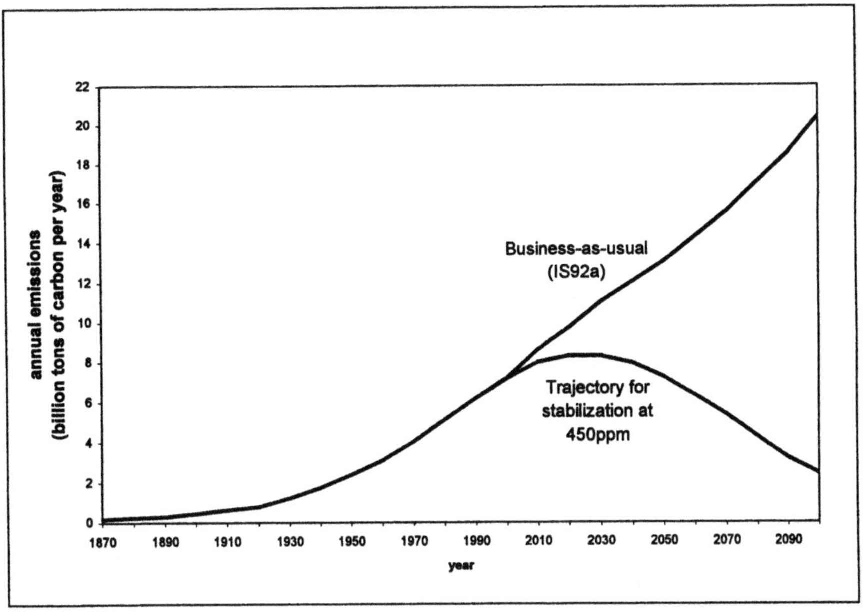

Figure 2: Global carbon emissions from fossil fuel combustion (1860-2100) – business-as-usual trajectory (IPCC IS92a scenario) and a trajectory for stabilization at 450 ppm

In light of these uncertainties, deferring action until there is firm evidence of climate change would embody a dangerous tampering with the climate system, and the ecological and social systems that rest upon it. The climate system is variable, complex, and inertial, making it hard to discern an incontrovertible "human fingerprint" before incurring impacts that might be irreversible and regrettable. Moreover, the longer we wait, the more we will have invested in a rapidly growing global industrial infrastructure that is based on the inefficient use of fossil fuels. We can act now to steadily reduce greenhouse gas emissions to levels consistent with a precautionary approach to the state of climate science, or we can defer action until the uncertainties have been "sufficiently reduced". If we take the latter course, continuing to economically expand in the present carbon-intensive mode, we are likely to find ourselves faced with the crippling burden of much greater reductions that must be achieved much more quickly, at much greater cost (Ha-Duong, Grubb and Hourcade, 1997; Amano, 1998).

Reckoning the far-reaching, complex, long-term and potentially irreversible ecological and socio-historical impacts of climate change in terms of individual consumer preferences from which the right prices could be derived, is an essentially meaningless if not impractical task. Using prices alone might be insufficient to effect the structural transition needed to avert global climate change.

3 Transportation and Social Costing: Context, Basis and Instrument

It has been amply established that transportation causes many negative environmental, health and amenity losses, even as it provides services to citizens and the economy. Among these impacts is climate change. For conventional economic theory, such impacts should be reflected in the costs of transportation (of vehicles, fuels, and the use of infrastructure). As current costs and prices do not reflect these impacts, decisions affecting travel demand, mode choice, and vehicle choice, result in more harm to the environment, public health and amenity than is "economically efficient." While this economic efficiency argument derives from a limited perspective on what constitutes legitimate bases for social policy, it nonetheless makes a strong pragmatic case that current markets allow some harms that should be corrected through prices.

It is important to distinguish between *basis* and *instrument* in environmental policy, how far we should go and how to get there. For neoclassical economic theory the both the basis and the instrument are in markets, prices and preferences. As we have discussed such a basis fails to reflect the impacts of climate change. Alternative bases for policy could derive from standards of environmental integrity and public health, ethical and aesthetic considerations, communal values and goals, sustainable development and inter-generational equity. With such *bases* for policy established, the reform of prices and costs might be effective *instruments* of policy. Pragmatically, then, prices modified to reflect "externalities" would provide incentives for different mode choices, vehicle purchases, and driving behavior, and for re-arranging tasks requiring access and mobility. For firms watching their bottom line, this calculus might come rather easily. But pricing is not the only effective instrument of policy, nor is its effectiveness an isolated matter.

The impact of the pricing instrument could be limited, in part because of the limited options available to consumers. If externalities were reflected in fuel prices, for example, it would represent only a small incremental cost of purchasing and driving automobiles; in our relatively affluent society the price elasticities of transport fuel use are rather low. The types of vehicles available, our infrastructure, land-use, urban design and culture have been influenced by the widespread use of automobiles (and vice versa), and the relative absence of other modes of access and mobility. Where is the infrastructure and urban design that would permit acceptable options for walking, cycling, public transit, station vehicles or alternative fuels? How would individual consumer preferences cause such requirements for increased choice to be developed? As with highways, urban land-use and other aspects of our current transportation system, these are matters of public policy that transcend price. They produce the physical and human contexts in which prices are formed and preferences operate.

The same environmental goals that could be addressed by price changes could also be met by alternative or complementary policies such as efficiency standards, R&D, infrastructure investments, emissions and carbon content standards, land-use changes, high speed rail, and transportation demand management. Indeed, such complementary policies could augment the impacts of price changes or reduce the price changes needed to achieve given environmental goals. At the same time, just as externalities costs could be used to modify fuel prices, they could also be used to motivate infrastructure investments, set efficiency standards, justify R&D expenditures, develop emissions and carbon content standards, influence driving and land-use conditions, and establish incentives such as feebates.

4 First Cause and Final Cause

Since the late Renaissance and the rise of modern science, especially physics, Aristotle's "final cause" has been rejected in favor of his "first cause" as the hallmark of scientific explanation. Teleological discourse, positing ends towards which things and events aim, has waned , while mechanical discourse, positing forces that push or pull upon things, has ascended. To be sure, the motion of matter might be best explained, at last for a few centuries, in purely reductive mechanical terms. That need not also be the case for human and societal development, for which the notion of purpose has at least proximate validity.

Yet much of the discourse, theory and applications of neoclassical economics, including externalities and social costing, emulates nineteenth century physics. Its achievements are elegant albeit stylized, with marginalism, optimality and a narrow conception of efficiency at is heart. Prices, markets and their related institutions, continue to be powerful and progressive historic forces, but these derive from other socio-historical phenomena, even as they influence them. While there is ample evidence that human beings and societies are not entirely free to make their own history, much of what we are (and could be) derives from purposes, visions, values and institutions that are shaped outside of marginal responses to prices based on instantaneous preferences. The aims of sustainable development, including climate protection, social and intergenerational equity, and forms of mobility, access and spatial organization that reflect the way we may wish to live, could be goals towards which we organize our polity, institutions and price systems.

5 Energy, Carbon and Pollution in U.S. Transportation

In 1990 the U.S. transportation sector consumed about 22.5 quadrillion Btu (Quads), almost entirely from petroleum, about 27% of total primary energy use in that year. Transportation energy use is projected to use about 32.8 Quads or about 29% of the U.S. total by 2010, reflecting its relatively rapid growth rate of 1.9% per year.[3] The contributions of the different modes to 2010 energy use are shown in figure 3.

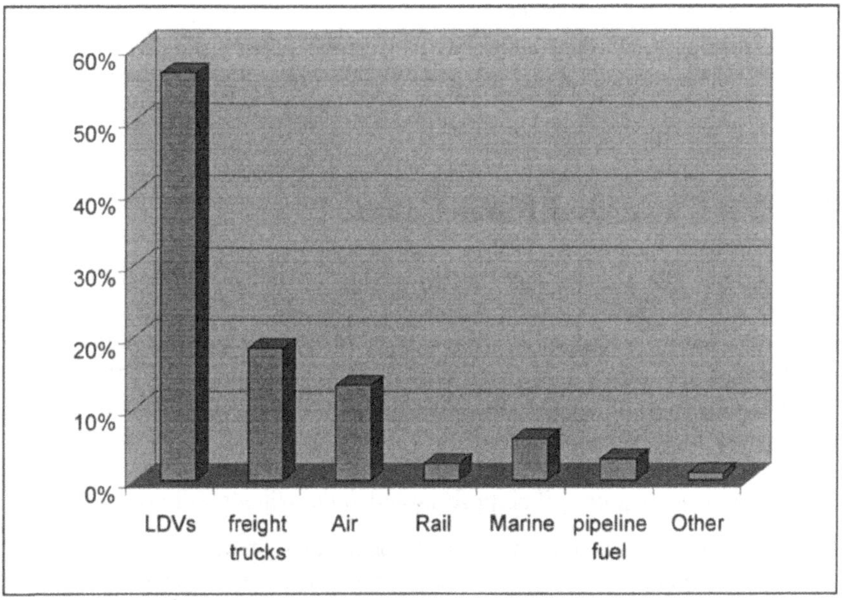

Figure 3: Energy shares of transport modes in the year 2010

Carbon emissions from transport are expected to rise from 433 million metric tons (MtC) in 1990 to about 628 MtC in 2010, an increase from 32% to 35% of total U.S. carbon emissions.

The projected growth in transportation sector energy use and carbon emissions far exceeds the historic growth rates in the 1970s and 1980s of just over one percent

---

3 There is an additional 20% energy use upstream in the fuel chain for refining; this adds another 4.4 Quads in 1990 and 6.5 Quads in 2010, which is generally reflected in the industrial sector energy use accounts.

per year. This increased growth rate is a result of many factors, including greater vehicle use, heavier and more powerful vehicles, faster speeds, and expanding freight movement and air travel, which on balance more than offset fuel efficiency improvements.

Table 1 summarizes the levels of pollutant and greenhouse gas emissions, and also summarizes transport emissions by mode. As can be seen in this table, emissions from on-road sources (cars, light trucks, buses, and freight trucks) make the largest contribution to national emissions.

Table 1: Transport emissions as percentage of national emissions, 1994

	Percentage of National Emissions					
	CO_2	CO	NO_x	VOC	PM-10	SO_2
Cars, Light Trucks, Buses and Freight	25%	62%	32%	27%	1%	1%
Aircraft	4%	1%	1%	1%	0%	0%
Railroads	1%	0%	4%	0%	0%	0%
Vessels	2%	0%	1%	0%	0%	1%
Off-highway	1%	15%	8%	9%	1%	0%
Transport Emissions as Percentage of Total US Emissions (%)*	33%	78%	45%	37%	2%	3%

* Percentages for carbon dioxide are for the year 1995. Totals may not add up due to rounding.

Source: Davis and McFarlin, 1996 and US Energy Information Administration, 1998.

Ongoing developments that can turn the tide of increasing petroleum use, carbon emissions, pollution and other negative impacts of transportation, if continued and augmented, include:

- advances in design and materials (e.g., fuel cell and hybrid electric vehicles);
- alternative vehicle fuels (e.g., cellulosic ethanol);
- transportation demand management, urban growth management and land-use planning (e.g., mixed use, light rail and transit);
- high speed inter-city rail, and
- better infrastructure for inter-modal travel and transport.

But, notwithstanding some successes along these fronts, there are many factors that impede progress. Integrated, strong and comprehensive public policy is needed to overcome the barriers to a sustainable transportation system. These barriers, which lay deep within the history, culture, infrastructure and material life of our society, were themselves created or strengthened by public policy. They are an example of the path-dependent nature of technological, environmental, social and economic change, by which certain options become locked-in and others locked-out, unless direct intervention expressing how we wish to live as a polity and society is undertaken.

6 The Social Costs of Transportation: An Example

As mentioned earlier, there are numerous costs of transportation - on health, environment, economy, and amenity – which are not accounted for in the market-based costs of driving, such as vehicle and fuels costs, insurance, etc. From the neoclassical perspective, accounting for such external costs in pricing, standards, investments or other policies, would help to ensure socially efficient choices amongst transportation alternatives; from alternative perspectives, it could move our transportation systems towards desirable social and environmental conditions.

In this regard, it is useful to consider an example to illustrate how prices might be modified. We consider two types of personal transportation strategies for the city of New York. The first strategy is the introduction of CNG vehicles, which could derive from fleet procurement, fuel mix requirements, incentives and/or other enabling policies. The second strategy is reductions in VMT, which could derive from various transportation demand-management policies, such as mode shift and carpooling incentives, land-use policies, and infrastructure development. A total of 100,000 recent vintage gasoline cars were considered, having a fuel efficiency in urban driving of 18 mpg, and a combined annual VMT of 4 billion miles.

We have modeled these strategies using EXMOBILE, a computer model developed at Tellus Institute to estimate impacts from such urban and regional sustainable transport strategies. EXMOBILE is based upon standard air quality models, and peer-reviewed methods and assumptions for exposure-response relationships and economic valuation of impacts. Table 2 summarizes the results using mid-range impact valuation for pollutants and \$25/ton for carbon dioxide.[4] In Figure 4, we summarize the cost of vehicle efficiency improvements (DeCicco, 1998). On this we have superimposed three lines: the pre-tax fuel price of about \$0.8/gal (about 4.4 cents/mile), air pollutant external costs (\$0.1/gal, or 0.6 cents/mile), energy security externalities (\$0.5/gal, or 2.6 cents/mile) as well as a carbon tax of

4 We have modeled these strategies assuming no ozone scavenging.

$25 per ton of CO ($0.25/gal, or 1.4 cents per mile). The combined effect of policies that incorporate these factors would lead to vehicle fuel efficiency close to 40 mpg.

Table 2: Emissions and externalities for VMT reduction and shifting to NGVs

VMT Elimination	Emission Benefits (000 tons/year)	External Benefits (million $)	External Benefits (cents per mile)
CO	101	8	0.2
NO_x	5	9	0.2
VOCs	7	2	0.1
Air Toxics	0.7	0.4	0.01
CO_2	2,153	54	1.3
Total:		73	1.8
Shift to NGVs			
CO	62	5	0.1
NO_x	4	7	0.2
VOCs	6	2	0.1
Air Toxics	0.7	0.4	0.01
CO_2	538	13	0.3

It is important to emphasize that this example considers recent vintage gasoline cars that have low pollutant emission factors relative to older cars and heavy-duty vehicles operating on diesel. Currently, diesel-fueled trucks and buses account for roughly 20% of total consumption by on-road motor vehicles. This, combined with the fact that diesel emission factors are several times larger than for gasoline vehicles, particularly for particulates and sulfur, makes it plain that health-related external costs for diesel-fueled heavy duty vehicles in urban areas are much larger than those for gasoline-fueled cars quoted above. In the case of NO_x, for example, emission factors for trucks and buses can be typically more than 12 times that for cars. To illustrate this, we calculated the external costs of heavy duty diesel vehicles in New York City, based on a scaling of emission factors for CO, NO_x, VOCs and air toxics, to be between 4.2 and 8.9 cents/mile; this is far higher than the 0.6 cents/mile found for these emissions from new gasoline cars. Including CO_2, particulates and sulfur would add additional costs.

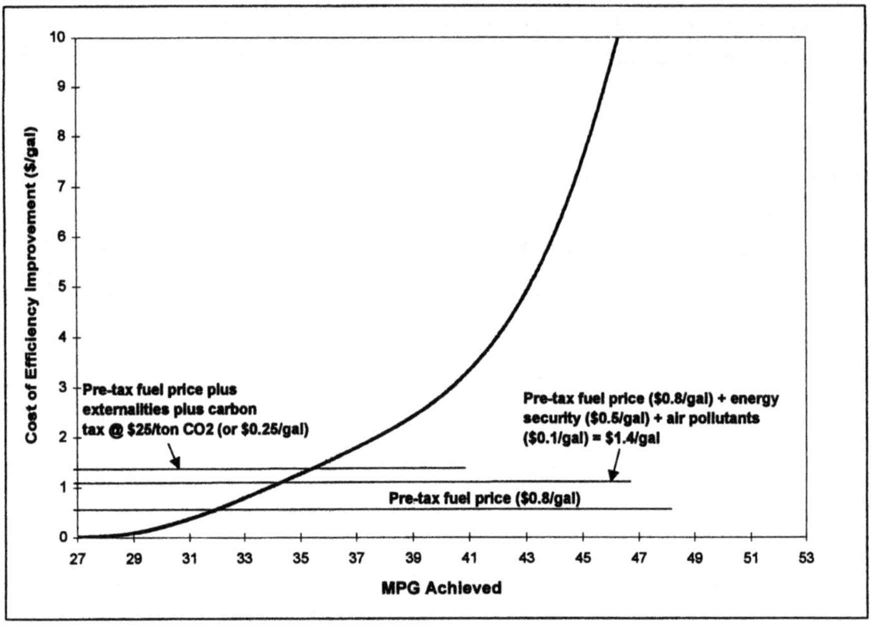

Figure 4: Effect on vehicle fuel efficiency of incorporating social costs

7 Policy Analysis and Results

Policies and measures can be targeted to overcome market barriers to more rapid innovation and diffusion of advanced energy-efficient and low carbon technologies, resources, and practices in U.S. transportation. In recent work (Bernow et al, 1998) we have analyzed three sets of policies, affecting energy efficiency, demand for mobility, and fuel type.

The vehicle efficiency initiative includes: progressively stronger fuel economy standards; an efficiency and emissions-based feebate system for vehicle purchases; R&D for improved design, materials and technologies; public sector market creation programs for cleaner and more efficient vehicles; and standards and incentives for freight trucks and other commercial modes. The mobility initiative includes urban/regional transportation demand management; congestion and emissions-based pricing; land-use and infrastructure planning for improved access to alternative and complementary travel modes; including transit, walking and biking; facilitation of high speed intercity rail; and pricing, planning and informational initiatives to promote intermodal freight movement. Finally, the transportation fuels policy includes: a progressively stronger cap on the carbon intensity of motor fuels; RD & D programs for renewable fuel production (especially cellulosic ethanol) and associated vehicle technologies; renewable fuels commercialization programs in various market segments, including public sector vehicle procurement programs.

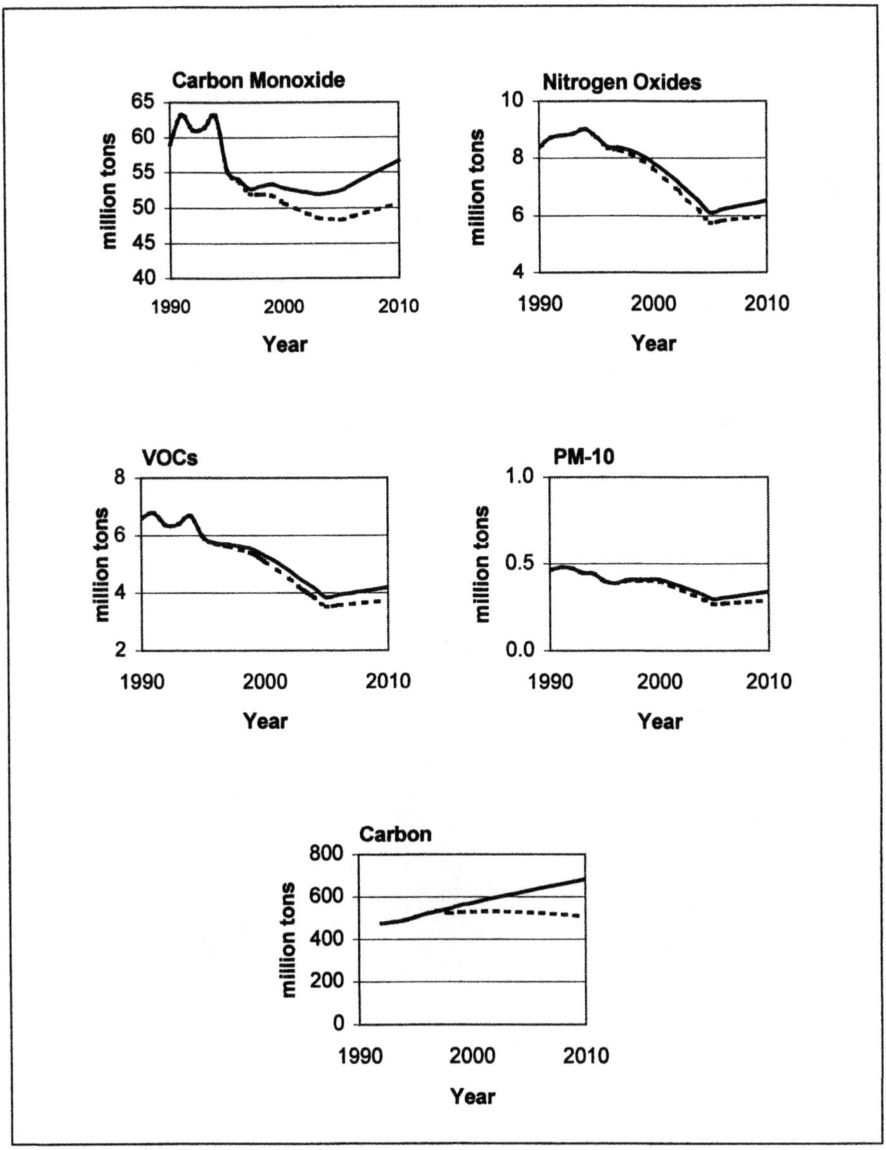

Figure 5: Emission reduction benefits of climate protection policies

The results of these analyses suggest that significant carbon reductions can be effected in U.S. transportation, with net economic benefits and pollution reduction co-benefits. Figure 5 shows that national climate protection policies achieve significant air pollutant reduction benefits by 2010. These benefits range from about 8% reduction for nitrogen oxides to a 13% reduction for particulates relative to business-as-usual. In the early years of the 1995-1010 period, both the base and policy cases show a decline in emission levels corresponding to the introduction of more stringent emission standards. Toward the end of the period, increases in VMT reverse this trend, resulting in growth in emissions of each pollutant.

Regarding carbon, Figure 5 shows that by 2010 total carbon emissions are reduced by roughly 24% to business-as-usual in that year. The emission reductions in the policy case are due to improvements in vehicle efficiency, mode shift and demand reduction, and increased use of low-carbon alternative fuels such as cellulosic ethanol.

The levelized costs and benefits under the national climate protection policies are shown in Figure 6. The costs incurred are about $6 billion. The benefits associated with these policies far exceed the costs and are on the order of about $28 billion.

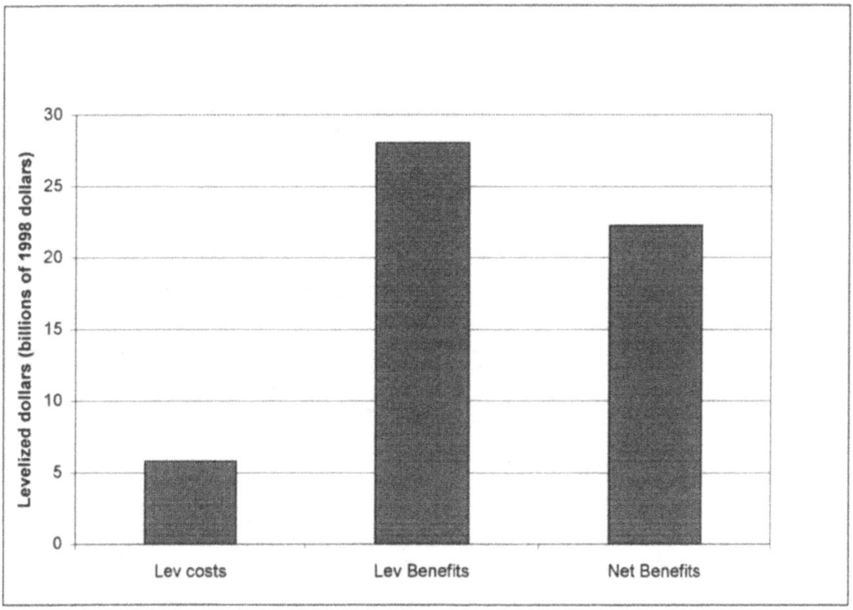

Figure 6: Levelized costs, savings and net benefits in the transportation sector under the climate protection scenario

References

Amano, A. (1997): On Some Integrated Assessment Modeling Debates. Paper prepared for the IPCC Asia-Pacific Workshop on Integrated Assessment Models, March 10-12, United Nations University, Tokyo.

Azar, C. (1996): Technological Change and the Long-Run Cost of Reducing CO_2 Emissions. Working Paper prepared for Centre for the Management of Environmental Resources.

Bernow, S./Dougherty, W./Duckworth, M./Kartha,S./Lazarus,M./Ruth, M. (1998): Policies and Mesasures to Reduce CO_2 Emissions in the United States. Tellus Institute and Stockholm Environment Institute – Boston.

Davis, S./McFarlin, D. (1996): Transportation Energy Data Book: Edition 16, Oak Ridge National Laboratory.

DeCicco, J./Lynd, L. (1997): Combining Energy Efficiency and Renewable Biofuels to Reduce Light-Vehicle Oil Use and CO_2 Emissions, in: Transportation, Energy, and Environment: How Far Can Technology Take Us?, edited by DeCicco and Delucchi, ACEEE.

Delucchi, M. (1991): Emissions of Greenhouse Gases form the Use of Transportation Fuels and Electricity, ANL/ESD/TM-22.

Delucchi, M. (1998): Summary of the Nonmonetary Externalities of Motor Vehicle Use: Report No. 9 in The Annual Social Cost of Motor-Vehicle Use in the United States, based on 1990-1991 Data. UCD-ITS-RR-96-3 (9). Institute for Transportation Studies, University of California Davis. September 1998.

Geller, H./Nadel,S./Elliott, R.(1998): Approaching the Kyoto Targets: Five Key Strategies for the United States. American Council for an Energy-Efficient Economy. Washington, DC.

Interlaboratory Working Group on Energy-efficient and Low-carbon Technologies (1997): Scenarios of U.S. Carbon Emissions: Potential Impacts of Energy Technologies by 2010 and Beyond. U.S. Department of Energy, Office of Energy Efficiency and Renewable Energy.

Koomey, J./Richy, R./Laitner, S./Merkel, R./Marnay, C. (1998): Technology and Greenhouse Gas Emissions: An Integrated Scenario Analysis Using the LBNL-NEMS Model. LBNL 42054. LBNL, Environmental Energy Technologies Division.

Rowe, R./Chestnut, L./Epel, J. (1996): Externality Benefits from Natural Gas Vehicles in New York, Hagler Bailly Consulting.

Schneider, S. (1988): Abrupt Climate Change, panel, Fourth Conference of Parties, Buenos Aires, 2-13 November

U.S. Department of Energy (USDOE) (1996): Assessment of Costs and Benefits of Flexible and Alternative Fuel Use in the U.S. Transportation Sector, Technical Report #14.

U.S. Energy Information Administration (1998): Annual Energy Outlook: 1998

Optimal Urban Transport Pricing and Sustainability

Margaret O'Mahony

Department of Civil Engineering
Trinity College, Dublin 2
Ireland

Stef Proost, Kurt Van Dender

Centre for Economic Studies
Catholic University of Leuven, Naamsestraat 69, B-3000 Leuven
Belgium

1 Introduction

External costs of transport are real costs not taken into account by consumers when they decide on transport usage. Transport activities are not sustainable when such externalities are not internalised. In this paper we integrate different sorts of urban transport problems in a consistent framework. With a partial equilibrium representation of urban transport markets we model external costs of air pollution, noise, accidents and congestion. The model, named TRENEN URBAN, which was developed within projects funded by the EU commission, is applied in case studies for Brussels and Dublin for assessment of the welfare effects of alternative policy instruments.

Section 2 describes the model approach. Section 3 provides more detail on the specification of the various model components. Results for the case studies of Brussels and Dublin are in sections 4 and 5. Section 6 concludes.

2 Model Approach

The basic approach of TRENEN URBAN is to look for the optimal combination of price and regulatory policies in the transport and environment domain via the optimisation of a welfare function. The welfare function includes private welfare and environmental welfare in monetary form. This optimum represents a market equilibrium with different types of taxes, public transport prices and environmental standards. In general, the optimum is the equilibrium where the difference between total benefits and total costs is maximised. Consider as an example the market for car kilometres (carkm) in a city as depicted in Figure 1. This figure represents the market for one particular period (peak) with one particular type of car (small gasoline car with catalytic converter).

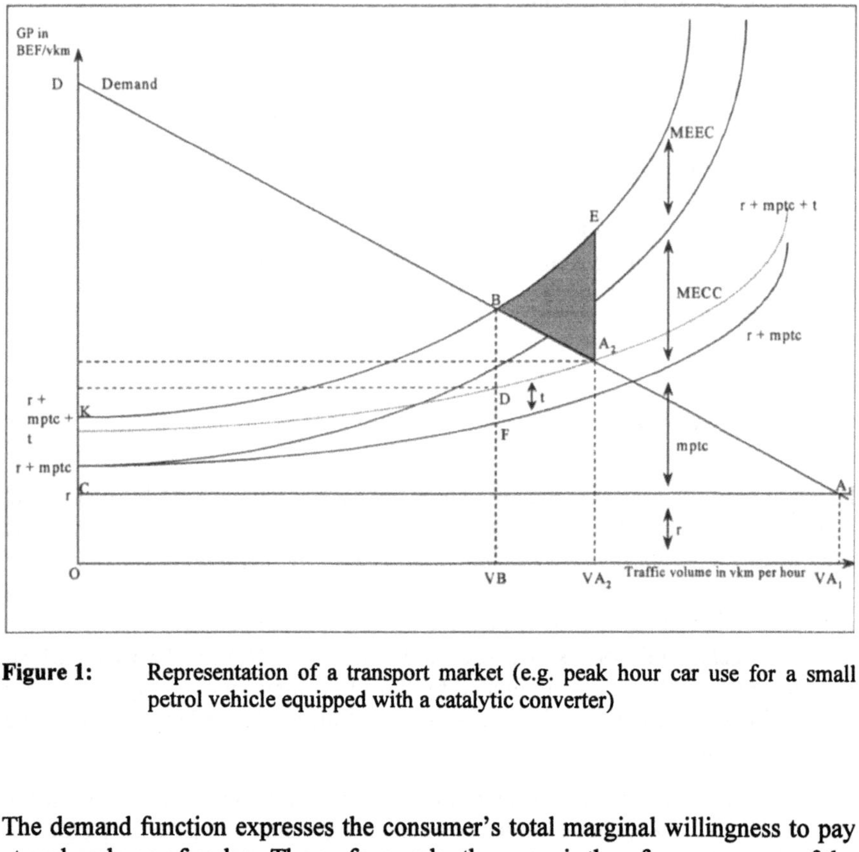

Figure 1: Representation of a transport market (e.g. peak hour car use for a small petrol vehicle equipped with a catalytic converter)

The demand function expresses the consumer's total marginal willingness to pay at each volume of carkm. The surface under the curve is therefore a measure of the total benefits of car use. At a very high price only the strictly necessary carkm are demanded but as prices decrease households use the car more.

The marginal resource cost curve gives the marginal resource cost of a carkm at each volume, such that the area beneath the curve is the total resource cost. In Figure 1 the marginal resource cost is constant and equals OC. The resource cost includes fuel costs, maintenance costs, vehicle depreciation, parking costs, and cost of other inputs, all on a per carkm basis. If there were no congestion and no externalities, the equilibrium volume of traffic would be VA_1, where car users' marginal willingness to pay equals the marginal resource costs. This would also be a welfare optimum because the difference between total benefits and total costs is maximised. The net benefit is measured by area DA_1C. A different type of pricing, giving a higher or a lower volume of transport would generate a smaller difference between total benefits and total costs because the willingness to pay decreases to a level below the resource cost when the volume increases beyond VA_1 and vice versa.

We now introduce the time cost of transport and work with the generalised price GP measured in Belgian Francs per vehicle kilometre (BEF/vkm). It consists of the sum of the resource costs r, the average time cost (mptc) and the tax t. Due to the limited capacity of the road network, time costs per carkm increase when traffic volume increases, i.e. congestion leads to traffic volume dependent time costs. When car users only pay the resource cost, the average congestion cost (mptc) and the tax t, we get equilibrium A_2. There are however externalities associated with this equilibrium. The first externality is congestion. A car user pays the average congestion cost (the time required to drive a carkm) but not the marginal congestion cost (the time loss caused to other drivers). The external congestion cost is represented by the distance MECC. It increases strongly with traffic volume. Other types of externalities like air pollution, noise and accidents costs are presented as proportional to traffic volume in the diagram where a constant cost per carkm is added to the marginal resource and time costs (distance MEEC). The highest cost curve is the social marginal cost of a carkm. The optimal point is equilibrium point B where all car users pay the marginal social cost of a carkm. Implementing point B rather than point A_2 generates a welfare gain equal to the area BEA_2. Total welfare is now equal to the area DBK.

The TRENEN model assesses instruments, like prices and standards, which bring the equilibrium from A_2 closer to B. Stricter emission standards tend to lower the air pollution costs (downward shift of the marginal air pollution costs) at the expense of higher resource costs (upward shift of the marginal resource costs). In fact several taxes on transport already exist, but these are not necessarily optimal. A model is required because of two types of complications. Firstly, many interrelated transport markets instead of just one have to be studied. With several types of fuels, cars and public transport modes, TRENEN URBAN consists of 20 interacting transport markets. The interactions work through money prices and time costs, because the same network is shared by the different transport modes (except metro). Secondly, policy instruments are not perfect and are subject to several types of constraints. It is difficult to tax cars as a function of their emissions and the level of congestion. A comparison of second best situations requires a quantitative approach trading off different types of inefficiencies.

Figure 2 presents the structure of the core of the model. The diagram contains three parts: a demand part, a supply part and an equilibrium price module. We start with the *demand part* on the left hand side of Figure 2.

A representative household has different transportation options. It can:

- vary its overall demand for transportation, i.e. choose between transport and other goods in maximising the utility level;
- choose the time of day for its travel (peak or off-peak);
- choose between motorised and non motorised transport;
- choose between two types of motorised transport (private or public mode);
- opt for metro or tram and bus, and for solo driving or shared driving (car pooling);
- if the car mode is chosen, choose for different sizes of cars;
- and, finally, choose between several types of fuel (diesel or petrol).

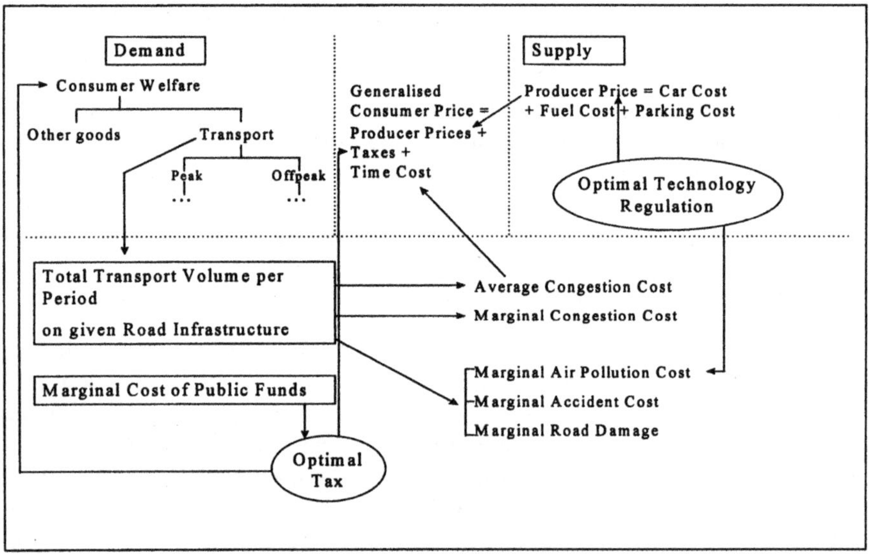

Figure 2: Flowchart of TRENEN II URBAN

Consumers choose between different types of transportation on the basis of their subjective preferences and the relative prices of the different transport alternatives supplied to them.

The *supply part* of the model (right hand side of Figure 2) represents the activities and choices made by the producers of cars and the suppliers of other inputs like fuel, car maintenance etc. Choices in the supply part of the model will be taken on the basis of profit maximisation, subject to government regulation on technology of vehicles. In this model transport infrastructure (roads, railway tracks etc.) is constant.

In the *equilibrium price module* (middle and lower part of Figure 2) generalised prices are computed for all transport modes. The generalised price consists of three components:

- a producer price for different types of vehicle km - this price is determined by the supply module;
- a transport time cost which is a function of the total traffic volume in equilibrium (time contains an average congestion cost);
- a tax (or subsidy) which has two functions: to raise tax revenue or to subsidise certain modes of transport and, secondly, to correct for external costs like air pollution, marginal congestion costs etc.

Besides taxes, the policy maker can also impose *environmental regulations* under the form of ad hoc constraints on the supply part of the model: minimal energy efficiency, banning certain types of fuels etc. This will increase the producer price but will decrease the external effects associated with the use of a vehicle.

3 Model Components

We discuss the representation of demand, supply, external costs, the congestion function and the marginal cost of public funds. A mathematical description of the model is in Ochelen, Proost, Van Dender (1998). Model results are presented for Brussels and Dublin in sections 4 and 5. The predicted transport situations in 2005 for unchanged policy conditions will serve as the reference equilibria. The applications discussed in section 4 and 5 do not include freight transport in the analysis.

3.1 Demand Representation

Four groups of consumers are examined: inhabitants and commuters are distinguished and a further distinction is made between those who have access to free parking and those who do not. Passenger transport demand is represented using a nested CES function (Keller, 1976). The CES function is easy to calibrate and requires a minimum of behavioural information: prices and quantities in a reference equilibrium together with substitution elasticities at each level. Nested logit functions are in theory a superior way to represent transport demand, but they are more data intensive and cannot be used easily for the computation of optimal taxes. The specific nested CES utility function used contains seven nests. The elasticities of substitution are determined:

- assuming that the lower down the tree, the easier one can substitute between the alternatives,
- such that they yield price elasticities consistent with the literature.

In determining the order of the nests we take in account the assumption of separability underlying the nested structure. All goods located on the same branch of a tree will react identically to a price change of a good on another branch of the tree.

3.2 Supply Representation

The supply part is kept very simple in this model. Its main function is to represent the resource costs of alternative transport modes. We distinguish between public and private transport.

3.2.1 Private Transport

For private passenger transport modes, a distinction is made between large and small cars, between diesel and petrol cars and between pooled and non-pooled cars. Resource costs are taken as constant per vehicle km for each of these categories. For petrol cars two technological options are available: standard technology including a normal 3-way catalytic converter and improved technology containing a pre-heated 3-way catalytic converter. The latter is more efficient in reducing harmful emissions in urban areas. For diesel cars there are also two possibilities. The improved technology adds a particulate filter to the standard technology.

The majority of car users do no pay for parking at the trip destination for two reasons: (1) high transaction costs, and, (2) free parking is a tax free benefit to employees. In TRENEN parking is modelled as follows. A parking firm supplies a parking space at a constant marginal cost. Payers for parking pay this marginal resource cost. Non-payers for parking pay nothing. The losses of the parking firm are paid, 40% by government (lost tax revenue due to the tax free benefit) and 60% by all consumers (Calthrop, Proost, Van Dender (1998)).

3.2.2 Public Transport

We consider two types of public transport, buses and trams, and underground. Buses and trams are defined as one mode because they are perceived by users as transport modes with the same quality. Buses and trams also (largely) use the same network and contribute to overall road congestion. Both public transport modes are represented by a linear cost function that contains a fixed cost and a proportional variable cost which differs by period: vehicle investment costs are fully allocated to the peak period. For the representation of economies of density in public transport, we adapt Mohring's (1972) framework to the requirements of TRENEN.

3.2.3 The Congestion Function

The model represents the city as a hypothetical one link system with homogenous congestion conditions. The congestion function is exponential. The precise functional form is based on extensive tests with detailed urban network models (O'Mahony, M., Kirwan, K, and McGrath, S, 1997).

3.2.4 External Costs

The methodology used in the estimation and valuation of the major external costs of transport is presented in detail in Mayeres, Ochelen, Proost (1996). Orders of magnitude, in the reference situation for Brussels in 2005, of the external congestion, air pollution, noise and accident costs are presented in section 4.

The values of time used in the calculation of marginal congestion cost are based on Hague Consulting Group (1990). The marginal external cost of air pollution caused by transport includes the damages linked to particulates, ozone formation, climate change and acidification. They are based on the EXTERN-E project of the European Commission. Marginal external air pollution costs per veh. km have been assumed constant in the model. Total air pollution costs can be reduced by choosing a cleaner car, a smaller car, a different, cleaner, transport mode or by reducing the volume of transport. More fuel-efficient cars were not introduced as a specific option. The external costs of noise are based on the subjective discomfort of all inhabitants of a city caused by vehicle noise. Using a detailed study of the noise production by traffic in Brussels we derived a formula giving the average sound level over a given period as a function of the volume and composition of the traffic flow. For the economic valuation we used hedonic pricing studies on the effect of noise on property values. In the case of accident costs one takes into account three types of costs: the willingness to pay of the victim to avoid an accident, the willingness to pay of the victims' family and friends to avoid an accident, and the direct economic costs of an accident (output loss for society, medical costs). From these costs one deducts the part that is internalised through insurance premia.

3.2.5 The Marginal Cost of Public Funds (λ)

It is assumed that all increases in indirect tax revenue are used to decrease labour taxes. Using information on the marginal costs of public funds by Snow and Warren (1996), marginal and effective tax rates from OECD (1996), and labour supply elasticities from Hansson and Stuart (1985), a value of 1.2 was calculated for the marginal cost of public funds in Belgium. This value was also applied to Dublin. Since the share of labour income in total income equals 70% approximately, the value of λ used in the applications is 0.066.

3.2.6 Calibration of Reference Equilibrium in Brussels, 2005

The Brussels region has 0.95 million inhabitants and 0.65 million commuters. For both categories, it was assumed that 30% pay for parking in the reference situation (Halcrow Fox, 1996). The peak period is 5 hours long (morning and evening peak), the off-peak is spread over 17 hours. The reference equilibrium is obtained by calibrating the model to the projected transport flows and prices in 2005, using the behavioural information contained in the elasticities of substitution. The money price is the sum of resource costs and taxes. The generalised cost is the money price plus time costs. Costs and prices are expressed per passenger km, using an occupancy rate of 1 for solo driving and 2.5 for carpooling in private transport, and 40 and 9 passengers per public transport vehicle for peak and in off-peak hours respectively.

A similar calibration procedure was used for the Dublin case study.

4 Results of a Case Study of Brussels

4.1 Introduction

In this section we compare, for 2005, the results of an unchanged policy and an optimised pricing policy for the city of Brussels. In the unchanged policy case the instruments used by government are fuel taxes, circulation taxes and subsidies to public transport covering the fixed cost and part of the marginal costs. In the optimised policy case all existing taxes are abolished, and replaced by a combination of road pricing with several cordons, fuel taxes and new public transport prices. The level of all these new taxes can be chosen freely, without any tax revenue constraint.

4.2 Reference Equilibrium

With unchanged policy in 2005, driving into the centre of Brussels, during peak hours, by non-pooled car from outside the larger ring of the city ('commuters'), will cost an estimated 3.4 ECU for the part of the trip inside Brussels, if policy and infrastructure remain unchanged with respect to 1995. This is the price in the case where the driver does not have to pay for parking space at his destination, e.g. when his employer provides free parking space. The price is a generalised price. It decomposes into a time cost of 1.55 ECU and a money cost of 1.85 ECU. A trip from inside the ring to an other point in the city ('inhabitants'), under otherwise equal conditions, will cost 2.5 ECU of which 1.4 ECU time costs and 1.1 ECU money costs. The length of the trips is 5.5 km and 4 km on average, respectively.

The cost of the same trips during offpeak hours is 2.3 ECU for commuters and 1.7 ECU for inhabitants.

The situation described is inefficient, for two reasons directly linked to the transport sector (cfr. Table 1 for an overview).

1. For both trips, the resource cost of parking is not charged to the drivers. This resource cost is 0.07 ECU/km for commuters and 0.17 ECU/km for inhabitants, 27% and 47% of the total resource cost per kilometre respectively. It is estimated that 70% of all trips take place under this condition. The resource cost of freely provided parking spaces is spread over society

2. Prices are below social costs. Social costs are the total cost of a trip to society. Apart from resource costs, they include marginal external costs. These marginal external costs are related to (in ECU/*km*, for the reference situation):

    - congestion (1.796 ECU in peak period, 0.003 ECU in offpeak),
    - air pollution (0.004 ECU in peak period, 0.004 ECU in offpeak),
    - accidents (0.032 ECU in peak period, 0.032 ECU in offpeak),
    - noise (0.002 ECU in peak period, 0.007 ECU in offpeak),
    - total per km: 1.834 in peak period, 0.0465 in offpeak; this amounts to ca. 7.3 ECU per inhabitant trip in the peak, 0.2 ECU per insider trip in the offpeak, 10.4 ECU per commuter peak hour trip, and 0.26 ECU per offpeak trip of a commuter.

The discrepancy between prices and social costs leads to an inefficiently high demand for transport. Since the discrepancies are different for different transport modes and time periods, the modal distribution and the time distribution of transport demand will be sub-optimal. The present size of marginal external costs is not a good guideline for policies, however, since price changes will induce demand reactions. This will lead to a new equilibrium in which marginal external costs are lower.

4.3 Optimal Pricing

In the optimal policy, prices are set such that they reflect marginal external costs as well as possible in all transport markets. Since resource costs are fixed per kilometre, taxes are used to arrive at these optimal prices. It is clear that implementation of such a flexible pricing policy will require a highly sophisticated tolling mechanism. Note that taxes are optimised in public transport as well as in private transport, and that the optimal taxes are not only determined by marginal external costs, but also by the marginal cost of public funds.

Table 1: Characterisation of the reference situation (Brussels, 2005)

Prices and costs (ECU/pkm)	Resource cost	Tax	Money price	Marginal external cost (per vkm)	Generalised price
Peak					
car, solo, small, petrol, free parking					
Inhabitants	0.361	0.089	0.280	1.834	0.614
Commuters	0.261	0.089	0.280	1.834	0.614
car, solo, small, petrol, paid parking					
Inhabitants	0.361	0.089	0.450	1.834	0.784
Commuters	0.261	0.089	0.350	1.834	0.684
car, solo, small, diesel, free parking					
Inhabitants	0.326	0.083	0.271	1.863	0.547
bust/tram (inhabitants)	0.080	0.039	0.12	0.092	0.587
Offpeak					
car, solo, small, petrol, free parking					
Inhabitants	0.359	0.083	0.271	0.047	0.419
bus/tram (inhabitants)	0.271	-0.151	0.12	0.014	0.521
Volume and composition of traffic	mio pkm	Share (%)	% carpool	Speed (km/h)	
Peak, private	3.846	41.6	29.6	23.1	
Peak, public	1.839	19.9		20.6	
Offpeak, private	2.839	30.7	25.4	49.7	
Offpeak, public	0.727	7.9		44.2	
Tax revenue (mio ECU/day)					
Private	0.508				
Public	-0.010				
External costs (mio ECU/day)	0.432				

The distinction between payers and nonpayers for parking is no longer relevant when all drivers have to pay for parking at their destination. We will mainly look at results of *optimal pricing* in this situation *with improved parking charges*.

Tables 2 and 3 summarise the results of the optimal pricing policy, when parking charges have been improved.

Table 2: Key results of optimal policy (case, 2005)

	welfare level	% welfare gain	% maximal welfare gain	Traffic level (mio/ pkm)	% peak, private traffic	% peak, public traffic	% offpeak, private traffic	% offpeak, public traffic	Other external costs (mio ECU/ day)
RF	54.60	0	0	9.252	41.6	19.8	30.6	7.8	0.432
FO	55.31	1.30%	97.3%	8.410	35.3	28.2	29.1	7.4	0.374

Our principal standard for policy assessment is welfare (cfr the definition of sustainability in the introduction): it is a quantitative measure (in our case, a monetary measure) of the net benefits yielded by a given economic equilibrium. It takes account of the benefits accruing to all consumers and producers, in the assumption that tax revenues are used by government to improve consumer welfare. The impact of negative externalities is accounted by subtracting the monetary value of these impacts from welfare.

The simultaneous introduction of improved parking charges and optimal pricing with respect to external costs leads to a welfare gain of 1.30% as compared to the reference situation. External costs of air pollution, noise and accidents ('other external costs', in the tables) decrease with 0.06 million ECU per day, a decrease with 13.4%. The change in congestion conditions is reflected in the average travel speeds. Whereas peak hour driving in the reference situation was at an average speed of 23km/h, the average speed is now 40km/h. This increase will be reflected in a decrease of time costs of trips. Offpeak speeds do not change significantly, because congestion is not problematic in the offpeak hours in the reference situation. The increase in travel speeds is related to the change in traffic level, and in modal and time distribution of traffic. Overall daily traffic drops with 0.842 million passenger car units, i.e. a 9% decrease. The share of peak traffic remains more or less constant (61.5% in reference situation and 63.5% in the optimum), but there is an important modal shift from private transport to public transport. Aggregated over peak and offpeak, the share of public transport rises from 27.6% to 35.6%. This effect decomposes into a small drop in the offpeak share of public transport, and a large peak share increase (+8.4%-point). In summary, the impact of optimal pricing on urban traffic in Brussel is that peak and offpeak traffic decrease, that the time distribution of total traffic remains more or less constant, and that the share of public transport in peak hours increases strongly. The combination of a decreased peak traffic level and a switch to collective modes leads to increased travel speeds.

Introducing optimal transport prices will lead to substitution of transport consumption for other consumption. All consumer groups consume more non transport goods in the full optimum. The order of magnitude of the increase is 2.5%. The total benefit of consumption to consumers (the consumer surplus) increases for all groups. For inhabitants who did not pay for parking in the reference situation, the increase is small. For this group, the per kilometre increase of private transport prices is so high that it largely offsets all other gains from the optimal policy.

Table 3a gives information on the optimal tax levels and compares them to the reference taxes. Recall that the taxes are the instruments used to bring about the optimal changes in traffic demand, and that the new taxes substitute all existing taxes in transport (fuel, registration taxes, etc.). Note also that it is assumed in this scenario that parking charges have been improved, so that all consumers now pay for the resource cost of parking. Hence, there is no need to use the tax instrument to correct for inefficiencies in parking charges.

Taxes increase for all modes, but more so for peak passenger car traffic and for offpeak public transport (where a subsidy is transformed into a net tax). In the case of peak passenger car traffic, the main incentive for the tax increase is the high marginal external congestion cost. For offpeak public transport, the tax increase is motivated by the large discrepancy between resource costs per passenger kilometre and prices per passenger kilometre in the reference situation: when all modes are priced optimally, there is no justification for subsidising public transport beyond covering the difference between average and marginal resource cost.

Optimal taxes are much more differentiated between transport markets than in the reference situation. There is a differentiation between peak and offpeak taxes. There is spatial differentiation: the per kilometre tax is higher for inhabitants than for commuters.[1]

Taxes are the instruments of the optimal pricing policy. The more relevant variable for the consumer is the generalised price of transport. Table 3b compares generalised prices in the reference situation and in the full optimum.

Generalised prices of transport increase, except in the case of peak public transport. Whereas the tax increase (Table 3a) is quite substantial, the increase in generalised prices is more moderate, even when parking charges are introduced for

1 On a per trip basis, the situation is reversed.

former nonpayers. The reason is that tax increases, causing money price increases, are partly offset by gains in travel speeds, which lead to lower time costs. The net generalised price increase during peak hours for private transport, due to internalisation of external costs, is approximately 40%. For public transport, an additional cause of decreasing time costs is the Mohring effect: when public transport demand increases, TRENEN assumes that the frequency of public transport services responds optimally. This leads to decreasing waiting times at public transport stops, when demand increases. This effect is partly responsible for the decrease in the generalised price of peak public transport.

Table 3a: Taxes in reference situation and optimal pricing (ECU/passenger km, % change w.r.t. reference case, 2005)

	ECU/pkm				% change			
	IN	IP	ON	OP	IN	IP	ON	OP
RF								
peak, car*	0.089	0.089	0.089	0.089	0	0	0	0
peak, bus	0.039	0.039	0.039	0.039	0	0	0	0
offpeak, car*	0.083	0.083	0.083	0.083	0	0	0	0
offpeak, bus	-0.151	-0.151	-0.151	-0.151	0	0	0	0
FO								
peak, car*	0.533	0.533	0.497	0.497	499	499	458	458
peak, bus	0.080	0.080	0.072	0.072	105	105	85	85
offpeak, car*	0.188	0.188	0.166	0.166	126	126	100	100
offpeak, bus	0.104	0.104	0.108	0.108	(index: 408	408	417	417)

* small petrol car driven alone
IN inhabitants nonpayers for parking
ON commuters nonpayers
IP inhabitants payers
OP commuters payers

Table 3c supplies additional information on the changes in price structure between reference situation and optimal pricing. The time cost component of the generalised price is seen to decrease strongly in peak hours, which follows from both the increase in the money price (tax increase) and the decrease in the time cost levels. For money prices, the opposite direction of effects holds (by definition). Tax rates increase, and they are now higher in the peak than in the offpeak (while the relation was opposite in the reference situation). Taxes were more or less equal in peak and offpeak in the reference situation, but the peak tax is higher in peak hours under optimal pricing. Since external costs are internalised in the generalised price, resource costs become smaller as a share of the generalised price.

Table 3b: Generalised prices for reference and optimal pricing (ECU/passenger km, index w.r.t. reference case, 2005)

	ECU/pkm				% change			
	IN	IP	ON	OP	IN	IP	ON	OP
RF								
peak, car*	0.610	0.780	0.610	0.680	0	0	0	0
peak, bus	0.587	0.587	0.570	0.570	0	0	0	0
offpeak, car*	0.419	0.589	0.419	0.489	0	0	0	0
offpeak, bus	0.521	0.521	0.483	0.483	0	0	0	0
FO								
peak, car*	1.085	1.085	0.949	0.949	78	39	56	39
peak, bus	0.501	0.501	0.475	0.475	-15	-15	-17	-17
offpeak, car*	0.694	0.694	0.572	0.572	65	18	36	17
offpeak, bus	0.797	0.797	0.783	0.783	53	53	62	62

* small petrol car driven alone
IN inhabitants nonpayers for parking
ON commuters nonpayers
IP inhabitants payers
OP commuters payers

Table 3c: Generalised prices in reference and optimal pricing (small petrol car driven alone by an inhabitant not paying for parking in reference), case, 2005 (ECU/pkm)

	Peak		Offpeak	
	RF	FO	RF	FO
Generalised Price	0.614	1.085	0.419	0.694
Time Cost	0.334	0.191	0.148	0.148
Money Price	0.280	0.894	0.271	0.546
Tax	0.089	0.533	0.083	0.188
Resource cost excl. parking	0.191	0.191	0.189	0.189
Resource cost of parking	0.170	0.170	0.170	0.170

In the optimal pricing policy taxes exceed marginal external costs. As explained before, this is for reasons of efficiency of the global taxation system. Marginal external costs for a small petrol car driven during peak hours are 0.407 ECU per kilometre (offpeak: 0.047 ECU/km). The optimal tax is between 0.497 and 0.596 ECU per kilometre (offpeak: between 0.17 and 0.19 ECU/km). The mark-up tax rate in terms of generalised prices (i.e. the difference between tax and marginal external cost, divided by the generalised price) is 15% in peak hours and 26% in offpeak hours.

Up to now, full optimal pricing was discussed in the context where all drivers pay for parking charges at the trip destination. Introduction of optimal pricing without improving parking charges at the same time leads to a welfare gain almost identical to the gain from optimal pricing plus improved parking charges. The reason is that the optimal tax instrument is flexible enough to correct for external costs and for parking pricing inefficiencies simultaneously. Issues of income distribution and of political feasibility make this policy less attractive however.

Improving parking charges is an important element of urban transport policy, and should preferably (presumably, can only) be implemented separately from the introduction of road pricing schemes (Calthrop et al., 1998). The importance of improving parking charges may be illustrated by comparing the welfare level of the reference situation to a situation where only parking charges are improved, while taxes and technology remain as they were. The welfare gain of this policy is ca. 0.42% with respect to the reference situation, which is approximately 32% of the maximal welfare gain. In other words, a third of the initial inefficiency on the urban transport markets is due to imperfect pricing of parking.

5 Results from a Case Study of Dublin

In Table 4 the key results from the full optimum scenario for Dublin are highlighted. We discuss two policy scenarios: one with perfect pricing instruments but with unchanged parking policy (FO1) and one where, in addition, all car users are forced to pay the resource costs of parking. (FO2) Compared with the reference situation the full optimum, FO1 (parking charge as in reference), returns a welfare gain of 0.47% of generalised income and a reduction in non-congestion external costs of 16%. There is a decline of 14% in the overall transport level. Demand for private transport across all consumer types decreases in the full optimum scenario with the share of private transport in the peak period dropping from 23.8% in the reference scenario to 22.6% in FO2 (resource cost of parking paid by user).

Demand for the bus mode decreases in the peak period and increases slightly for commuters in the off-peak period. Demand for the rail mode decreases in both peak and off-peak periods for inhabitants and for commuters. These reductions can be attributed to the increase in taxes which public transport users face in the full optimum scenario. The slow modes (walking and cycling) also indicate an unexpected reduction in demand but this relates to the overall decline in consumption of transport. The share of private transport drops in the off-peak period as well as in the peak period, whereas the share of public transport only drops in the peak period and shows an increase of 16% in the off-peak period.

Table 4: Key results for Dublin case study

	% Welfare Gain	External Cost (non-congestion)	% Peak Private	% Peak Public	% Off-peak Private	% Off-peak Public
REF1		1.009	23.78	7.26	53.42	15.54
FO1	0.47	0.85	22.61	5.91	53.51	17.97
FO2	0.45	0.847	22.58	5.91	53.42	18.09

In the full optimum scenario there is a significant increase in taxes across all modes of transport. For a small petrol car with only one occupant in the peak period the tax rises from 1.02 ECU/trip to 4.89 ECU/trip for an inhabitant and 1.93 ECU/trip to 7.24 ECU/trip for a commuter. In the off-peak period the tax on private transport increases by 69% for inhabitants and by 59% for commuters between the reference and full optimum scenarios.

Public transport no longer receives a subsidy in the peak period in the full optimum scenario. An inhabitant using the bus in the peak period receives a subsidy of 0.38 ECU/trip in the reference scenario but in the full optimum scenario this consumer is charged a tax of 0.99 ECU/trip, because she also contributes to the different external costs. In the off-peak period the tax on buses rises from 0.04 ECU/trip to 1.07 ECU/trip for an inhabitant and from 0.05 ECU/trip to 0.91 ECU/trip for a commuter. Overall, however, the taxes imposed on public transport per passengerkilometre are still considerably lower than those on private transport due to the high occupancy rates of these vehicles.

6 Conclusions

In this paper we have given an operational meaning to the concept of sustainable transport for an urban area. Sustainable transport was defined as transport that fully pays for its marginal social cost. External costs taken into account include congestion, noise, accidents and air pollution. With case studies for Brussels and Dublin we have shown drastic price changes are necessary to achieve sustainable transport.

Acknowledgments

TRENEN II URBAN was developed at CES, within the TRENEN II STRAN project (1996-1998). This project was funded by DGVII of the European Commission under the Transport RTD Programme of the 4th Framework Programme. The point of departure for TRENEN II URBAN was the TRENEN I model, developed within the TRENEN I project (1994-1995), funded within the JOULE II Programme of DGXI of the European Commission.

We thank the participants of the 4th International Social Cost and Sustainability Conference (New York, 1998) for their comments.

References

Calthrop E./Proost S./Van Dender K. (1998), Parking Policies and Road Pricing, Urban Studies, forthcoming

Hague Consulting Group (1990), The Netherlands' 'Value of Time' Study: Final Report, Den Haag, Hague Consulting Group.

Halcrow Fox (1996), Transport Research APAS - Urban Transport VII-28: Pricing and Financing of Urban Transport, ECSC-EC-EAEC, Brussels-Luxembourg.

Hansson I./Stuart C. (1985), Tax Revenue and the Marginal Cost of Public Funds in Sweden, Journal of Public Economics, 27, 331-353

Keller W.J. (1976), A Nested CES-Type Utility Function and Its Demand and Price-Index Functions, European Economic Review, 7, 175-186.

Mayeres I./Proost S. (1997),Optimal Tax and Investment Rules for Congestion Type of Externalities, Scandinavian Journal of Economics, 99, 2, 261-279.

Mayeres I./Ochelen S./Proost S. (1996), The Marginal External Cost of Urban Transport, Transportation Research D, 1, 2, 111-130.

Mohring H. (1972), Optimization and Scale Economies in Urban Bus Transportation, American Economic Review, 591-604

Ochelen S./Proost S./Van Dender K. (1998), Optimal Pricing for Urban Road Transport Externalities, Center for Economic Studies Discussion Paper Series, 98.26, Leuven

OECD (1996), The OECD Observer - OECD in Figures - Statistics on Member Countries, OECD-ADOBE

O'Mahony M./Kirwan K./McGrath, S. (1997). Modelling the Internalisation of External Costs of Transport, Transportation Research Record, 1576, 93-98.

Small K.A. (1992), Urban Transport Economics, Harwood Academic Publishers.

Snow A./Warren R. S. (1996), The Marginal Welfare Cost of Public Funds: Theory and Estimates, Journal of Public Economics, 61, 289-305

PART III

PRICING STRATEGIES AND SUSTAINABLE MOBILITY

Goal Driven Design of a Sustainable Transport System

Wolfgang Schade, Werner Rothengatter, Astrid Gühnemann, Karsten Kuchenbecker

IWW - Institut für Wirtschaftspolitik und Wirtschaftsforschung
University of Karlsruhe, Kollegium am Schloß, Bau IV, 76128 Karlsruhe
Germany

Abstract. The paper describes and summarises the results of a research project[1] focussing on the development of a methodology to design a sustainable transport system. In the project a goal driven procedure for planning an environmentally sustainable transport system as part of the federal transport infrastructure planning in Germany has been developed. To demonstrate the feasibility of the procedure, it has been applied in a case study for Baden-Württemberg, a federal state in the south-western part of Germany.

The foundation of the new concept is the political definition of environmental goals that are aimed at achieving sustainability. Transport policy scenarios are designed that include various regulatory policy measures as well as infrastructure measures for all transport modes. Afterwards, the transport system is evaluated in terms of its environmental effects. This evaluation is undertaken on network level with consideration of multimodal effects. This procedure is repeated until one of the scenarios achieves the given environmental goals. If several scenarios fulfil the goals, a subsequent evaluation procedure will be carried out, which aspires to find the economically optimal scenario.

The environmentally sustainable scenario is used to calculate shadow prices for the achievement of the environmental goals. This is done by evaluating the cost of those measures that are necessary to change the development of the environmental effects within the trend scenario towards the achievement of the environmentally sustainable scenario.

The results of the case study have demonstrated that a multimodal and network-wide assessment of the environmental impacts of transport infrastructure plans

---

1 The project was undertaken on behalf of the German federal environmental agency (Umweltbundesamt) by the project partners IWW, Karlsruhe; ifeu, Heidelberg; Kessel+Partner, Freiburg; PÖU, Hannover; PTV, Karlsruhe (IWW et al. 1998).

and projects is possible. This allows for an integration of environmental regards into the early stages of the transport planning procedure.

1 Introduction

At present, the project proposals for the German federal transport infrastructure plan (Bundesverkehrswegeplan = BVWP) are assessed by means of a cost-benefit analysis (CBA), which includes the evaluation of several environmental effects (BMV 1992). Supplementary, for certain projects an ecological risk analysis is performed to assess spatial impacts on nature and biodiversity. Its results add to the decision-making in the form of qualitative statements.

However, some weak points of the present planning process can be stated with regard to a comprehensive and early consideration of the environmental impacts associated with the implementation of the infrastructure plan: the projects are neither assessed as a network nor in comparison to the other transport modes, there is no systematic integration of the results from the ecological risk analysis, the list of impacts evaluated in the CBA is incomplete, local impacts are weighted much higher than global effects, and the monetary values used in the CBA partly do not correspond with recent research results.

Therefore, the research project presented here has been designed to overcome these shortcomings by introducing new concepts for a network level assessment that is interlinked with project oriented CBA. In the first part of the project, approaches for the enhancement of the monetary evaluation of environmental effects as part of the BVWP have been developed. In the second part, a goal driven procedure for the design of environmentally sustainable transport plans has been developed that allows for an evaluation of the environmental impacts of transport in a multimodal and network based integrative assessment at an early stage of transport planning. The third part of the project deals with a case study for Baden-Württemberg to demonstrate the feasibility of the goal driven procedure and to receive first results for shadow prices of the applied environmental goals, which can be used in project appraisal (IWW et al. 1998).

2 Enhancing the Monetary Evaluation of Environmental Impacts within the BVWP

In the research project monetary evaluation approaches have been developed for environmental impacts, which are not included in the present economic assessment for the federal transport infrastructure plan and which are not yet analysed in supplementary studies for the federal ministry of transport.[2] These comprise the following effects:

- Tropospheric ozone,
- carcinogenic pollutants,
- additional anthropogenic greenhouse effect,
- outdoor noise by transport and
- effects on nature and landscape.

For some of the impacts new methodologies have been developed and applied. For others it is suggested to assess them according to state-of-the-art cost values and practices. In the case of tropospheric ozone, carcinogenic pollutants and outdoor noise the results are achieved with direct cost evaluation methods. For gaseous emissions the resulting cost values are presented in Table 1.

Table 1: Cost values to enhance the current monetary evaluation of the BVWP

Gaseous Emission	Evaluation Methodology	Cost Value	Unit of Measurement
NO_x	Damage costs for human health and vegetation	320 (1990) 406 (2010)	DM per ton
VOC	Damage costs for human health and vegetation	320 (1990) 525 (2010)	DM per ton
Benzene	Unit risk considering mortality and effected population	100	DM per ton per mio inhabitants
Particulates	Unit risk considering mortality and effected population	1750	DM per ton per mio inhabitants
CO_2	Avoidance cost for long-term reduction (2050) of CO_2 emissions	400	DM per ton

In the case of nature and landscape the assessment of projects for the federal transport plan should include the evaluation of specific aspects of nature and landscape based on social conventions on the desired state of the natural environment. Three complementary environmental approaches can be derived from this central requirement:

1. Avoidance cost approach: A monetary valuation of avoiding impairments on designated areas can be based on the costs of project alternatives or variants,

2 The actual assessment procedure for the German federal transport infrastructure plan is described in a report from the German ministry of transport (BMV 1993).

which bypasses the area, respectively on the additional costs for technical avoidance or abatement measures.

2. Compensation cost approach: I.e. the translation of the requirement for the compensation respectively substitution of functions which are lost by the utilisation of ground through the construction of transport infrastructure. This leads to costs for the acquisition of areas, primary reconditioning of an area for specific biotope types, necessary (re-)cultivation measures and costs due to the loss of ecological functions over a limited time period.

3. De-sealing cost approach: This requirement means that in future no additional areas are to be sealed by the construction of transport infrastructure. This implies de-sealing of sealed areas if new sealing happens because of new construction of infrastructure. Corresponding cost values have been specified for different types of infrastructure.

and

3 Basic Methodology of the Goal Driven Approach

The environmental effects of traffic can reach levels above which unpredictable risks arise for human health and life or for the existence of natural habitats. Environmental quality goals are stated to limit environmental impacts to values below such levels. If these goals are exceeded, the direct valuation by damage costs or willingness to pay approaches is no longer appropriate. It is therefore necessary to supplement the direct valuation method by an approach that - in the case of established target values and when translated into prices - is capable of influencing traffic behaviour in such a way that the exceeding of target values is avoided. Such a methodology has been developed with the goal driven approach.

Methodologies applied for environmental assessment should consider the severity of risks that are pursued by human activities like transport. If irreversible damages may occur, it is recommended to apply a strict precautionary principle, which is accomplished by fixing environmental targets and determining measures that are necessary to meet these targets. This principle is covered in the proposed goal driven procedure for the development of environmentally sustainable transport plans.

The starting point of the goal driven methodology are environmental targets for critical environmental effects (see Figure 1). On this basis, scenarios for different sets of transport policy measures (transport policy scenarios) are designed in such a way that the environmental targets are fulfilled. The scenarios consist of infrastructure measures as well as regulatory policy measures.

After the definition of transport policy scenarios, these have to be operationalised for a multi-modal transport forecast and a prognosis of local, regional and global environmental impacts. Based on the results, it has to be assessed whether the environmental targets are reached by means of the assumed measures. If not, the transport policy scenarios have to be modified and re-assessed until an environmentally favourable scenario is found. If more than one transport policy scenario fulfils this criterion of environmental validity, it is possible - by applying economic evaluation models - to determine the scenario that is economically most efficient. In this manner, an environmentally sustainable transport plan can be developed that outlines, next to the infrastructure projects, those complementary policy measures that are necessary to comply with environmental goals.

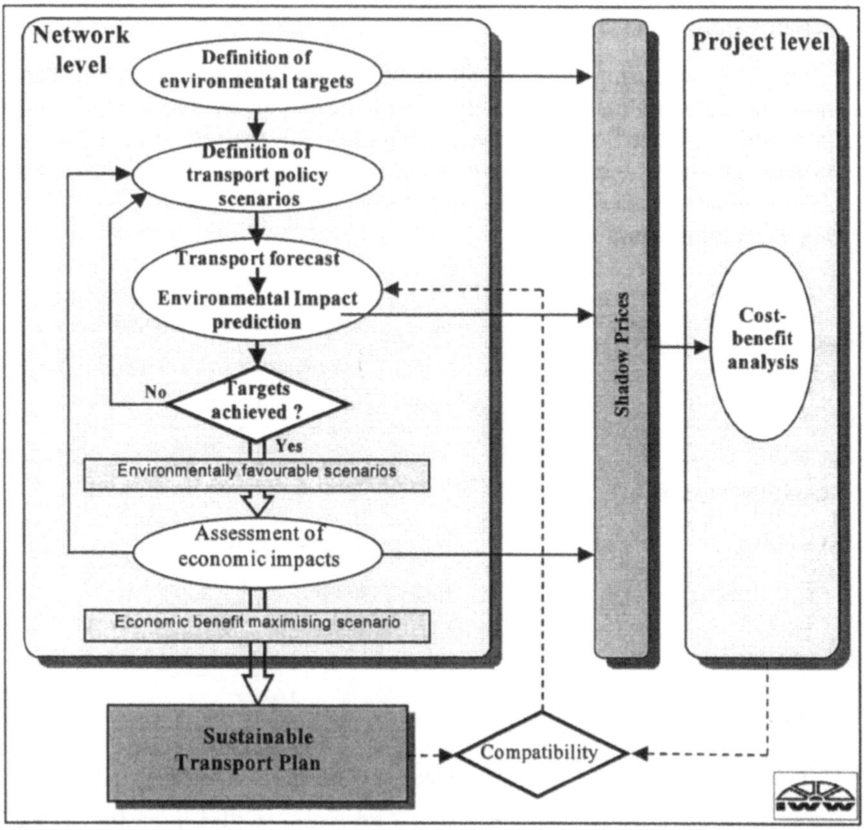

Figure 1: Methodology for the design of environmentally sustainable transport plans

For the design of transport infrastructure plans a large number of project proposals has to be evaluated as a basis for the necessary investment decision. Because of the huge amount of potential combinations of measures it is not possible to assess each possible combination of projects on the network level under the assumption of complementary measures. Therefore, the single projects can subsequently be evaluated in a cost-benefit analysis, applying so-called shadow prices, which are derived from the optimal transport policy scenario. By the use of the shadow prices the assessment results received on the network level can be integrated into assessments on the project level (see also Chapter 3.2).

3.1 Deriving Shadow Prices with a Linear Programme

The derivation of shadow prices can be achieved by calculating solutions of a linear programme with a target function that maximises benefits under consideration of constraints that might represent budget or resource constraints (GÜHNEMANN/ROTHENGATTER 1998).

The whole infrastructure plan should maximise the economic benefits. These benefits are given by the target function z with the sum of the specific benefits of all activities multiplied by their usage intensities. But the resources, which are needed to undertake activities, are restricted, which is reflected by the constraints.

Benefit maximisation:

$$\max \rightarrow \quad z = \sum_j u_j x_j$$

j:	activity $j = 1, \ldots, n$
x_j:	usage intensity of activity j
u_j:	specific benefit of activity j
z:	total benefit (output)

Resource constraints:

subject to

$$\sum_j r_{ij} x_j \le R_i$$

$$x_j \ge 0$$

e.g. for CO_2

$$\sum_{j=allmodes} ef_{CO_2,j} x_j \le 0.2 * CO_{2Emission1990}$$

i:	resource $i = 1, \ldots, k$
r_{ij}:	resource input per unit j
R_i:	availability of resource i
$ef_{CO_2,j}$:	emission factor for CO_2 [g per km]
x_j:	distance travelled in modes j in the target year [km]

As shown above, the constraints could represent the restrictions given by the environmental goals. E.g. for carbon dioxide we have the example constraint that the quantity of emissions in the target year are restricted to 20% of the emission level in the base year 1990. By solving the linear programme, an optimal value for the total benefits z is achieved with the given intensities x_{jo} for the activities j. Now we could intensify the restriction for one resource, for instance lower the restriction R_i for CO_2 by one ton within the corresponding constraint. The other restrictions are treated ceteris paribus. Then we receive a different solution for the linear programme. The difference represents the shadow price of one ton CO_2 emissions. Since the benefits are expressed in monetary units, we can create a direct translation mechanism from tons of emissions used within the resource constraint into monetary units used in the benefit maximisation function.

Because of complexity of the transport models and the environmental models it would only have been possible to operationalise the models within a linear programme with a major loss of detailed information. Therefore, this theoretically convincing approach of deriving shadow prices for environmental goals and their effects could not be applied. Instead, a simplified methodology was developed, which is explained within the description of the case study (see Chapter 4.6).

3.2 Linking Direct Costs and Shadow Prices

As mentioned above, the currently applied project-oriented assessment and the proposed network level assessment are linked by the use of shadow prices for the economic evaluation at the project level. For the economic evaluation of environmental effects, composed cost functions are developed (see Figure 2). They consist of two parts. In the first part, if environmental burdens are below the environmental goals, cost values derived from direct cost evaluation methods are applied (see Chapter 2). For this part of the cost function it can be argued that environmental damages and economic benefits are substitutional. For the second part, if environmental burdens exceed the environmental goals, cost values according to the shadow prices are applied. For this part of the cost function it is argued that environmental damages that violate the environmental goals are not negotiable because they are in conflict with a sustainable development.

A further argument for the use of composed cost functions is that the residual risk, which is remaining even if an environmental target is met, can be considered. For instance, if the target value for particulate matter is not overrun, the shadow price for particulate matter would be zero. But also below the target, these emissions might cause damages, which have to be evaluated within the cost-benefit analysis. Therefore, below the environmental targets the cost values determined by direct evaluation method are applied (see Table 1).

The next reason to use cost functions is that the sensitivity for environmental impacts varies in space for local impacts. Therefore, for these impacts cost functions are applied, which consider the spatial difference by differentiated cost values.

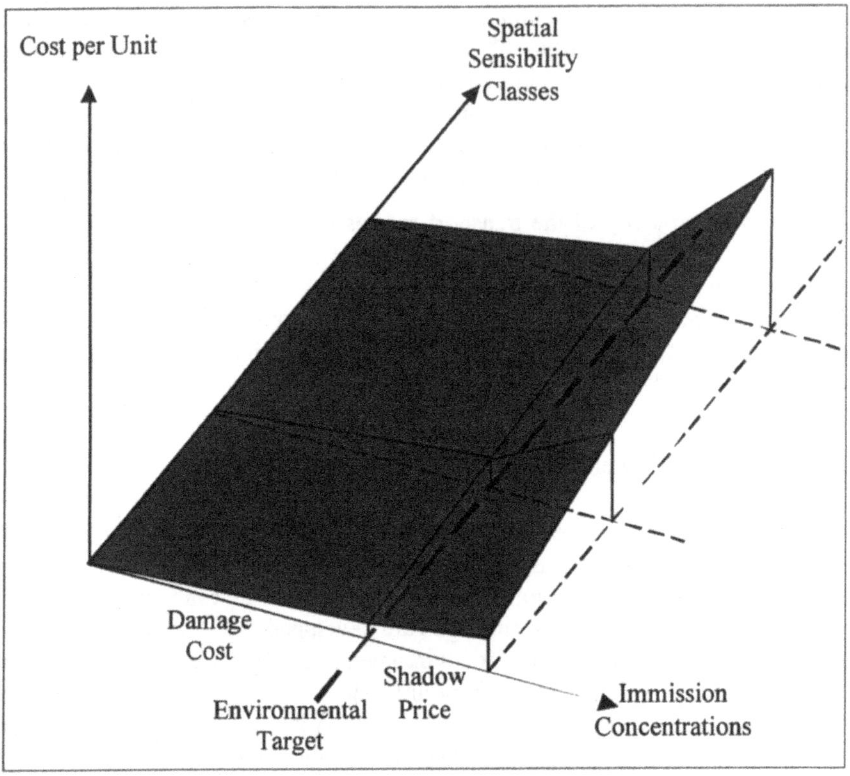

Figure 2: Linking damage costs and shadow prices: the composed cost function

4 Application of the Goal Driven Procedure in a Case Study

The feasibility of the developed procedure has been shown in the project through its application in a case study for the transport networks of the German federal state of Baden-Württemberg. For the forecast of environmental effects, some new development was necessary for the modelling of local effects of transport for a complete network. In the following the necessary steps of the applied models are briefly explained, and the results of the modelling are presented.

4.1 Definition of Environmental Targets

The objective of the design of environmentally oriented transport plans is to contribute to the formation of a sustainable transport system. To achieve this, the concept of sustainability has to be transformed into a set of measurable indicators to describe the state of the environment, and into target values to assess the development of these indicators. The following requirements have to be met by the operationalisation of the environmental goals:

- spatial differentiation,
- differentiation by transport modes,
- definition of reference levels e.g. relating to a certain base year,
- necessity of consistency of the environmental goals with regard to the severity and reversibility of the environmental impacts.

Table 2 summarises the indicators and corresponding environmental targets used in the project. The proposed environmental targets have been derived from lists of environmental criteria for sustainable development published by the German federal environmental agency (UBA 1997). These values represent safe minimum standards to prevent irreversible environmental damage.

Table 2: Indicators and target values for environmental impacts

Environmental Impact	Indicator	Environmental Target 1992 - 2010
Global warming	CO_2 emissions in transport	-30%
Tropospheric ozone	transport related emissions of	
	NO_x	-80%
	VOC	-70%
Atmospheric pollution	ambient concentration of	
	benzene	≤ 2.5 μg/m³
	particulate matter	≤ 1.5 μg/m³
Noise	daytime level for noise exposure of inhabitants	≤ 65 dB(A)
Nature protection	further fragmentation of protected areas	not allowed
	further sealing	not allowed

4.2 Definition of Transport Policy Scenarios

A crucial point in the development of environmentally sustainable transport plans is the selection and combination of transport policy measures. Not only the environmental, but also economic and social needs for an efficient transport system have to be taken into consideration. The selection of measures in this project refers to a catalogue of transport related measures which was compiled by the UBA (UBA 1997). The strength and direction of the effects expected by the application of particular measures is estimated in a first qualitative assessment on the basis of experiences from other projects (IVT, IWW et al. 1995).

After assembling promising measures to a catalogue (called "*framework scenario*") this has to be operationalised, and the impacts analysed by means of the transport and environmental models. In view of the results from the impact analysis it might be necessary to either 'adapt' particular measures within one framework scenario or to design a new framework scenario with a different combination of policy measures.

For the case study within this project three different transport policy scenarios have been set up next to a base scenario 1992 and a trend scenario 2010: a scenario based on the H'-scenario from the latest German federal transport plan and two framework scenarios. The focus of framework scenario 1 (*FS1*) lies on regulatory policy instruments (e.g. stricter speed limits) that aim at a forced introduction of technological developments. Technological measures amongst others refer to emission reduction technologies and a decrease in average fuel consumption for car fleet to $5\ ^{l}/_{100km}$ gasoline resp. $4\ ^{l}/_{100km}$ diesel. Additionally, measures influencing the private costs of transport participants are assumed.

Framework scenario 2 (*FS2*) is based on the results and experience gained in FS1. Certain measures with only little influence on the impacts or with too strong effects have been removed from the catalogue of FS1, or have been conceptually modified. Furthermore, it was necessary to take further measures to reach the fulfilment of the environmental targets. Besides a reduced infrastructure extension, several measures are taken in FS2 that influence the transport behaviour.

4.3 Transport Forecast

The transport forecast model uses a systems approach. The transport forecasts for passenger and freight traffic have been performed multi-modally by means of models already applied in the German federal transport infrastructure planning. Basis of the forecasts have been the transport demand matrices set up for the BVWP'92. The project partners used detailed network models for the modes road, rail, air and inland waterway transport. In contrast to federal transport infrastructure planning, the spatial differentiation has been refined (121 districts corresponding to NUTS-IV regions in Baden-Württemberg), induced traffic was explicitly taken into account, and the traffic data are directly linked to the environmental data via a grid model (5x5 km^2 squares).

On this basis, the influence of the determining factors of transport on the key transport variables e.g. traffic volume has been predicted in a multistage process. For this research project it was important that the applied models are capable of mapping the changes in transport caused by the assumed measures and to provide data for the succeeding forecast of environmental impacts in the necessary accuracy and differentiation. Results of the transport models are shown in Figure 3.

4.4 Forecast of Environmental Impacts[3]

The baseline for the environmental models are the traffic loads on the transport networks resulting from the transport models (see Figure 3). For the modelling of local and regional environmental impacts the environmental burdens by other sources and the characteristics of the affected regions play an important role besides the variables of the transport activities. In a net-wide analysis it is necessary to describe this spatial data with an accuracy that is adequate for the level of federal infrastructure planning. In this project the observed region has been overlaid with a grid using a resolution of 5x5 km^2, whose elements were assigned specific region types based on the analysis of individual indicators e.g. population density, share of nature reserves. The traffic loads resulting from the transport forecast can also be assigned directly to the grid elements via the digitised transport networks. For each grid element, subsequently the environmental impacts have been determined on the basis of the traffic loads and the regional characteristics, and have been compared to the environmental goals.

3 The presented figures have been taken from IWW et al. (1998) and GÜHNEMANN (1998) as well as a detailed description of the applied transport models and environmental models can be found within those two references.

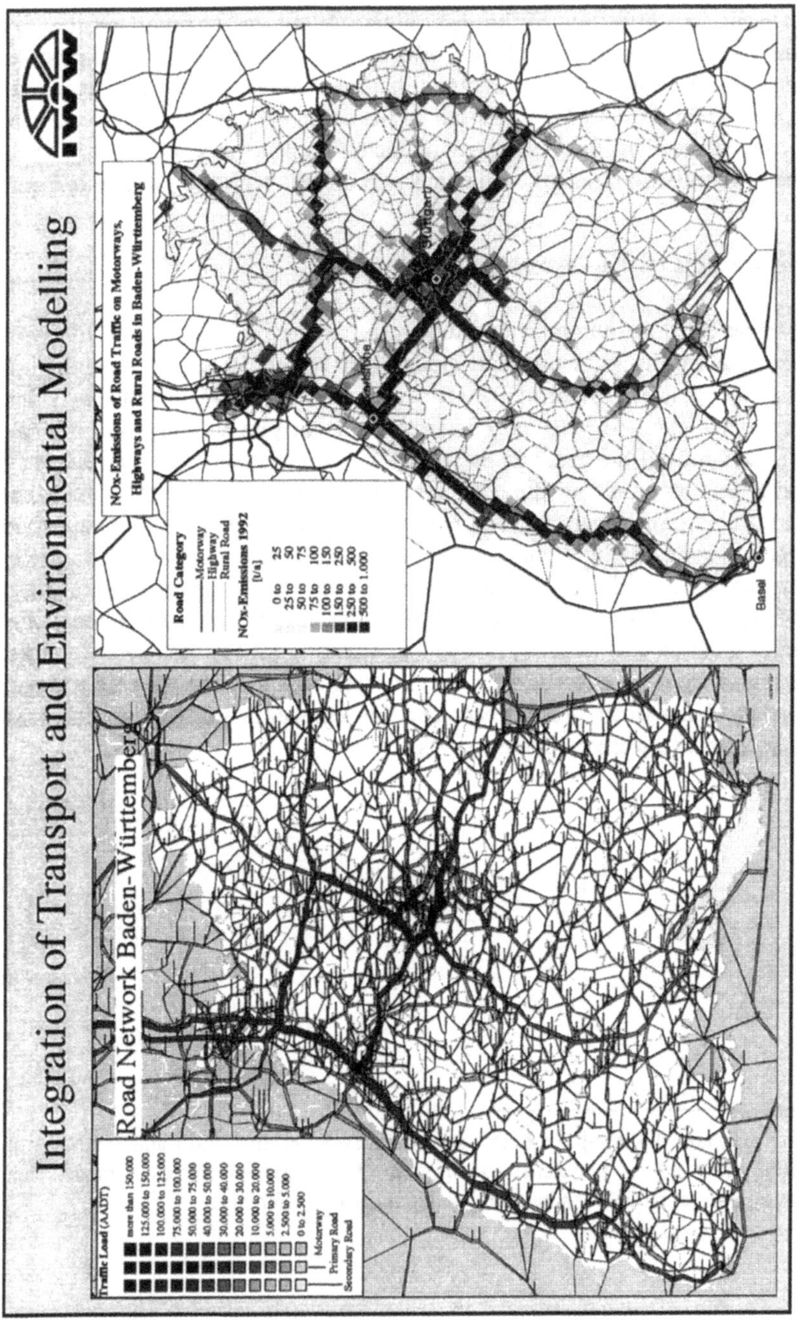

Figure 3: Traffic loads and NO_X-emissions of road traffic in Baden-Württemberg

4.4.1 Gaseous Emissions

The emission factors needed for the calculation of transport emissions[4] have been determined in this project for road and rail transport using the program TREMOD (IFEU 1997) that has been developed on behalf of the German Environmental Protection Agency (Umweltbundesamt). The following differentiation for the emission factors has been applied for road traffic: 6 air pollutants, 2 kinds of fuels, 4 vehicle categories, 4 road categories, 3 congestion classes and 3 gradient classes. By linking the emission factors and the traffic loads the road transport emissions have been calculated for each network segment. These again could be aggregated by grid elements (see Figure 3) or regions. Supplementary the emissions of road vehicles during the cold start phase play an important role especially in urban areas. These have been specified for cars and light-duty vehicles and added to the emission for urban traffic. The evaporative VOC-emissions are estimated in relation to the population densities and distributed across the grid squares.

The basis for the calculation of rail transport emissions are average energy consumption values specified for different train categories. Emission factors have been determined for the direct emissions from diesel engines, and for the emissions of power generation related to rail transport. In the field of inland waterway transport four types of ships with different dead-weight tonnage have been considered. For these the gaseous emissions have been determined via the fuel consumption for different driving situations and via emission factors related to the consumption of fuels.

As a result it can be stated that the dominant emissions of road traffic can be cut down considerably by modal shifts to rail transport and by technical measures. A level of emissions is reached such that with FS2 a transport plan has been found that achieves the pre-set environmental target levels in most points regarding the transport emissions.

4.4.2 Ambient Air Quality

Since the environmental impacts of carcinogenic air pollutants are a local problem, the target values for benzene and diesel particulates are given as concentration values. Therefore, a model to predict ambient air quality has been developed. The concentrations of air pollutants have been modelled separately for background concentration and the excess concentrations due to transport activities. On the level of federal transport planning detailed dispersion models had to be excluded from choice because of the high data volume and data processing requirements. The excess concentrations by road transport in rural areas have been cal-

---

4 The emissions from production, maintenance and disposal are not considered in the project apart emissions from fuel production.

culated according to MLuS-92 (FGSV 1996). In urban areas a simplified approach using typical housing structures has been applied based on a model developed by Lohmeyer (HEUSCH/BOESEFELDT 1997). The background concentration was given for different types of regions and has been extrapolated according to the development of emissions until the year 2010. By the reduction of air pollutant concentrations that has been achieved in the framework scenarios, it can be accomplished that the target value of 1.5 µg/m³ for particulates (see Figure 4) and 2.5 µg/m3 for benzene is reached in most of the regarded grid areas.

Those areas remaining in FS2 where supplementary measures to improve ambient air quality have to be taken are the city centres and central urban areas. In these areas, the background pollution by the subordinate network and other sources already contributes with a high share to the concentrations reached.

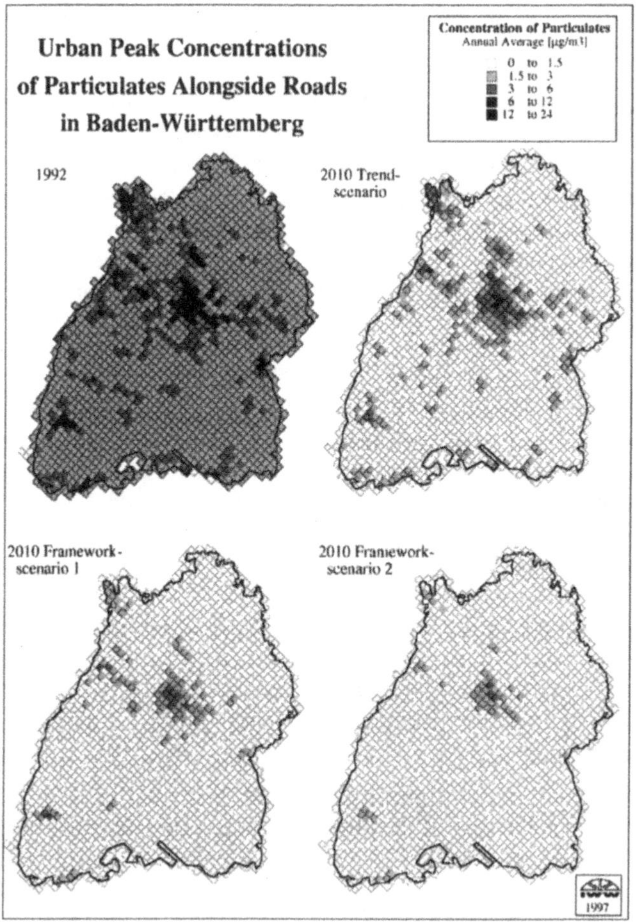

Figure 4: Concentrations of particulates in the different scenarios

4.4.3 Noise

Due to the variety of local influencing parameters, the modelling of noise disturbances can only be performed on the network level by the use of screening models. To predict noise disturbances by road transport, in a first step the reference noise level along roads is calculated based on the traffic load according to the noise protection manual for roads in Germany: RLS-90 (BMV 1992). The number of inhabitants that are exposed to noise above a certain level is then determined via the application of typical housing structures in accordance to the revised methodology of the federal transport planning (HEUSCH/BOESEFELDT 1997). In addition, noise disturbances by rural traffic have been modelled, too. In the case of rail transport the modelling of noise alongside tracks is based on a model provided in the German noise legislation (16. BImSchV). Subsequently, for each network section a corridor is determined within which a defined noise level is exceeded, and by using the population densities the number of affected inhabitants is calculated. The target noise level has been set to 65 dB(A) at daytime.

The results from the case study reveal that in the base year 1992 about 10% of the population in Baden-Württemberg is exposed to road transport noise and about 2% to rail transport noise above 65 dB(A) at daytime. In many areas the noise exposure due to road transport can be reduced below the aspired target value by the measures taken in FS2. The increase of rail traffic in FS1 and FS2 brings about a higher noise exposure along certain railway sections (see Figure 5). In FS2 these noise impacts are partly compensated by an improved equipment of trains.

4.4.4 Impacts on Nature and Landscape

The impacts of the transport infrastructure on nature and landscape can forecast on the network level by using indicators that express an environmental risk. Such indicators are the land take by the networks, the segmentation of conservation areas and the relevance of infrastructure construction for exclusion areas. The first two indicators can be derived by overlaying the transport networks with the spatial data. By the abandonment of constructing new roads with a low expected traffic density in FS2 it is possible to reduce the impacts by ground sealing and segmentation of areas compared to the other scenarios.

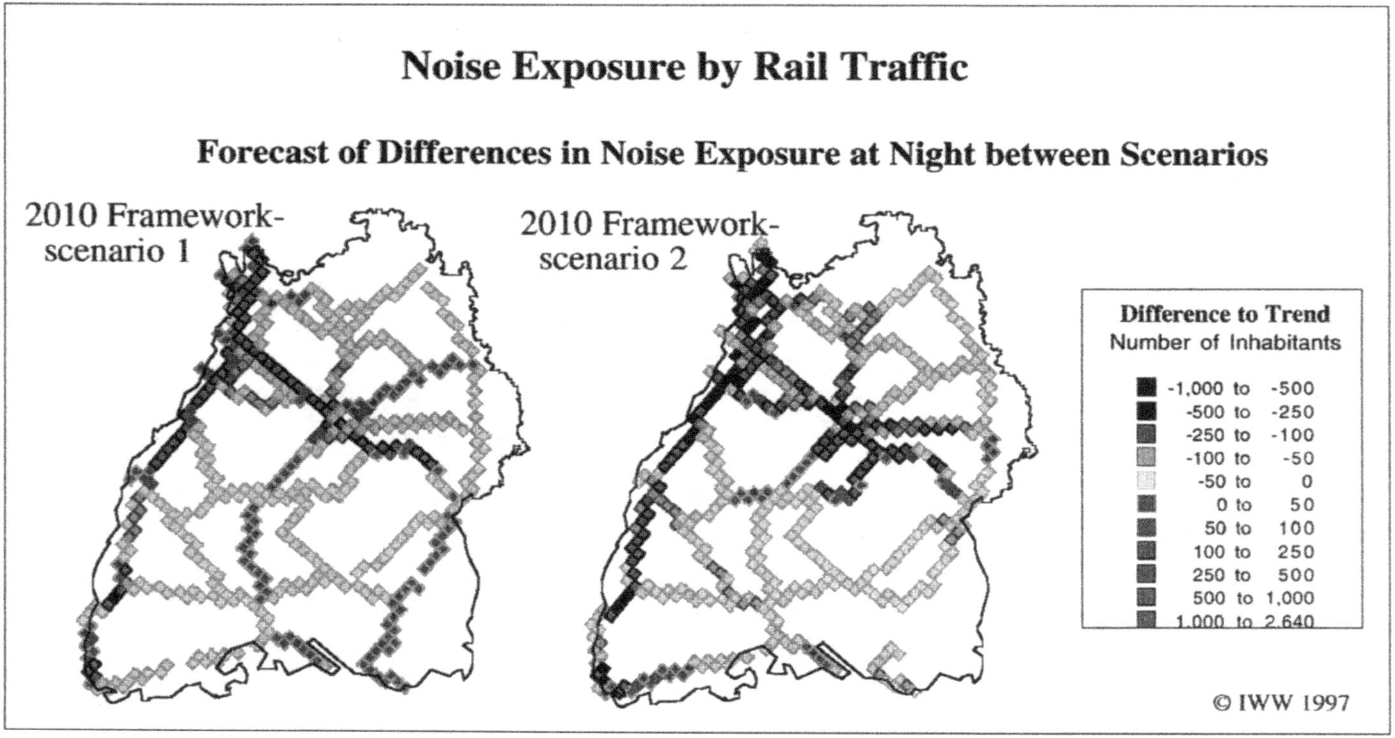

Figure 5: Differences in affected inhabitants by rail transport noise over 65 dB(A) in Baden-Württemberg

Land take in areas of high environmental relevance shall be avoided in the earliest possible stage of transport planning by the definition of exclusion areas (UBA 1997) in which further infrastructure construction is not allowed. Such exclusion areas should be at least all areas that are protected by international, national or regional legislation. To show the feasibility of the procedure, in this project the nature protection areas of Baden-Württemberg have been used. For each grid square the proportion of nature protection areas on the total area has been calculated. If this proportion lies above a defined value a considerable risk for impacts on the protected area by infrastructure construction can be assumed. By overlaying the transport networks with grid elements accordingly classified it was possible to identify those new infrastructure projects for which a high risk of land take in exclusion areas can be already stated on the network level (see Figure 6).

Subsequently, it has been calculated how high the costs would be for avoiding these risks by bypassing the areas in the case of new construction, or by supplementary mitigation measures in the case of upgrading infrastructure. In the example of Baden-Württemberg, this leads to additional infrastructure investment and operation costs of 80 mio DM/year in FS1, that can be reduced to 40 mio DM/year in FS2.

4.5 Economic Evaluation

Once transport policy scenarios have been found which fulfil the environmental targets, the economic assessment takes place, which concentrates on those effects that describe the economic efficiency in the narrower sense, and which comprise changes in operating costs, infrastructure costs, travel time costs and accident costs. The quantification of these costs can be performed by means of standardised assessment methods as applied in German transport infrastructure planning (BMV 1993). Additionally, costs due to changes in the mobility behaviour have been evaluated in monetary terms (see Figure 7). The cost increase in FS2 compared to FS1 turns out to be quite moderate. The cause for this is that the set-up for FS2 aimed at reducing the economical shortcomings by the assumed measures.

4.6 Simplified Methodology for Deriving Shadow Prices

The scenario costs presented in Figure 7 are the base for the calculation of shadow prices. Instead of applying a linear programme as described in Chapter 3.1 a simplified methodology was developed to distribute the cost to the different environmental targets. The result are the shadow prices for the achievement of the environmental targets (see Figure 8).

In the described methodology the costs of global measures have been assigned to the air pollutants. The goal of bypassing exclusion areas and the noise effects have been handled separately because in these cases local measures are necessary.

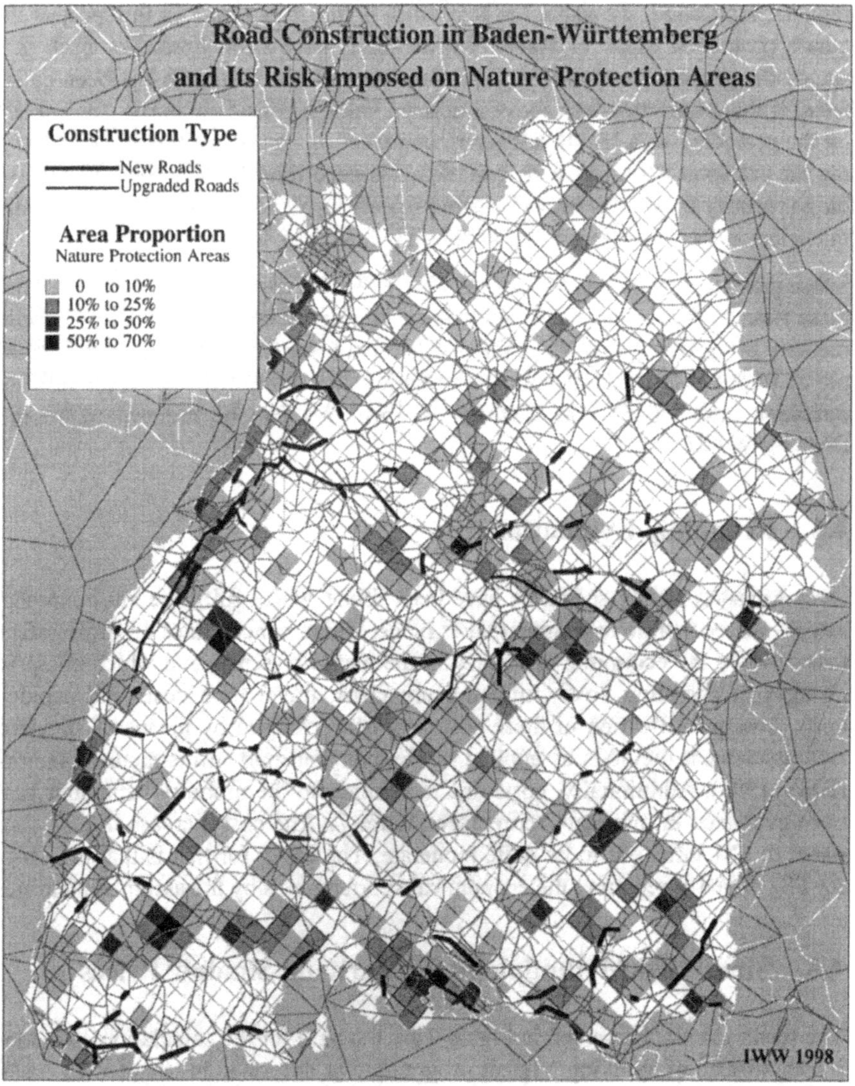

Figure 6: Risk for effects on nature and landscape by new infrastructure projects

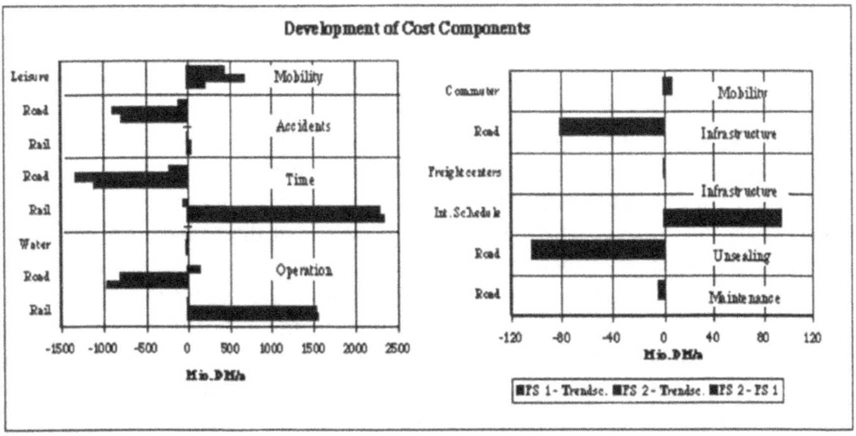

Figure 7: Development of cost components between the scenarios (Trend, FS1, FS2)

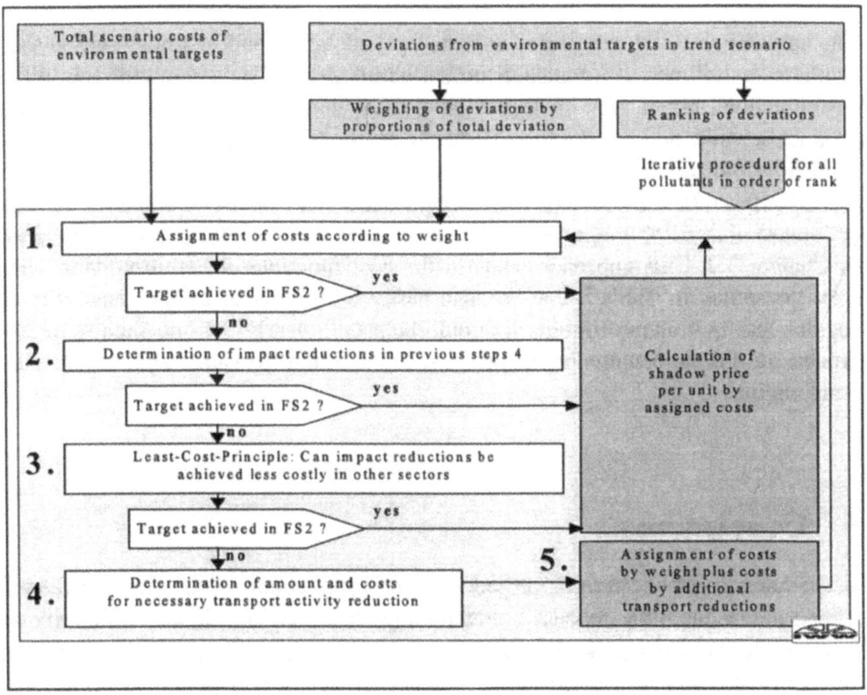

Figure 8: Simplified methodology for the determination of shadow prices

If the environmental target for a pollutant is already achieved in the trend scenario, no further measures have to be taken for the reduction of this particular environmental impact. The shadow price equals zero. For all other impacts the following procedure has been applied: In the first step, the proportional deviation between the results of the trend scenario and the target values were calculated for each impact. The impacts were then weighted and ranked in the following procedure according to this deviation. In the following steps, the target exceedings were assessed for the impacts separately, and in the order of their ranks. Following the least-cost principle, additional measures were assumed until the target value for the regarded impact has been met. In the first step, the scenario costs were assigned to the air pollutants proportional to their weights. In the second step, the effects of measures taken for the reduction of previously regarded impacts have to be considered. In step 3 it has to be evaluated whether the specific impact can be lowered with less costs in a different sector, e.g. power generation. If the previous measures were not sufficient to reach the target fulfilment, additional measures were necessary in step 4 that directly reduce the transport activity of the transport participants, and which were also monetarily valued. From this procedure the cost values listed in Table 3 result for the assessment of individual projects.

The application of the simplified approach to calculate shadow prices can be substantiated as follows: If a transport infrastructure project leads to a violation of an environmental target, new measures have to be taken on various levels to again produce a valid policy scenario. These measures lower the economic benefit of the whole transport plan by a certain amount - the shadow price of the environmental impact. The direct and indirect approaches are linked to consider the risk of impacts that still remains below the defined environmental targets as described in Chapter 3.2. This approach leads to the cost functions for environmental impacts presented in Table 3 that are also partly differentiated by the sensitivity of regions and by transport mode. It should be stated clearly that the shadow prices depend on the environmental targets, on the selected measures and on the analysed region.

5 Conclusions

In the context of the research project for the improvement of the German federal infrastructure planning process a methodology has been developed, which allows to integrate the assessment of environmental impacts into the planning process at an early stage and in a multi-modal manner. Hence, a transport investment plan can be designed that corresponds to the requirements of environmental sustainability, and at the same time improves the economic and spatial functionality of the transport system.

Table 3: Cost functions for the evaluation on project level e.g. within a CBA

Environmental Impact	Spatial and Modal Differentiation			Cost function	Unit of Measurement
CO_2	global			400	DM/ton
NO_x	global			17.850	DM/ton
VOC	global			525	DM/ton
Particles	projects in grid squares, within which the target values of 1.5 $\mu g/m^3$ is achieved in the trend scenario			1.750	DM/(ton inner-urban emissions * mio inhabitants)
	projects in grid squares, within which the target values of 1.5 $\mu g/m^3$ is achieved in FS2 first			2.550	
	projects in grid squares, within which the target values of 1.5 $\mu g/m^3$ is exceeded in FS2			4.050	
Benzene	projects in grid squares, within which the target values of 2.5 $\mu g/m^3$ is achieved in the trend scenario			100	DM/(ton inner-urban emissions * mio inhabitants)
	projects in grid squares, within which the target values of 2.5 $\mu g/m^3$ is achieved in FS2 first			2.000	
Noise	less than 67 dB(A)	road	Motorways	41	DM p. inhabitant
			rural roads	41	affected of noise
			urban roads	41	above 65 dB(A)
		rail		4.420	
	less than 70 dB(A)	road	motorways	109	
			rural roads	109	
			urban roads	109	
		rail		9.665	
	above 70 dB(A)	road	motorways	2.321	
			rural roads	3.656	
			urban roads	5.324	
		rail		20.680	

The proposed approach has the advantage that not only scenarios can be assessed and compared regarding their environmental effects, but that at least one transport policy scenario has to be explicitly designed, which is in accordance with established environmental policy goals. By the application of the shadow prices, which are derived from the optimal transport policy scenario on network level, a harmonisation of the aspired environmental targets and the cost values used in project appraisal is achieved. Simply spoken, the major difference between the former forecasting approach of federal infrastructure planning and the goal driven approach is: in forecasting approaches the infrastructure plan is the *input* of the assessment procedure while in goal driven approaches the infrastructure plan is the *output* of the assessment procedure.

An essential part of the methodology is the setting of environmental standards. For this, it is appropriate that the values proposed by the responsible decision-makers are derived in co-operation with national and international bodies and panels of experts to obtain environmentally *and* socially acceptable goals.

In view of the current developments for strategic environmental assessment (SEA), i.e. the environmental assessment of policies, plans and programmes, the results from this research project can provide an important contribution with respect to methodological aspects. It has been shown that for the assessment of the environmental impacts of transport plans appropriate models are available, that allow for a multi-modal evaluation of the global, regional and local impacts of policy measures. Based on these findings it seems adequate to analyse the present assessment procedure of the German federal transport infrastructure planning before its re-edition in the next millennium, and to revise it thoroughly with regard to environmental protection and spatial planning.

References

BMV (Bundesminister für Verkehr) (Hrsg.) (1992): „Richtlinien für den Lärmschutz an Straßen“ (english: “Guidelines for Noise Protection alongside Roads”), Ausgabe 1990 (RLS - 90), berichtigter Neudruck. Bonn.

BMV (Bundesminister für Verkehr) (1993): „Gesamtwirtschaftliche Bewertung von Verkehrswegeinvestitionen - Bewertungsverfahren für den Bundesverkehrswegeplan 1992“ (english: “Assessment of Transport Infrastructure Investments on a National Economic Basis - Assessment Methods for the Federal Transport Infrastructure Plan 1992”), Schriftenreihe des BMV, Heft 72, Bonn.

FGSV (Forschungsgesellschaft für Straßen- und Verkehrswesen) (1996): „Merkblatt über Luftverunreinigungen an Straßen – Teil: Straßen ohne oder mit lockerer Randbebauung“ (MLuS 1992) (english: “Leaflet on Air Pollution by Road Transport - Part: Roads in Medium-Density or High-Density Populated Areas”), Ausgabe 1992, geänderte Fassung 1996.

Gühnemann, A. (1998): “Methods for Strategic Environmental Assessment of Transport Infrastructure Plans”, dissertation thesis, Karlsruhe.

Gühnemann, A./Rothengatter, W. (1998): „Strategic Environmental Assessment of Transport Infrastructure Investments”, paper presented on the WCTR 1998 in Antwerpes, Karlsruhe.

Heusch/Boesefeldt (1997): „Ergänzung und Aktualisierung der Verfahren zur Bewertung von Fernstraßenprojekten für die Bundesverkehrswegeplanung“ (english: “Completion and Updating of Assessment Methods of Motorway Projects for Federal Transport Infrastructure Planning”), Schlußbericht, Im Auftrag des Bundesministeriums für Verkehr, Aachen.

IFEU (1997): „Daten- und Rechenmodell, Energieverbrauch und Schadstoffemissionen aus dem motorisierten Verkehr in Deutschland 1980 bis 2020“ (english: “Data- and Arithmetical Model, Energy Use and Emissions of the Motorised Transport in Germany from 1980 until 2020”), Heidelberg.

IVT, IWW et al. (1995): „Wissenschaftliche Begleituntersuchungen zum Generalverkehrsplan Baden-Würt.“ (english: “Accompanying Scientific Examinations on the Transport Master Plan of Baden-Württemberg”), mehrbändig, Karlsruhe.

IWW/IFEU/K+P/PÖU/PTV (1998): “Entwicklung eines Verfahrens zur Aufstellung umweltorientierter Fernverkehrskonzepte als Beitrag zur Bundesverkehrswegeplanung” (english: “Development of a Procedure for the Design of Environmentally Sustainable Transport Plans as a Contribution to Federal Transport Infrastructure Planning”), Schlußbericht vom März 1998, im Auftrag des Umweltbundesamtes (F+E Vorhaben 10506001), Karlsruhe.

UBA (1997) Umweltbundesamt, Abteilung Umwelt und Verkehr: „Maßnahmenplan Umwelt und Verkehr-Ein Konzept für eine nachhaltig umweltverträgliche Verkehrsentwicklung in der Bundesrepublik Deutschland“ (english: “Action Plan, Environment and Traffic - Concept for the Development of Environmentally Sustainable Transport”), Berlin.

Distance-Based Vehicle Insurance - A Practical Strategy for More Optimal Vehicle Pricing

Todd Litman

Victoria Transport Policy Institute
1250 Rudlin Street, Victoria, BC, V8V 3R7, Canada

Abstract. Automobile insurance premiums are currently a fixed cost with regard to annual vehicle mileage. Distance-based insurance would be more equitable and economically efficient, providing a number of specific benefits including increased road safety, reduced traffic congestion and pollution, road and parking facility cost savings, insurance affordability, and increased consumer welfare. This paper discusses different distance-based pricing strategies, and evaluates the benefits that would result from their implementation. Per-Mile Premiums is found to provide the greatest benefits. This means that the exposure unit is changed from the vehicle-year to the vehicle-mile or -kilometer. Other rating factors are incorporated into this price unit, so higher-risk vehicles are charged more per mile than lower-risk vehicles. This strategy requires "odometer audits" to provide accurate mileage data. The incremental cost of such audits is estimated to be about $7.50 per vehicle year. Total benefits are predicted to be many times greater.

Keywords. *Vehicle insurance, transportation demand management (TDM), equity, affordability, traffic safety, consumer welfare*

1 Introduction

What would be the consequences if gasoline were sold like automobile insurance?

With gasoline sold by the car-year, vehicle owners would make one annual advance payment that allows them to draw gasoline unrestricted at their fuel company's stations. Each vehicle's fuel price would be calculated based on the average cost of supplying gasoline to vehicles with similar user profiles. This would cause problems similar to those occurring with automobile insurance.

Unmetered fuel would encourage increased driving. Some drivers who minimize their vehicle use would simply drop out of the system because their costs are unrealistically high per-mile. This would cause a spiral of increased fuel consumption and higher costs per vehicle. Of course, above average fuel users would object to any change in this system because of the benefits they enjoy. This price structure would increase everybody's costs, encourage inefficient travel patterns, and leave some users (particularly low-income drivers) without realistic travel options.

There is growing interest in using pricing instruments to address various transport problems. Although most discussion of optimal pricing focuses on internalizing externalities (EC, 1997), converting appropriate fixed costs into variable costs provides benefits of equal magnitude (Litman, 1998a). When all costs are considered (including non-market costs such as users' travel time and environmental impacts), about a third of automobile costs are external, and almost a quarter are internal but fixed, as illustrated in Figure 1.

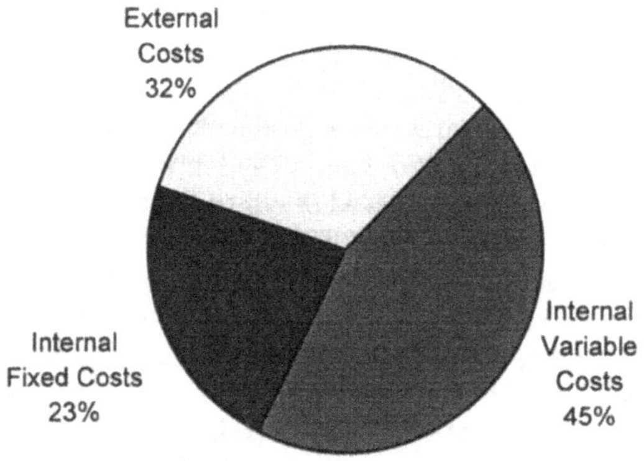

Figure 1: Distribution of automobile costs (Litman, 1998b)

Figure 2 shows the average distribution of motor vehicle expenses (financial costs). Most are considered fixed with respect to vehicle travel. This price structure encourages excessive driving since vehicle owners perceive minimal savings when they reduce their mileage.

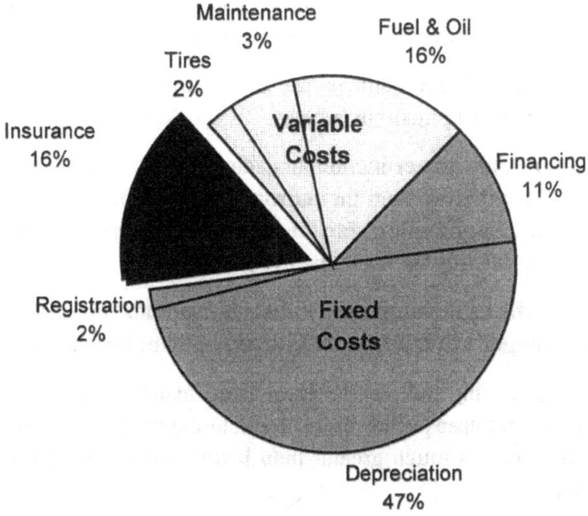

Figure 2: Typical financial costs of an intermediate size car (Litman, 1998b)

Variable costs as a portion of total costs have declined significantly over the last several decades, as indicated in Figure 3.

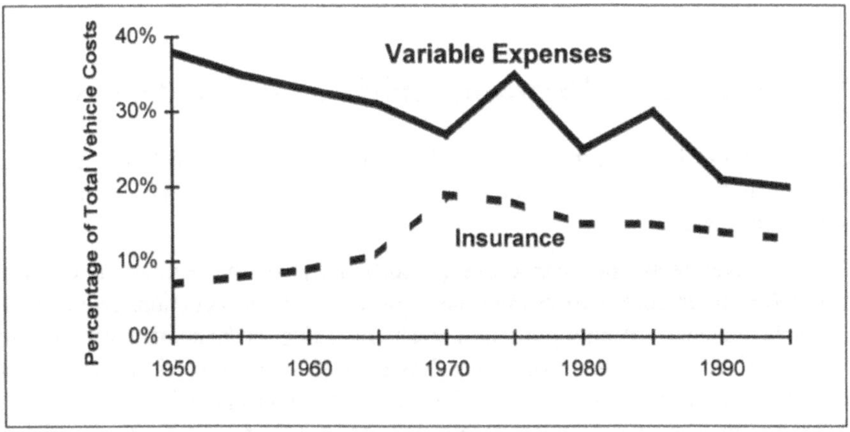

Figure 3: Variable costs as a portion of total costs (MVMA 1995, p. 58)

Current insurance pricing does not effectively represent marginal crash costs (Vickrey, 1998). This creates a number of problems:

- It is economically inefficient. It fails to convey to drivers the true costs they impose, and deprives drivers of a chance to save money by avoiding costs.
- It is unfair. Low-mileage vehicles are overcharged and high mileage vehicles undercharged their true insurance costs.
- It is regressive, since lower income households tend to drive their vehicles less than average. It violates even the narrowest definition of vertical equity: poor households are charged more for the same good (per-mile vehicle insurance) on average than wealthy households.
- To provide "affordable" unlimited-mileage insurance coverage, low-risk drivers are overcharged while higher-risk drivers are undercharged their true costs.
- The excessive driving that results from fixed insurance pricing (about 10% of vehicle travel) increases other motor vehicle externalities. Thus, the total economic inefficiency is much greater than just the direct distortions in the insurance market.

Distance-based pricing converts insurance from a fixed cost into a variable cost with respect to vehicle travel. This "marginalizes" crash compensation costs, making premiums more actuarially accurate. It provides a positive financial incentive to reduce mileage by returning to individual vehicle owners a greater share of the insurance cost savings that result when they drive less. These insurance savings are currently dispersed among all vehicles in a rate class.

2 Relationship Between Vehicle Travel and Crashes

Common sense indicates that a vehicle's crash risk is related to how much it is driven. All else being equal, increased driving increases crash risk (CAS, 1996, p. 35; Bath, 1993).

Vehicle travel reductions can cause proportionally *larger* declines in crashes. About 70% of crashes involve multiple vehicles, so travel reductions reduce both a vehicle's chances of both *causing* a crash and *being hit by* another vehicle. An average driver is culpable (at-fault) in less than 50% of the crashes they are involved in. As a result, a 10% reduction in a driver's chance of *causing* crashes reduces total insurance claims by only 5%, but a 10% reduction in a vehicle's travel reduces that vehicle's claim rate by 10%, and total claims by up to 17%, since it reduces risks to other road users.

Low-mileage vehicles as a group tend to have higher crash rates per mile than higher-mileage vehicles for the following reasons (Janke, 1991):

- People with specific high-risk attributes related to age and physical disability are over-represented in the lowest vehicle-mileage categories, while high-mileage drivers are likely to self-select to be relatively capable drivers.
- Newer, mechanically safer vehicles tend to be driven more each year than older vehicles.
- Urban drivers tend to have higher crash rates and lower annual vehicle-mileages.
- High vehicle-mileage drivers tend to do a greater share of their travel on safer, grade-separated highways.
- There may also be other types of offsetting behaviors, by which higher-mileage drivers take more precautions to limit their risk.

However, differences in crash rates *between* high- and low-mileage drivers does not indicate changes in crash rates that would occur from changes in average vehicle travel, since most risk factors (such as those listed above) are held constant. Although some vehicles may average one crash every 50,000 miles, and others every 500,000 miles, a reduction in an individual vehicle's mileage can be expected to provide a proportional reduction in crashes, rather than shifting them into a different risk category.

In the past, insurers and other road safety experts actually had little information on the relationship between individual vehicles' annual mileage and crash rates. Since 1993, motor vehicles in the Greater Vancouver region have been required to undergo "AirCare" emission tests prior to their annual registration. More than 1 million vehicle-years of odometer readings have been recorded. These odometer readings have been matched to the insurance claim records of specific vehicles, providing a unique database of the relationship between crashes and claims. Figure 4 shows their distribution by annual kilometre category.

Figure 5 illustrates the crash rates for these vehicles. It shows that both culpable and non-culpable crashes tend to increase with vehicle use in the most common annual-kilometre ranges (0-40,000 km/yr).[1]

---

1 The low crash rates in the 50,000+ kilometre category is believed to result, in part, from data errors.

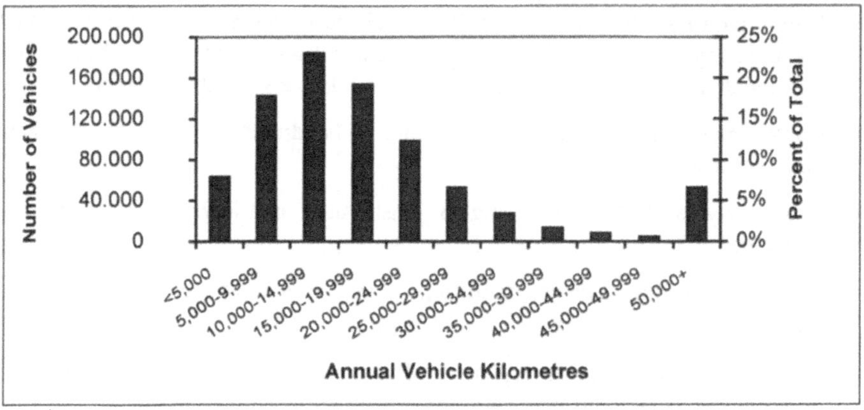

Figure 4: Distribution of annual vehicle kilometres (ICBC, 1998)

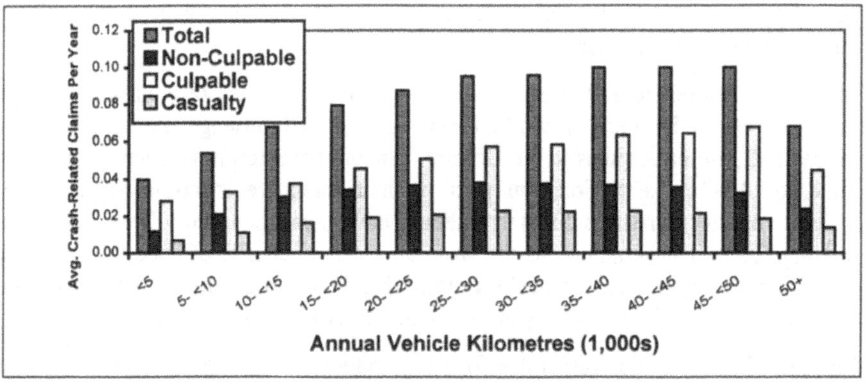

Figure 5: Crash rates by annual vehicle-mileages (ICBC, 1998)

Figure 6 shows the crash rates for various major categories. Figure 7 illustrates crash rates for "RoadStar" rate classes. In nearly all cases crash rates increase with annual vehicle mileage.

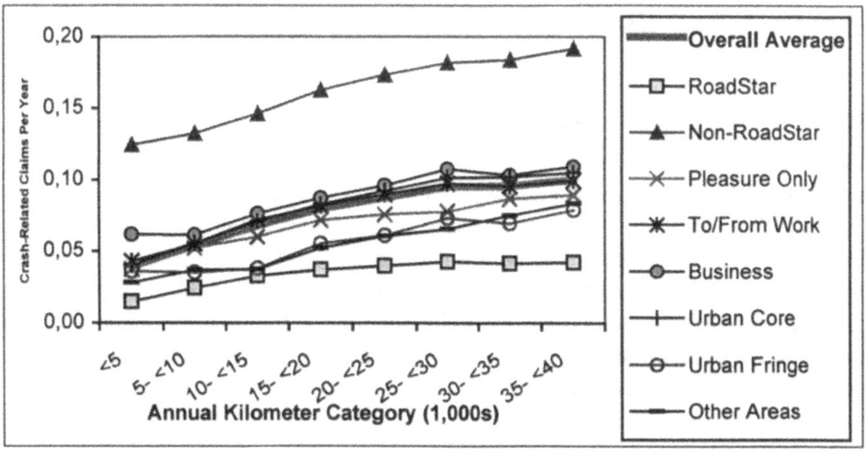

Figure 6: Crashes per year by major category (ICBC, 1998)[2]

The evaluation by rate class indicates that distance-based pricing is essential for actuarial accurate pricing. Lower-mileage vehicles are currently subsidizing the insurance costs of higher-mileage vehicles within their rate (price) class.

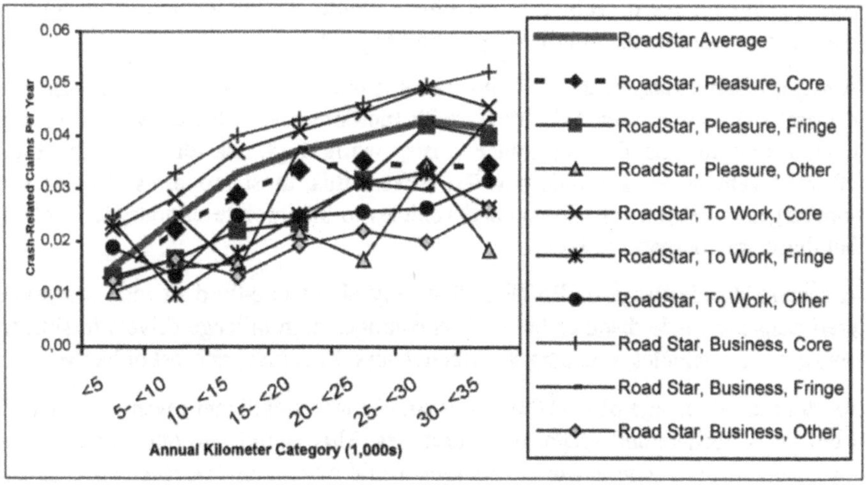

Figure 7: Crashes per year for selected rate classes (ICBC, 1998)

2 RoadStar refers to vehicles with at least nine continuous years without a culpable claim

3 Distance-Based Insurance Pricing Options

3.1 Mileage Rate Factor (MRF)

Vehicle insurance could become more distance-based by placing greater weight on mileage in existing rate structures, based on premium payers' self-reported estimates of their future travel (Hundstad, Bernstein and Turem, 1994). However, vehicle owners cannot predict with certainty how many miles they will drive, and they tend to underestimate their annual mileage if given a financial incentive. As a result, Mileage Rate Factor is inaccurate and can only apply a portion of the actuarially justified weight on mileage.

3.2 Pay-at-the-Pump (PATP)

Pay-at-the-pump uses a surcharge on fuel sales to fund basic insurance coverage (Tobias, 1993; Sugarman, 1993; Wenzel, 1995). Proposed fuel surcharge range from 15-50¢ per gallon, depending on the level of coverage. Collision and comprehensive coverage, alternative fuel vehicles (including diesel), and coverage for driving in other jurisdictions would require insurance purchased as it is now. Various administrative systems have been proposed for PATP. Some would establish government-operated insurance companies, others have insurance companies bid on blocks of vehicles, and others would distribute funds to insurance companies based on the number of policies they sell.

A major disadvantage with PATP insurance is that it does not directly incorporate drivers' risk factor. Low-risk drivers with fuel-intensive vehicles would overpay their actuarially-justified insurance costs, while high-risk drivers with fuel-efficient vehicles would underpay. To address this, most proposals also include surcharges on higher-risk drivers and vehicles to incorporate various risk factors, but these are not distance-based.

A second disadvantage of PATP is that only about one-third of total insurance premiums are made distance-based. It encourages high mileage drivers to shift to non-gasoline vehicles, reducing its effectiveness for achieving most objectives.

Another disadvantage of PATP it that it could cause significant revenue "leakage" from cross-borders and illegal fuel purchases. This would introduce a new inequity, since drivers who evade the charges would have their insurance costs subsidized by drivers who pay them.

PATP provides universal liability coverage (at least for gasoline vehicles) which makes it attractive in jurisdictions with high rates of uninsured driving. However, there are other ways to address this problem. For example, less than 1% of insurance claims involve uninsured vehicles in British Columbia due to the successful integration of vehicle insurance and licensing transactions (vehicle owners must pay for insurance to obtain license tabs). Distance-based insurance reduces the cause of uninsured motoring by making insurance more affordable. More insurance revenue would be lost through fuel surcharge evasion than would be recovered from uninsured motorists in most jurisdictions.

3.3 Per-Mile Premiums (PMP)

This strategy means that vehicle insurance is sold by the vehicle-mile or –kilometer rather than the vehicle-year (Butler, 1992; Litman, 1997). Other rating factors are incorporated into this price unit, so higher-risk vehicles would be charged more per mile than would lower-risk vehicles. Table 1 shows an example of this price structure.

Table 1: Per-mile premiums for selected rate classes

	Pleasure Use, Urban Core	Pleasure Use, Urban Fringe	To Work, Urban Core	To Work, Urban Fringe	Business Use, Urban Core	Business Use, Urban Fringe
RoadStar	$0.020	$0.016	$0.027	$0.016	$0.026	$0.017
Non-RoadStar	$0.125	$0.094	$0.111	$0.087	$0.108	$0.088

Per-Mile Premiums requires "odometer auditing" to collect accurate vehicle-mileage data. Odometer audits would be performed when a vehicle's insurance is renewed, in most cases once a year. Odometer audits involve five steps:

1. Check speedometer and instrument cluster for indications of tampering.
2. Record tire size and check that it is within the specified range.
3. Attach a small seal to the ends of mechanical odometer cables to indicate if it is removed. This is unnecessary on most newer vehicles that have electronic speedometers.
4. Check odometer accuracy and calibrate with a dynamometer. This step is optional, or could be performed on a spot-check basis.
5. Record odometer reading and forward results to the vehicle licensing agency.

Odometer audits typically require 5 to 10 minutes, or less if performed with other vehicle servicing, with incremental cost of $5 to $10 (assuming chargeout rates of $60 per hour). Governments would certify odometer auditors and incorporate odometer data into the vehicle registration database. Odometer auditing certification programs could be self-supporting through fees. Odometer auditors would typically be existing vehicle service stations and emission inspection stations, and some insurance agencies might become certified as a marketing strategy.

Most odometer fraud could be detected through this auditing, either through physical evidence or by discrepancies in readings. Odometer audit should provide data comparable in accuracy to what is used in other typical commercial transactions, and far more accurate than self-reported information currently used by insurance companies. Odometer auditing would create significant additional benefits. Used vehicle buyers could obtain accurate mileage histories, and transport planners could use the data for modeling. Other vehicle charges could become distance-based at little extra cost. It would be particularly easy to prorate vehicle registration fees, which average about $130 per vehicle year in the U.S.

4 Comparison of Distance-Based Insurance Options

4.1 Actuarial Accuracy

Actuarial accuracy requires pricing that incorporates mileage and other risk factors. Both Mileage Rate Factor and PATP are significantly constrained in their ability to accurately price crash risk. Mileage Rate Factor is constrained by the weight that can be placed on mileage before self-reported estimates of future travel are unacceptably understated. PATP is constrained because it uses fuel consumption as a surrogate for vehicle travel and then incorporates rating factors through fixed (not distance-related) surcharges on vehicle registration fees and drivers' licenses, resulting in a trade-off between actuarial accuracy and distance-related pricing.

Per-Mile Premiums is unconstrained in incorporating risk factors. Nearly any rating factor can be incorporated into the vehicle-mile price unit. It is inherently more actuarially accurate than the alternative pricing strategies.

4.2 Implementation Costs

Mileage Rate Factor using self-reported estimates of future travel has the lowest implementation costs, but costs would increase to gather more accurate data. PATP would have moderate to high transition costs, since it requires establishing a new system to fund basic insurance. It could reduce some administrative costs for vehicles with only basic insurance, but most drivers would need additional coverage, resulting in little overall savings.

Per-Mile Premiums requires a new rate plan and an odometer auditing system. The majority (85-95%) of audits would probably be performed with other scheduled servicing with an estimated incremental cost of $5 per vehicle year, while a minority (5-15%) would pay a $10 fee, plus another $10 in travel and time costs, resulting in an average incremental cost of about $7.50 per vehicle year.

4.3 Travel Impacts

Distance-based insurance pricing provides vehicle owners with a new opportunity to save money by reducing their driving. The magnitude of these savings varies, from an average of about 0.9¢ per mile for Mileage Rate Factor, to 1.8¢ per mile for PATP, up to about 5¢ per mile for Per-Mile Premiums, or 6¢ if registration fees are also prorated. This increase in potential savings effectively increases the variable cost of driving (offset by a reduction in fixed costs) as indicated in figure 8.

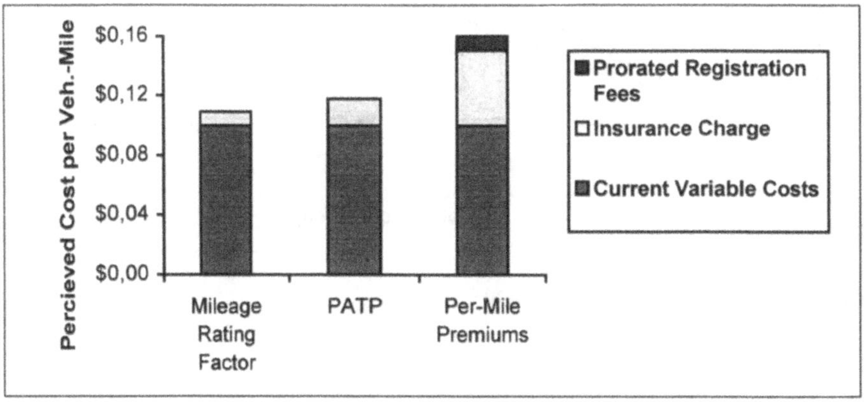

Figure 8: Distance-based insurance impacts on variable vehicle costs

Figure 9 illustrates how the strategies increase the perceived variable cost of driving.

There is abundant empirical evidence that pricing effects travel (Oum, Waters and Yong, 1992; Johansson and Schipper, 1997). Consumers consolidate trips, shift modes, change destinations, and foregoing lower-value trips in response to financial incentives.

Distance-based insurance could lead to slightly increased vehicle ownership since it reduces fixed costs. However, vehicle travel would probably not increase significantly. Most additional vehicles are likely to be second vehicles, such as an old truck or a collector car. These would substitute for, rather than add to, existing travel. Only drivers who purchase their first vehicle due to reduced fixed insurance costs would increase vehicle travel, and their annual mileage should be low otherwise they would experience no savings. As a result, increases in vehicle travel are likely to be overwhelmed by reductions in travel among existing vehicle owners.

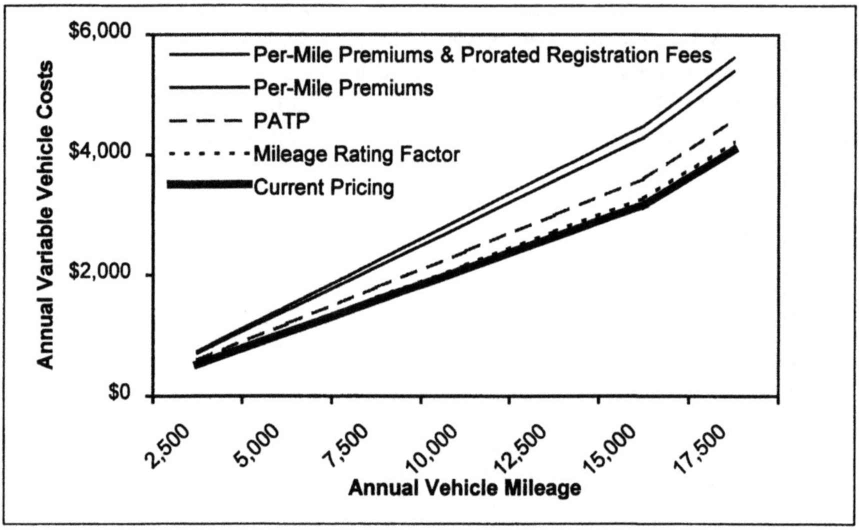

Figure 9: Variable costs compared

Some people suggest that Per-Mile Premiums may have little impact on travel because payments are infrequent, resulting in many months separating an individual trip decision and its incremental insurance cost. However, these charges involving hundreds of dollars per year, and therefore highly visible to consumers. In a similar pricing situation, there is little evidence that households using oil or wood fuel purchased annually are less motivated to conserve heat than homeowners using gas or electric heat which is paid monthly or bi-monthly. Most drivers are likely to respond to this financial incentive, although perhaps somewhat less than a more frequent fee.

Using standard elasticity values, such as those in Table 2, the travel impacts of these price changes can be estimated, as summarized in Table 3.

Table 2: Travel reductions estimates (Deakin and Greig Harvey, 1997)

Mileage Fee	Vehicle Travel Reduction	Mileage Fee	Vehicle Travel Reduction
1¢	-2.3%	6¢	-12.6%
2¢	-4.5%	7¢	-14.5%
3¢	-6.6%	8¢	-16.3%
4¢	-8.7%	9¢	-18.0%
5¢	-10.7%	10¢	-19.7%

Table 3: Predicted travel impacts

	MRF	PATP	PMP	PMP & Prorated Registration Fees
Increased variable cost	9%	18%	50%	60%
Travel reduction	1%	6%	10%	12.5%
Avg. annual per-vehicle miles reduced	120	720	1,200	1,500

4.4 Crashes and Crash Costs

Distance-based pricing can reduce vehicle crashes at least as much as vehicle travel declines, and probably somewhat more, as discussed earlier. Mileage Rate Factor should reduce crashes by only about 1%. PATP should reduce crashes about 6%. Per-Mile Premiums should reduce vehicle travel by about 10% and provide an extra incentive for higher-risk drivers to reduce their vehicle use, resulting in by far the greatest reductions in crashes and associated costs.

4.5 Energy and Emission

Mileage Rate Factor would provide little reduction in energy consumption or emissions. PATP would reduce fuel consumption, and fuel related emissions such as CO_2, by up to 15% (depending on fuel switching and fuel sale "leakages"), but other emissions (such as NOx and particulates) would decline by smaller amounts. Per-Mile Premiums would reduce energy consumption and all emissions by 10-12%.

4.6 Congestion and Facility Cost Savings

Reductions in vehicle travel tend to reduce traffic congestion, and road and parking facility costs. Mileage Rate Factor would provide little benefit. PATP would reduce vehicle travel by about 6%, providing modest benefits. Per-Mile Premiums would reduce travel by 10-12%, and therefore provides the greatest benefits.

4.7 Consumer Benefits and Costs

Distance-based insurance allows consumers to purchase just the amount of crash risk they can afford, rather than providing an all-or-nothing price option. Any vehicle travel foregone as a response to distance-based pricing represents consumers' lowest value trips that they willingly give up in response to their additional financial savings.

Figure 10 shows how total costs vary under the different pricing strategies. None have a great impact on *total* costs since insurance is just one of many vehicle expenses.

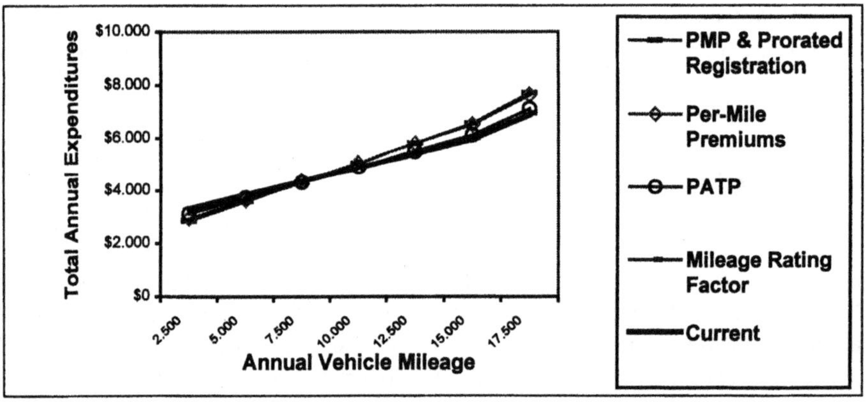

Figure 10: Comparison of total costs by annual mileage

Most consumers would save money with Distance-Based Insurance. Even high-mileage vehicle owners who pay more for *insurance* would save on average in *total vehicle costs* because they drive less in response to this new opportunity to save money. For example, vehicles currently driven 15,000 miles annually are predicted to reduce their mileage to about 13,500 on average under Per-Mile Premiums (a 10% reduction), resulting in net financial saving of $75 or more. The true "cost" is therefore the reduced consumer surplus from 1,500 miles of marginal (low value) vehicle travel foregone.

4.8 Equity

Current insurance pricing is unfair (horizontally inequitable) since premiums are not actuarially accurate, and regressive (vertically inequitable) since lower income households tend to drive less than average and so overpay compared with higher income households. Mileage Rate Factor provides small equity benefits. PATP replaces one type of inequity (overcharging low vehicle-mileage drivers in each rate class) with other inequities: overcharging lower-risk drivers with fuel inefficient vehicles who do not have access to untaxed fuel. Per-Mile Premiums is most equitable because it accurately reflects crash costs and provides the greatest savings to lower income households.

4.9 Affordability

Distance-based insurance increases affordability by allowing consumers to purchase just as much accident risk as they can afford. This reduces the need for distortive cross-subsidies in current pricing that are justified to provide "affordable" unlimited-mileage insurance even to high-risk drivers. Mileage Rate Factor converts only a small portion of fixed costs to variable costs and so provides minimal affordability benefits. PATP provides moderate benefits since about two-thirds of insurance costs would still be fixed. Per-Mile Premiums shifts the most fixed costs to variable charges and so offers the greatest affordability benefits.

4.10 Economic Efficiency, Productivity and Development

Distance-based insurance directly increases economic efficiency by making prices more accurately reflect marginal costs. It can also increase economic productivity indirectly by reducing motor vehicle externalities (congestion, crashes, roadway costs, pollution, etc.) and by shifting consumer expenditures away from petroleum to goods that have greater employment generation.

Mileage Rate Factor provides small economic benefits. PATP does not reflect marginal crash costs, and so does not increase economic efficiency directly, but moderately reduces vehicle externalities. However, PATP imposes significant economic costs to a particular jurisdiction by increasing cross-border and illegal fuel sales. Per-Mile Premiums provides the greatest economic benefits by most accurately reflecting marginal costs and providing the greatest reduction in vehicle externalities. Odometer auditing would provide additional economic benefits by creating data that can reduce odometer fraud, assist transport planning, and allow other vehicle fees to become distance-based.

4.11 Public Acceptability

One public opinion survey found a modest majority of support for distance-based insurance pricing as a TDM strategy (Viewpoints Research, 1995). Of the three options there was least support for PATP. Mileage Rate Factor may have the advantage that it requires the least change from current practices, but consumers may be uncomfortable with pricing that is based on unverified data. Public acceptance of Per-Mile Premiums appears to depend on policy makers' ability to demonstrate that incremental costs (including consumer inconvenience) are significantly smaller than benefits, and that it is equitable. If this can be done there is evidence that the public would accept this option.

5 Summary of Benefits

Table 4 evaluates the three strategies in terms of the eleven criteria. Mileage Rate Factor has the lowest implementation costs and ties for public acceptability. PATP ties for energy and emission reductions. Distance-Based Pricing is best for ten criteria.

Figure 11 summarizes estimated monetized benefits and costs in British Columbia. This analysis indicates that all three options provide benefits that exceed incremental costs. Per-Mile Premiums has the greatest net benefits, with an estimated Benefit/Cost ratio greater than 50. Any one of the five monetized benefits would justify the incremental costs of this strategy.

6 Conclusions

Distance-based insurance has many potential benefits: increased equity, reduced crashes, increased economic efficiency and productivity, increased consumer surplus and choice, insurance affordability, reduced traffic congestion, reduced road and parking facility costs, and reduced pollution. It takes a more rational approach to achieving insurance affordability by allowing consumers to purchase just as much accident risk as they can afford. This reduces the need for highly distortive cross-subsidies in current pricing to provide "affordable," unlimited vehicle-mileage insurance even to high-risk drivers.

Table 4: Summary of impacts (✓ = Best)

	Mileage Rate Factor	PATP	Per-Mile Premiums
Actuarial Accuracy			✓
Implementation Costs	✓		
Travel Impacts			✓
Crash Reduction			✓
Energy Use & Emission Reduction		✓	✓
Congestion & Facility Cost Savings			✓
Consumer Surplus			✓
Equity			✓
Affordability			✓
Economic Efficiency			✓
Public Acceptability	✓		✓
Total Bests	**2**	**1**	**10**

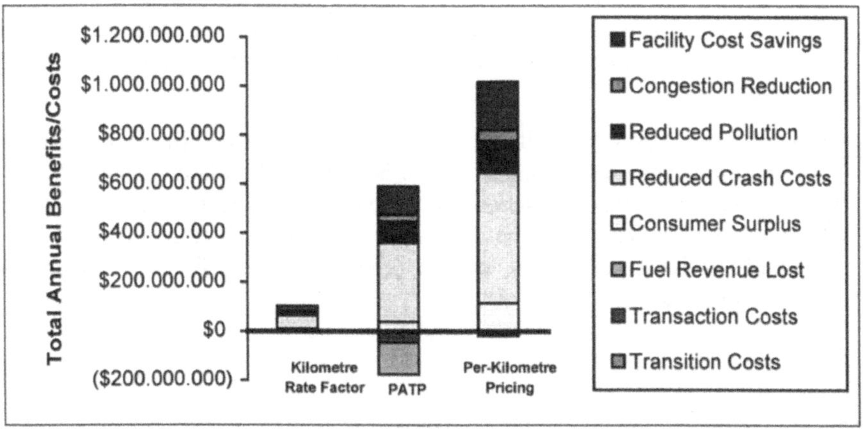

Figure 11 Summary of total benefits and costs

Of the three strategies considered:

- *Mileage Rate Factor* is easiest to implement but is highly constrained. Only a small portion of the actuarially accurate weight can be placed on mileage before self-reported estimates of future vehicle travel become unacceptably distorted.

- *Pay-at-the-Pump* is not actuarially accurate because payments are based on vehicle fuel efficiency, not risk factors. Only about a third of insurance payments would be distance-based, and cross-border and illegal fuel purchases could become major problems. It would cause the largest reduction in fuel consumption, but smaller vehicle travel reductions. PATP appears to be regressive. It would eliminate uninsured driving, but there are more effective ways to address this problem.

- *Per-Mile Premiums* is most actuarially accurate. Virtually any risk factor can be incorporated into this price structure. It is the most fair (horizontal equity) and would provide the greatest financial benefit to lower income households (vertical equity). It converts the greatest amount of fixed costs into variable costs, resulting in the greatest reduction in vehicle travel. This makes it most effective at achieving nearly all identified objectives. It is particularly effective at reducing vehicle crashes.

  This pricing strategy requires odometer auditing to provide data that is comparable in accuracy to that used in other common commercial transactions. By creating an accessible database of each vehicle's annual odometer readings, total odometer fraud should decline. The incremental cost of odometer auditing is predicted to average about $7.50 per vehicle year. This is about a quarter of the total incremental costs of current emission inspection programs, which provide only a fraction of the total benefits that Per-Kilometre Premiums could provide.

  Consumers appear to be willing to consider distance-based pricing, despite the fact that most have only a vague idea of how it could be implemented, excessive estimates of implementation costs, and underestimates of total benefits. Since it could provide net benefits to most households there seems to be considerable political potential if the full benefits can be effectively communicated to citizens.

References

Bath, Stephen. Influence of Socioeconomic Factors on the Exposure to Crash Risk for Young Drivers, Traffic Safety Research Dept., ICBC (North Vancouver), April 1993.

Butler, Patrick. Operation of an Audited-Mile/Year Automobile Insurance System Under Pennsylvania Law, National Organization for Women (Washington DC; www.now.org), 1992.

CAS. Foundations of Casualty Actuarial Science, 3rd Edition, Casualty Actuarial Society (Arlington; www.casact.org), 1996.

Deakin, Elizabeth and Greig Harvey, "The STEP Analysis Package," in Guidance on the Use of Market Mechanisms to Reduce Transportation Emissions, USEPA (Washington DC; www.epa.gov/omswww/market.htm) 1998, Appendix B.

EC, Towards Fair and Efficient Pricing In Transport, European Commission (Brussels; http://europa.eu.int/en/record/green/gp9512/ind_tran.htm), 1997.

Hundstad, Lyn, Robert Bernstein, and Jerry Turem. Impact Analysis of Weighting Auto Rating Factors to Comply with Proposition 103, California Dept. of Insurance (Sacramento), 1994.

ICBC. Various data. Insurance Corporation of British Columbia (Vancouver), 1998.

Janke, Mary. "Accidents, Mileage, and the Exaggeration of Risk," Accident Analysis and Prevention, Vol. 23, No. 3, 1991, pp. 183-188.

Johansson, Olof, and Lee Schipper, "Measuring the Long-Run Fuel Demand for Cars," Journal of Transport Economics and Policy, Vol. 31, No. 3, 1997.

Litman, Todd. "Distance Based Vehicle Insurance as a TDM Strategy," Transportation Quarterly, Vol. 51, No. 3, Summer 1997, pp. 119-138.

Litman, Todd. Socially Optimal Transport Prices and Markets, Victoria Transport Policy Institute (Victoria; www.islandnet.com/~litman), 1998a.

Litman, Todd. Transportation Cost Analysis; Techniques, Estimates and Implications, Victoria Transport Policy Institute (Victoria; www.islandnet.com/~litman), 1998b.

MVMA. Facts and Figures, Motor Vehicle Manufacturers Association (Detroit), 1995.

Oum, Tae Hoon, W.G. Waters II, and Jong-Say Yong, "Concepts of Price Elasticities of Transport Demand and Recent Empirical Estimates, Journal of Transport Economics, May 1992, pp. 139-154

Sugarman, Stephen. "Pay at the Pump" Auto Insurance, Institute of Government Studies Press (Berkeley), 1993.

Tobias, Andrew. Auto Insurance Alert, Fireside (New York), 1993

Vickrey, William. "Automobile Accidents, Tort Law, externalities, and Insurance: An Economist's Critique," Law and Contemporary Problems, 33, 1968, pp. 464-487.

Viewpoints Research. "A Comprehensive Overview of TDM Public Opinion Research," Greater Vancouver Regional District (Burnaby), 1995.

Wenzel, Tom. Analysis of National Pay-as-you-Drive Insurance Systems and other Variable Driving Charges, Energy & Environment Division, Lawrence Berkeley Laboratory (Berkeley), July 1995.

Wilde, Gerald. Target Risk, PDE Publications (Toronto), 1994.

Your Driving Costs; 1995-1996, Canadian Automobile Association (Ottawa; www.caa.ca), 1995.

Valuation of Road Pricing on Selected European Roads

Lionel Clement[1]

ISIS
4 Rue des Cuirassiers, 69 428 Lyon Cedex 03
France

Yves Crozet

Université Lyon 2, Laboratoire d'Economie des Transports, Lyon
France

Jean-Michel Gambard

ASFA, Paris
France

1 Introduction

In Europe roads carry 2,565.4 thousand million passengers-miles, and 741.3 thousand million tons-miles[2]. These figures are very close to the US figures (see table 1).

The continuous growth in social costs linked to the increase of traffic, led European policy makers to develop a strategy that corresponds to the payment of the infrastructure used.

For policy makers, pricing is only one instrument among others (others are: regulation, traffic control, infrastructure and land-use planning), but it has an important interest to adapt demand and supply from an economic and social point of view. This paper focuses only on one part of the social cost: external costs in the

1 Thanks to Monika Bauz for checking and English translation. Thanks to Büro Dr. HERRY and Heusch Boesefeldt for their case study.

2 A, B, CH, D, DK, E, F, FIN, GR, I, L, N, NL, S, TR, UK (CH and TR are not part of the CEC)

transport sector. Internal costs (for individuals and for the sector) are not taken into account.

Table 1: Road transport in Europe and in USA

	European Union (1996)	USA (1995)
Passenger (thousand Mio p-miles)	2,565.4	2,863.9
Freight (thousand Mio t-miles)	741.3	835.9

Source: EU, DGVII, Eurostat

Table 2: Road transport growth in Europe

	Annual growth rate (1970-1996)
Passenger	3.2%
Freight	3.9%

After setting out the issues at stake related to external costs in Europe, a brief reminder of the European policy on infrastructure charging is given and the link with the EUROTOLL Project established. Although pricing based on marginal social cost is supposed to be generalized at the European level within 5 years, it is actually difficult to implement. Thus, the system will progressively be introduced according to three steps laid down in the White Paper of the European Commission which has recently been published. But how can we evolve from the existing situation to the internalization of external costs? The study based on the micro-economic theory and applied to the transport sector for a congested infrastructure shows that the implementation of toll or the variation of existing toll can be used as a tool towards pricing schemes that take into account external costs. However, the principles, difficulties and unexpected effects linked to the implementation of such tools are numerous and have to be well discerned. In this sense, the impacts of pricing strategies based on toll are investigated in an in-depth manner within four case studies of the EUROTOLL Project. The analysis shows their positive effects on traffic volumes, user behavior, etc. Thus, toll and toll variation can be efficient instruments and lead to a modification of the traditional approach of pricing in order to facilitate the achievement of the European objectives.

2 External Costs: What is at Stake in Europe?

External costs are considered as a very important issue in Europe. For ECMT the bottom threshold to consider for the implementation of a policy concerning external costs is that the costs can be assessed at around 4-5% of the GIP without taking into account all effects (geographical cut effect, climate changes, etc.). Thus, the percentage is contained in a range of 230-300 billion ECU for 1993 (approximately 195-250 billion USD). ECMT specifies that external environmental and accident costs amount to 1 ECU per liter of oil (around 0.85 USD), which corresponds to the current price of 1 liter of 98 unleaded gasoline in France.

The external costs estimates vary according to local circumstances and evaluation methods used. However, it is useful to have a look at the overall size of external costs and their breakdown across modes (see table 3)

Table 3: External costs of transport

	Road				Rail			
	Passenger (ECU/1000 Passenger-km)		Freight (ECU/1000 ton-km)		Passenger (ECU/1000 Passenger-km)		Freight (ECU/1000 ton-km)	
1995 values	IWW/ INF RAS	Green Book	IWW/ INF RAS	Green Book	IWW/ INF RAS	Green Book	IWW/ INF RAS	Green Book
Original base year	1991	1994	1991	1994	1991	1994	1991	1994
Country	EU 17	EU	EU 17	EU	EU 17	EU	EU 17	EU
Accidents	35.7	18.3	24.5	13.2	2.1	3.1	1.0	2.0
Noise	4.9	2.5	14.0	3.3	3.4	2.5	5.1	1.8
Air pollution & climate	14.6	15.3	25.9	17.3	5.6	2.5	2.0	1.5
Total	**55.2**	**36.1**	**64.4**	**33.8**	**11.1**	**8.1**	**8.1**	**5.3**

Source: QUITS, DGVII, Final Report

Despite the differences, the share of road transport total costs exceeds by far those of rail in both the IWW/INFRAS and the Commission's Green Book estimates.[3] According to ECMT congestion costs are very difficult to assess and the methods used cannot be considered as reliable, because the value-of-time level has been taken into account in the calculation. Moreover, congestion is limited to urban areas. The previous values are still being discussed in Europe and they reflect the methods used for their assessment.

3 Pricing in Europe

3.1 Transport Market

In a competitive market, prices may have numerous functions:

- Allocation of resources, which means distribution efficiency, to avoid rationing
- Production of goods at their lowest price
- Welfare of the economy when the price is equal to the marginal social cost[4] (consumers buy worthwhile goods).

The European road transport market, as for other countries outside Europe, is not really competitive and presents a high level of average costs compared to marginal costs for infrastructure (average increase return to scale and marginal decrease return to scale).

In the case of the European transport market:

- Prices do not properly include external costs.
- The customer approach is not well developed.
- It would be important to develop the network because there is a waste of resources (including both nodes and links aspects).
- Uniformity between European countries has to be reached.

3 Considering the other modes, the IWW/INFRAS study mentions that air traffic induces considerable costs whereas inland navigation external costs are very low.

4 Social cost to the sector = internal cost + external cost (uncovered infrastructure costs + harmful costs)

3.2 Road Pricing and Policy Objectives in Europe: Current Situation

The well known approach concerning road pricing and policy objectives can easily be summarized (see table 4). Charges for roads are usually in the form of an annual license or vignette (period license) and fuel tax. Some European countries (France, Italy, Portugal, Spain) have developed a significant tradition in the toll field with generalized distance-related toll implemented on their highway network (for both light and heavy vehicles). The public-private partnership has thus become usual in these countries. Others European countries (Greece, Austria, Belgium, Norway) use toll, but not in such a homogeneous way (sensitive corridor, tunnel,...).

Table 4: Kind of road pricing and objectives

	STATE			OPERATORS
	General taxation	**Specific taxation**	**Fuel taxes**	**Toll without variation**
All infrastructures investment	x			x
Road maintenance and improvement		x not proportional		→ Motorways x
Internalization of external costs			x not strictly proportional	

Thus, *toll is only one kind of road pricing* the main role of which is to reimburse the loans taken out for the building of road infrastructures in the frame of public/private partnerships, and to finance road maintenance and improvement.

3.3 Infrastructure Charging in Europe: Future Situation

Two important papers recently published must be considered, to have a good understanding of the European policy in terms of infrastructure charging, and to understand how valuations realized in EUROTOLL are embedded in this frame.

I) The report of the High Level Experts Group concerning pricing of infrastructures in Europe (European Commission, DGVII, June 1998[5])

This report tries to give an orientation to adapt the level and structure of prices so that they are in accordance with the transport efficiency and sustainability:

- User must pay real cost
- Discrimination: all users are equal
- Modes have to be considered together (general equilibrium approach rather than simple equilibrium in the frame of the economics theory)
- Tariffs must be differentiated (Level of costs, Level of service)
- Efficiency of the infrastructure use.

Recommendations are given to:

- introduce external effects in pricing,
- encourage users to use the most appropriate combination for their trip (interconnection and interoperability),
- develop private-public partnership,
- build a common accounting frame for pricing principles,
- take into account CBA for efficient infrastructure investment,
- build a step by step implementation program.

II) The "White Paper"

The "official" viewpoint of the EC is presented in the "White Paper" entitled "Fair payment for infrastructure use" (July 1998). It puts forward the diversity of the countries' charging systems and the need to set up a gradual and progressive harmonization of these systems. In the line of the High Level Experts Group report, it proposes that the charging system be based on the "users pay" principle taking into account all the external costs (i.e. "marginal social cost", but Member States can continue to support the provision of public services). The EC does not impose a centralized Community charging scheme and proposes a step-by-step approach for the implementation. In this "White Paper" the EC *"...does not lay down principles for infrastructure"* and gives orientation concerning the use of the Cost Benefit Analysis.

---

5 See bibliography. This report was launched to help the EC to clarify their view on pricing following the "Green book" published in 1995.

For the road sector the EC encourages the Members States to develop kilometers related electronic kilometer charging for the adoption of interoperable systems for HGVs (existing toll, Eurovignette) in the first phase (1998-2000)[6]. The EC also encourages the Member States to develop urban road pricing schemes to deal with external costs, including congestion. In the second phase (2001-2004) distance related charges should be extended to include external costs in addition to infrastructure costs. In the last phase (after 2004), marginal social cost based charges for HGVs and commercial passenger transport should be generalized.

3.4 Reality: How to Implement a Marginal Social Costs Pricing Scheme?

Marginal social cost is highly recommended, but not easy to implement directly for numerous reasons:

- calculation[7],
- flexibility,
- desegregation by class of users,
- technological aspects (tools),
- electronic collection systems,
- unity budget constraints[8],
- etc.

In this way, how can we evolve from the existing situation to the internalization of external costs?

One possibility is the implementation of toll (at a certain level) and the variation of existing tolls on roads already tolled. EUROTOLL, a European research project can give interesting orientations about this subject (even if its main topic is not the internalization of external cost).

---

6 EC specifies that they will propose an environmental classification of HGVs to better reflect the cost due to vehicle use.

7 A lot of progress has been made in the last years (see ECMT report in the bibliography). The most difficult to calculate is the level of marginal costs in accordance with the traffic variation (for congestion).

8 Takings are voted before expenses and they are assigned to priority tasks of central or local government, which are not necessarily those which have generated the revenus.

3.5 EUROTOLL and Pricing Policy in Europe

EUROTOLL is a reference project in the Directorate General for Transport (DG VII) in the field of road pricing within the European Union 4th Framework Program for Transport Research and Development. The aim is to undertake an in-depth investigation into the effects of road pricing and toll strategies on road mobility and transportation factors.

EUROTOLL is based on ten interurban/suburban case studies in France, Germany, Italy, Austria and the United Kingdom, and involves operators, engineering consulting companies and universities. The project uses an innovative approach combining conceptual and practical research through three main stages:

- define concepts re tolling strategies, user reactions,
- perform the case studies and operate the concepts,
- learn from case studies and consolidate the conceptual research.

The research work carried out within the EUROTOLL project case studies addresses the following transport policy goals:

- sustainable mobility
- increased network efficiency
- increased network accessibility
- increased network safety
- fair pricing and harmonization

The work carried out within EUROTOLL can be replaced in the frame of the internalization of external cost in the transport sector by considering theoretical schemes.

4 Toll: Theoretical Schemes

Realizing the important role which may be played by toll in the internalization of social costs in the transport sector is based on the understanding of three theoretical schemes:

- Fundamental scheme
- Economic and management tolls
- Scheme taking into account all external costs.

These schemes correspond to a theoretical road (highway or not) largely used in peak hour periods.

4.1 The Fundamental Scheme

In the figures below two types of demand are considered:

1. Demand 1: off-peak hour demand
2. Demand 2: peak hour demand.

In the case of untolled roads we can see that a change in the demand conditions (from off-peak to peak hours) leads to a situation with congestion, which means higher cost for the collectivity (external costs are more important) (see figure 1).

If we introduce toll as a new component of the cost (i.e. price for users), we will have the following situation (supply conditions change because of the introduction of toll) (see figure 2). The difference between C1 and C1' is equal to the toll.

The introduction of toll will lead to a decrease in the traffic volume (from T1 to T'1) which will prevent from congestion problems, if their is no alternative route.

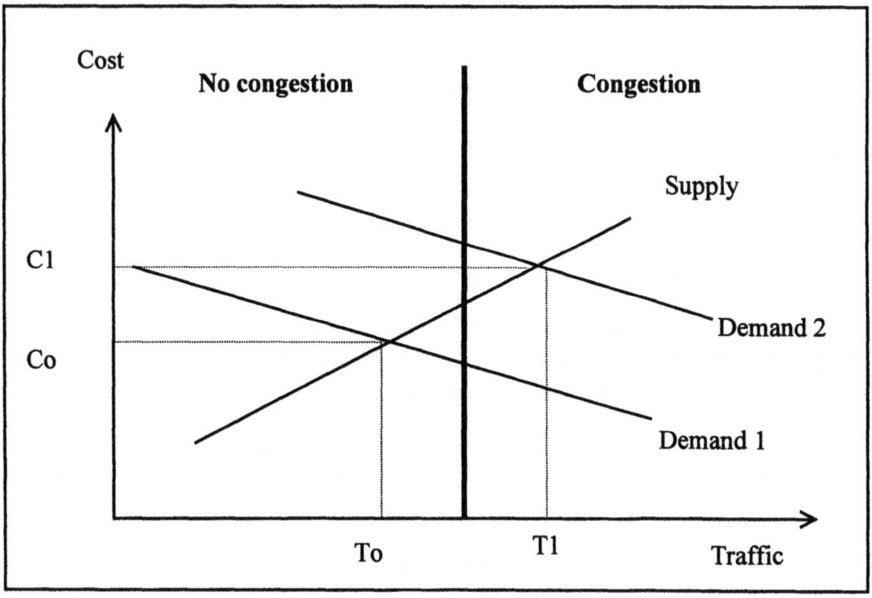

Figure 1: Supply and demand for untolled roads

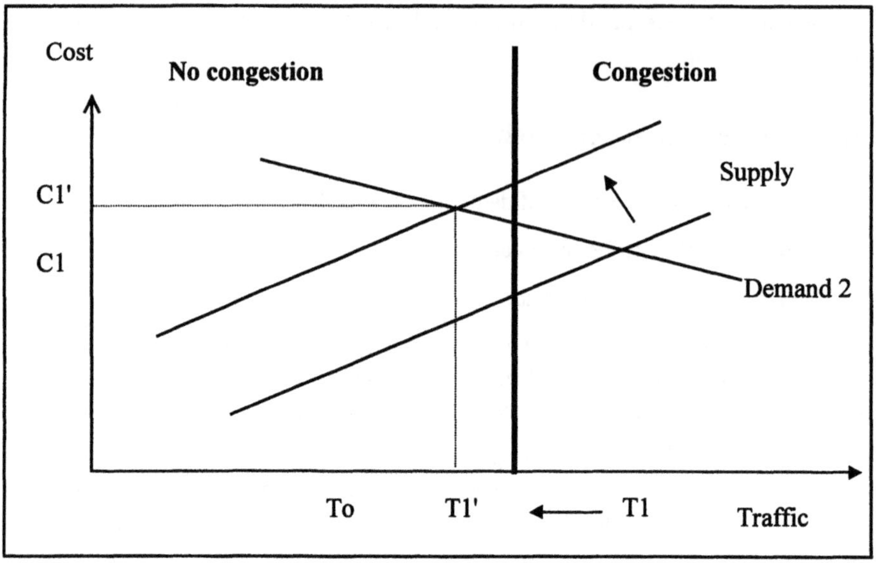

Figure 2: Supply and demand for a toll road

4.2 Economic and Management Tolls

Two types of toll can be distinguished:

1. Economic toll: Toll used to pay some fixed costs, plus investment costs and maintenance costs
2. Management toll: Toll used to change the level of demand

In the following graphs, we consider the marginal cost function corresponding to the price to be paid by the user in accordance with the traffic variation. So, two kinds of marginal cost can be distinguished:

- Operator Marginal Cost (OMC): corresponds to the costs borne by the operator due to an increase in one traffic unit. This marginal cost is linked to supply.
- Social Marginal Cost (SMC): corresponds to the costs borne by the collectivity (congestion, accident, noise, air pollution, etc.) due to an increase in one traffic unit.

Thus it is possible:

- **not to take into account social costs** (here: external costs). In this case, an Economic Toll may be implemented corresponding to the level of the OMC (see figure 3).
- **to take into costs due to congestion**. In this case, an management toll could be implemented to change the level of the demand, to be in accordance with the equilibrium between supply and demand (E), and between marginal cost and price (see figure 4).

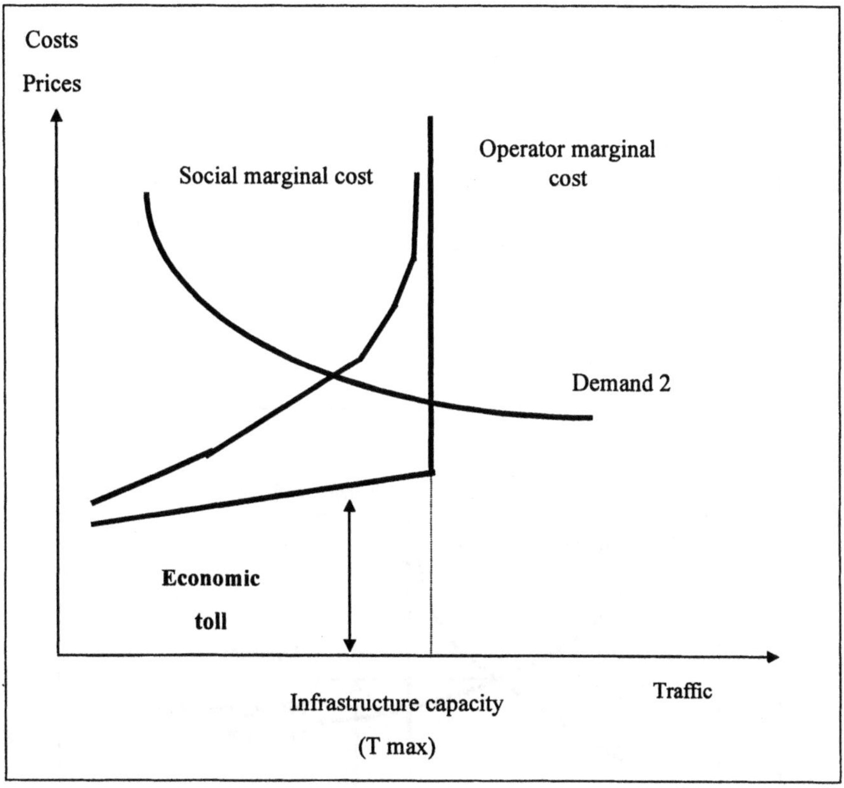

Figure 3: Economic toll

If we want to take into account external costs of transport (more or less), we can introduce a variation of the management toll.

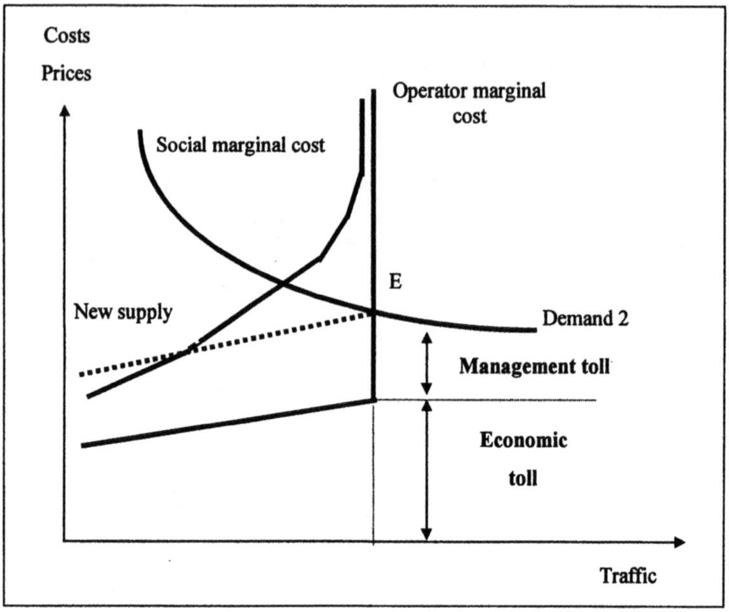

Figure 4: Management toll

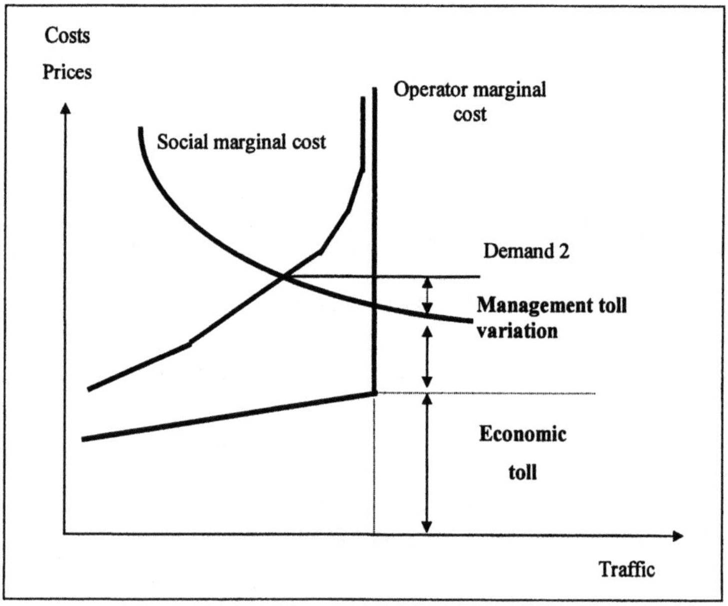

Figure 5: Management toll variation

5 Why EUROTOLL Can Provide Important Elements with Respect to European Pricing Issues?

5.1 EUROTOLL: Field of Investigation

EUROTOLL is studying toll variation as a tool to understand the impacts of proper price signals:

1. on transport demand (short term impacts on traffic, acceptability, etc.)
2. on the supply management.

The case studies developed in EUROTOLL are close to the second theoretical frame (4.2), but they are also strongly linked to the third (4.3). Because there was a lack, in terms of applied research, concerning the differentiation of targeted pricing (the price does not necessarily reflect the social cost of trips in the transport market) some real or trial cases have been analyzed. In this sense, it seems that time or space toll variation is a good tool to go further in the internalization of social cost into the transport market (external costs there).

5.2 Types of Toll Variation

In the frame of the previous theoretical schemes, toll variation as studied in EUROTOLL, has to be considered *as an economic toll plus or minus a management toll variation.*

It is easy to understand what the implementation of toll means. However, several possibilities for toll variation exist and have to be highlighted:

- spatial toll variation: for one Origin/Destination pair, toll is higher for some routes.
- time toll variation: for the same route, toll is different according to the time of the day.
- spatial and time toll variation: for one Origin/Destination pair, some routes are cheaper in off-peak periods.
- toll variation by vehicle category.

EUROTOLL investigates the first three types of toll variation.

6 Principles, Difficulties and Desired Effects of Toll Variation Encountered in Eurotoll

6.1 Basic Principles to Implement Toll Variation

- Very good knowledge of the level and the features of traffic (peak and off-peak periods, user information to develop, Essential Road Users (targeted demand), marketing approach, technological systems to broadcast information, optimization of revenues/expenses, etc.)
- Compensatory measures. If toll variation is implemented for peak periods, the operators' revenues will be better but the user surplus will certainly be lower than previously. To alleviate this social loss the access to the corridor (or network) has to be introduced, at another time or for another route, i.e. distinguish between GREEN PERIODS and RED PERIODS.

Example (see figure 6):

1. red period: demand during peak hours (economic toll + management toll at level x)
2. green period: demand during off-peak hours, (economic toll - management toll at level y, such as y<x or y=x)
3. white (other) periods: demand in average hours, (average of red and green period, economic toll).

6.2 Difficulties Linked to the Implementation

They may be numerous:

- public image of operators,
- edge effects,
- increase of noise,
- operators' revenues:

  before operation:
  level of revenues x - operating expenses

  after operation:
  level of revenues y - operating expenses - costs of operation

- handling of alternative solutions: paths, design of periods, etc.

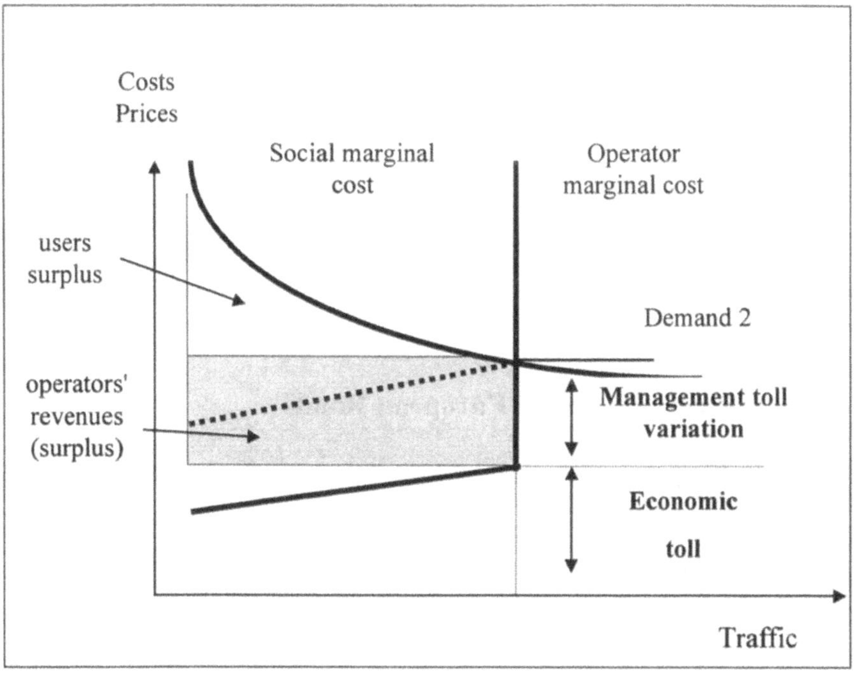

Figure 6: Surplus variation

6.3 Desired Effects of Toll Variation

- *For users in red periods who do not change their habit:*

  -Better level of service
  -Gains in time
  -Gains in comfort

- *For the collectivity*

  -Avoid that high marginal costs are not recovered
  -Decrease of external effects (congestion, pollution, noise)

- *For operators*

  -Smooth off-peak period traffic curve
  -Optimize the exploitation (efficiency of the network)
  -Possibility to increase revenues (time is money)

Now, focusing on practical examples will give us more concrete results concerning impacts of road pricing strategies.

7 Results from EUROTOLL Case Studies

With respect to the topic addressed in this paper, four EUROTOLL case studies can be considered and provide interesting results about the impact of road pricing strategies.

7.1 Features of Selected European Roads

The two first case studies are in operation, and two second are trials. Both concern congestion contexts (periodic or daily).

7.1.1 Case Studies in Operation

Table 5: Three EUROTOLL corridor toll variation case studies in operation (periodic congestion context)

Case Study	Target	Measure	Location	Targeted users	Purpose	Modes
A1 - A10/A11 (France)	*Reduce congestion by smoothing peak hours*	• Peak-off peak-hour toll • Information + VSM	Interurban/ Suburban	Week-end returns	Leisure	LV*, and LV*, HV**
A5/A6 (France)	*Reduce congestion* *On A6: traffic transfer from A6 to A5*	• Variable tariffs/routes • Information campaign	Interurban	Occasional Long distance trips	Leisure	LV*

* LV = Light Vehicles
** HV = Heavy Vehicles

7.1.2 Trial Case Studies

Table 6: Two EUROTOLL scenarios case studies (daily congestion context)

Case Study	Transport Demand Strategy	Site	Location	Targeted users	Purpose	Modes
A12/A13 (Austria)	*Toll variation Day, night*	Corridor	Interurban	Long distance trips	All	LV*, HV**
Stuttgart (Deutsch -land)	*Road pricing implementation* *Simplified global structure of fares and increase of car pricing by means of toll*	Access corridor and Network	(Sub)urban	Short distance trips	Commuting, business	LV*, PT***

*   LV = Light Vehicles
**   HV = Heavy Vehicles
*** PT = Passenger Traffic

7.2 Cross Analysis of Case Studies Results

Potential impacts of road tolling schemes can be shown in the following categories. These are not always linked to the problem of externalities but are important to consider in the frame of a future implementation of a Transport Demand Management (TDM) pricing strategy:

- demand reactions (response of road users to the imposition of toll charges, including the sensitivity of traffic demand to charging levels)
- social and individual road user acceptance (evidence on the degree of acceptability of tolls by users according the willingness to pay surveys, etc.)
- user information (ensuring that road users are informed of tariffs)
- internalization of external costs (reflecting how the costs imposed on other road users and non-users are affected by tolling schemes including accidents and other environmental effects)

- marketing aspects (measures aimed at increasing the awareness of tolling schemes, including publicity campaigns)
- management of congested networks (implications for the reduction or transference of traffic congestion according to time, period or location as a consequence of the tolling scheme implementation).

The aim of this section is to give some global results concerning these categories.

7.2.1 Price Sensitivity / Demand Reactions

Four main demand reactions can be considered. For each of them, some dimension have to be considered (see table 7).

Table 7: Demand reactions

Main demand reactions considered	Dimension
• Route change	• Explaining factors
• Mode change	• Toll effects
• Time change	• Marginal price variation effects
• Frequency change	

For example, according the third dimension: Level of marginal price variations in relation with demand reactions (ceteris paribus). Even if the impact of TDM pricing strategies upon demand is depending on numerous factors, marginal price variation is an interesting single indicator. Table 8 shows that the impact of toll variation upon demand is high (in a relative point of view), when the reaction link to the TDM strategy is route change.

Table 8: Interdependence of demand reactions and marginal price variations

	Route change	Mode change	Time change	Frequency ch.
Marginal price variation	high	low	Variable	null
Case study	A5/A6	A13/A13	A1-A10/A11	A12/A13

In the same way, the desired route change on the base of tolling will be effective if:

- toll differences are correctly defined,
- additional route length is not too important,
- level of service (LOS) on the main route is close to C or D,
- LOS on the parallel route is better than on the main route,

7.2.2 Social / Individual Acceptance

Social and individual acceptance depend on numerous factors, and the main consequences have to be considered.

Table 9: Factors of individual and social acceptance

Depending on numerous factors:	Main consequences:
• policy goals and transport targets • clearness and fairness of measures • trip features • who pays the toll • ...	• awareness: to be considered • information: to be adapted • differentiation into several levels: to be developed (LV/HV; distance, time,...)

Awareness means, for tolling strategies: is public and individual awareness about TDM strategy developed or not? Thus, toll measures have to be prepared to be clearly and fair. For example, for A1-A10/A11, only 21 to 27% of people were not aware of the TDM strategy. Information plays a key role in social and individual acceptance of toll measures.

As nothing is uniform, differentiation needs to be introduced according:

- Light Vehicles (LV) / Heavy Vehicles(HV)
- Distance
- Time
- Purpose
- etc.

7.2.3 User Information

The impact of user information has to be assessed in general and regarding pricing strategies and demand management. Table 10 shows that results in terms of user information will then be very different.

Table 10: EUROTOLL results: diversity of results in terms of user information

Periods concerned	TDM strategy	EUROTOLL case study	Main objective	Type of information mean	Main support	Learnings
Holidays and W.E.	**Tolling strategies and information**	A5 / A6	Shift traffic from A6 to A5	Pre-trip	Press, radio, leaflets, ...	On-trip information is not adapted in this case
W.E. returns		A10 / A11	Spread the demand	On-trip	Leaflets,signpost	Large number of round trips increased the efficiency of the strategy

7.2.4 Marketing Aspects (Learnings)

Marketing aspects are very important for the success of a tolling strategy. We list here six aspects in the toll variation case:

- the tariff scheme must be understandable
- the tariff scheme must be linked with the measure to induce advantages for users
- effects in terms of travel time or free flowing must be highlighted because they cannot be easily assessed by users
- LV and HV are two different marketing target groups
- only policy objectives which will have an impact on people's understanding have to be selected
- external supports are crucial for success (public agencies, consumer associations, etc.)

7.2.5 Internalization of External Costs

The implementation of toll variation leads to the necessity to list and assess all direct and indirect impacts on user behavior regarding external effects. This means that we have to assess expected positive impacts, risks and secondary effects.

Positive impacts, such as:

- pollution and noise (example: decrease of pollutants emission for A1, transfer of traffic on rail for A12/A13)
- safety (example: increase of safety due to stops on rest areas and better LOS)
- congestion

Secondary effects, such as:

- unforeseen and opportunists users behaviors (example: users stop on emergency lanes to wait for cheaper period)
- reduction of the global congestion of the whole network may involve micro congestion on spot points,...

7.2.6 Management of Congested Networks

The EUROTOLL case studies show that toll variation is a good tool for demand management but it depends on user acceptance and understanding. In case of a congested network, the pricing measures which may be implemented will bring about various effects and user reaction according to the reference situation:

- toll or pricing already in operation / no toll in operation
- urban/interurban context

In the following section we present elements concerning pricing measures leading to the change of existing toll, firstly when the objective is to spread demand in time, secondly when the objective is to spread demand in space.

Demand spreading in time:

Main principles are:

- toll fare higher in peak hours
- toll fare lower in off-peak hours

Transferable results concerning traffic are:

- transfers depend on user awareness, acceptance and level of toll variation

- transfers to the parallel network are significant or not (function of its attractivity)
- transfers allow to lead to a decrease in congestion in peak periods
- transfers need to be encouraged by information campaigns

Demand spreading in space:

Main principles are:

- toll fare higher on congested routes
- toll fare lower on non congested routes.

8 Conclusion: Toll with Variation: a Simple Means to Support the Internalization of External Cost in the Transport Sector

There are three main principles re tolling. The first one is the most common, and the two others are real tools to complete the set of road pricing types with regard to pricing objectives:

- **Financial leverage tool (infrastructure financing, road maintenance and improvement)**
  The tariff is a compromise between the maximization of financial revenues and the collective surplus.
- **Traffic and demand management (spreading of peak periods and reduction of traffic)**
  Toll can be used as a means of traffic management. In an interurban context, the experiences in France show the possibilities for innovative traffic management on corridors with dense traffic and for network optimization.
- **Internalization of external cost (environmental conservation).**
  Although no experience of tolling strategies devoted to environmental conservation currently exists, we tried to demonstrate, in this paper, that the issue can be addressed through toll variation in order to achieve the European objectives re pricing principles.

Table 11: Types of road pricing and objectives: new approach

	STATE			OPERATORS	
	General taxation[9]	**Specific taxation**	**Fuel taxes**	**Toll without variation**	**Toll with variation**
All infrastructures	x			x	
Road maintenance and improvement		x not proportional		x	Motorways
Spreading of peak periods					x
Reduction of traffic					x
Internalization of external costs			x not strictly proportional	**GIVE IT PROPORTIONAL**	x

References

CAPRI, Current position and proposed outline of the concerted action, State of the Art, Concerted Action on Transport Pricing Research Integration, Deliverable 1, Status : Restricted, May 1998, 30 p.

Collombier L., Comportement des usagers face à la modulation tarifaire sur l'autoroute A1, TFE de l'ENTPE, 29/06/1995, 158 p.

Crozet Y., External costs and internalization, paper for the Seminar on tolling strategies and experiences, Eurotoll, Lyon 7 and 8 of July 1998, 8 p.

9 Income taxes. Specific taxation: vignette, card for car ownership.

DG VII, High Level Group report on the pricing of the transport infrastructures, Chaired by Mr. Blonk, EC, DG VII, June 1998, 12 p.

DRAST, Les transports en Europe, Ministère de l'Equipement du Logement des Transports et du Tourisme, Février 1997, 70 p.

ECMT, Policies for Internalization of External Cost, Efficient Transport in Europe, ECMT, 1998, 261 p.

ECMT, Statistical trends in transport, 1965-1994, ECMT, 1998, 251 p.

European Commission, Fair payment for infrastructure use: A phased approach to a common transport infrastructure charging framework in the EU, "White paper", DGVII, 22 July 1998, 47p.

EUROTOLL, Internalization and external Cost and Tolling, Deliverable R3, Status: Public, August 1997, 34 p.

EUROTOLL, Results of Case Studies, Deliverable R11/I, Status: Confidential, June 1998, 150 p.

Fournier P., Monsigny M., Road pricing via tolling, Paper for the 8th WCTR, Antwerp, July 1998, 21 p.

Gambard J.M., Road tolling, a concept with a future in Europe, Paper for the Road Financing Conference, ENPC, Paris, November 1998, 7p.

Monsigny M., Herry M., France and Austria : convergence towards efficient road infrastructure financing, Paper for the Road Financing Conference, ENPC, Paris, November 1998, 8p.

Quinet E., Touzery L., Triebel H., Economie des transports, Economica, 1982, 282 p.

Quinet E., Analyse économique des transports, PUF, 1990, 302 p.

Constitutional Constraints on Social-Cost Pricing

Daniel Lazare

130 W.86th St., #8A, New York, NY 10024
USA

Over-reliance on auto and truck transport is a growing problem throughout the industrial world. Yet no nation is so completely and thoroughly dependant on automotive transport as the United States. In 1994, Americans drove a total of 8,898 miles (14,317km) for every man, woman, and child. This was better than two and half times that of the Japanese (5,440km per person) and roughly double that of the French (7,976km per person), the British (7,020km), or the Germans (6,477) – a discrepancy that, thanks to the plummeting price of gasoline in the U.S., is undoubtedly growing worse (Federal Highway Administration, 1995: VII-2, VII-5). The U.S. transportation sector, not surprisingly, consumes two to three times as much energy per capita as the Japanese, French, British, or German transportation sectors, while total rail passenger travel in America is anywhere from 34 to 91 percent less than in those four countries, even though its population is three to four times greater (OECD, 1994: 6-7, 21-21, 38-39).

Over the years, any number of theories have been advanced to explain this discrepancy. Americans, for example, are often said to drive more than Europeans because distances in the U.S. are so much greater. At first glance, this would seem to make sense. At 27 people per square kilometer, the U.S. is far more thinly populated than any country in Continental Europe. Yet American auto dependency is exceptional even by the standards of lightly settled countries elsewhere in the OECD. Canada has 90 percent fewer people per square kilometer, yet Canadians still drive 24 percent fewer kilometers per year (OECD, 1994: 6-7, 21-21, 38-39). Australia has an even lower population density - 2.2 people per square kilometer – yet Australians drive even less - just 5,989km per capita as of 1995 (McLennan, 1998: 602). In addition, overall population densities are misleading since Americans, in large measure, do not live in the wide open spaces out West, but in crowded urban corridors where population densities are commensurate with those of the rest of the industrialized world. As the agricultural share of the workforce has declined – farming now accounts for just 3.7 percent of U.S. employment (U.S. Bureau of the Census, 1997: 415) – America has seen a long-term population shift from the more agriculture-dependent interior to coastal regions where the economy is more financial, industrial, and service-oriented. By 1987, this trend had reached the point where 52.9 percent of the population was living within

80km of one of the nation's four coasts – the Atlantic, the Pacific, the Great Lakes, and the Gulf of Mexico. This means that better than half the people was living on just 10 percent of the land, where population densities, as a result, were fully comparable to those of the European Union (OECD, 1991: 248). When it comes to population density, Americans live like Europeans, yet drive like Montanans or Coloradans.

Another common explanation for the discrepancy is that Americans drive more because they can afford to due to higher levels of per-capita wealth. Yet a glance at OECD income tables shows this to be untrue as well. As of 1994, GDP per capita in the U.S., based on then-current exchange rates, was about 29 percent ahead of that of the British, virtually on par with that of French, and 16 percent behind the level of Germany, where vehicle-kilometers per capita are substantially less (OECD, 1994: 24-25). Thus, higher levels of driving do not correlate with higher levels of income. (Indeed, as Newman, Kenworthy, et al. have shown, auto usage tends to decline as per-capita income rises above a certain level and people grow increasingly concerned with environmental issues and the quality of life (Kenworthy et al., 1997: 5-13).) Finally, it is often said that American drive more due to an abundance of domestic oil supplies. But while this might have been true three or four decades ago, it is no longer the case now that the U.S. has ceased being a net oil exporter. Canada produces approximately twice as much oil per capita as its neighbor to the south, yet its citizens drive fewer kilometers per year, as we have seen, while its transport sector consumes roughly 22 percent less energy (Kenworthy et al., 1997: 6-7, 18-19).

Americans' exceptional driving habits, on the other hand, *can* be attributed to the low retail price of motor fuel in this country. Retail gasoline prices in this country are extraordinary – an average of just 26.6 cents per liter (US$1.01 per gallon) as of July 1998 versus 86.6 cents in Germany, US$1.04 in France, and US$1.19 in Britain (International Energy Agency, 1998: 56). As the boom in sport utility vehicles shows, prices have reached the point where fuel is now a negligible factor in U.S. driving costs. Given a virtual consensus from one end of the political spectrum to the other, moreover, they are likely to remain that way in the years to come as government marshals its full resources to keep them at rock-bottom levels or, if possible, to drive them even lower.

But this still begs the question why. When gas prices momentarily spiked up to 32.8 cents per liter ($1.24 a gallon) in April 1996, a small panic broke out in Washington. President Bill Clinton worried that "there are not going to be as many people driving as far to do whatever it is they're going to do this summer," while Congress moved to repeal a 1.1-cent-a-liter gas tax adopted just three years earlier (Anonymus, 1996). Yet Americans were paying a fraction of what Europeans were paying at the time, while today Americans are paying even less. The issue, therefore, is why U.S. politicians are so hypersensitive when it comes to even the smallest perturbations in the price of this one commodity and why, barring major political changes, they are likely to remain that way for decades to come.

This paper argues that a long-term policy that cannot be successfully explained in terms of geography, per-capita income, or natural resources and that transcends mere partisan differences of Republican versus Democrat can be more readily understood in terms of political structure. American driving habits are unique, this paper contends, because the American political environment is unique. No other advanced industrial society conceives of the relationship between the individual and the state in quite the same way or defines democracy so exclusively in terms of the rights of the individual. While all industrialized nations are familiar with the tension between individual and collective interests, no other advanced industrial economy sees the two as mutually antithetical to quite the same degree. While political leaders throughout the First World have taken aim since the late 1970s at the allegedly smothering influence of the welfare state, none has gone as far as President Clinton has in elevating hostility to government to the level of a founding national principle. As he declared in 1994 in introducing a new Supreme Court nominee: "You know, this country got started by people who wanted a good letting alone from government. I think he understands that." (Ifill, 1994) It is difficult to imagine any comparable world leader asserting that the purpose of society was to promote anything quite so anti-social.

This unique political environment is the result of an equally unique history. The United States is far and away the oldest major republic in the world. Switzerland, the second oldest in the OECD, dates from 1874, when its current constitution was adopted. The U.S. Constitution, by contrast, is nearly a century older, having been drafted in 1787, ratified in 1788, and implemented in 1789 when George Washington took the oath of office in the then-capital of New York. Despite such events as the Civil War of 1861-65 in which 600,000 lives were lost, the quasi-revolutionary New Deal of the 1930s, or the civil rights revolution of the 1950s and '60s, the ideas underlying both the Constitution and the republic have changed remarkably little in the 210 years since. America is an essentially Euclidian society in which virtually everything in it derives from certain founding principles which, because they are held to be "self-evident" (to quote the Declaration of Independence), have gone largely unexamined. It is impossible to understand any aspect of American policy, up to and including transportation, without understanding how those two-century-old principles continue to guide, shape, and animate American political thought.

One founding principle, for example, is that of limited government. Although nowhere does the phrase "limited government" appear in the Constitution of 1787, the concept is implicit throughout the document. Until the Thirteenth, Fourteenth, and Fifteenth Amendments, adopted in the aftermath of the Civil War, the Constitution was an exercise in what the political philosopher Isaiah Berlin defined as "negative liberty," i.e. the freedom of the individual vis-à-vis the state. Article I of the Constitution placed limits on the power of the legislative branch, Article II limited the power of the executive, while the Bill of Rights, as the first ten amendments are known, limited the power of the entire federal government vis-à-vis the states and the people. While the Preamble, the famous introductory paragraph that begins with the phrase, "We the People," sets forth all the things government should accomplish, e.g. "establish justice, insure domestic tranquility, provide for the common defense," and so forth, the bulk of the document is devoted to all the things the national government could not do, such as establishing a national church, abridging freedom of speech, or interfering in any way with the institution of slavery. The concept of "positive liberty," meaning the freedom of the *demos* as a whole to use government to modify its political environment at will, was viewed with deep apprehension by virtually all the founders with the notable exception of Alexander Hamilton.

This two-century-old concept of limited government implies several things. It implies government, for example, that is not just limited in scope, but limited in terms of speed of response and ability to innovate in the face of unforeseen developments. Given that it is a people's government that the Constitution seeks to define, it implies that the people, far from being sovereign, are limited in their ability to govern themselves or even to modify the Constitution made in their name. (The U.S. Constitution's amending process is notoriously slow and difficult.) Finally, it implies that democracy itself is limited. Where virtually every other national constitution in the First World defines the state as democratic (not counting Britain, of course, which lacks a written constitution altogether), the U.S. Constitution, significantly, does not. Nowhere does the world "democracy" or any of its variants appear in the body of the document or in any of its by now twenty-seven amendments. The reason, simply, is that the founders viewed democracy with suspicion and saw no need to include a term they viewed as synonymous with license and disorder. Curiously in terms of modern political theory, they saw freedom and democracy as mutually opposed. The greater the level of democracy, the more freedom would be vulnerable to the passions of the mob. For one to flourish, the other had to be limited and constrained.

To this end, the founders created a state apparatus designed in great measure to nullify and frustrate democracy by fragmenting the *demos* and turning it against itself. They did this by dividing the political realm horizontally between the federal government and the states and then vertically among the legislative, executive, and judicial branches. They further divided political power by splitting the legislative branch into two chambers of roughly equal weight, the House of Representatives, which is elected according to population, and the Senate, in which each of the 50 states has two representatives each regardless of population differentials nowadays of as much as 67 to one. The result was a system of built-in countervailing tendencies. If one ruling institution pulled in one direction, the aim was designed to allow, if not encourage, the others would pull in the opposite. The goal was not to foster majority rule, but to frustrate it by preventing the majority from gaining control of the entire apparatus. The founders saw this as important because they were essentially pessimistic about the majority's ability to take charge of society and reorganize it on a rational basis. As James Madison, the single most important figure at the 1787 Constitutional Convention, put it a few months later in the Federalist Papers: "...democracies have ever been spectacles of turbulence and contention; have ever been found incompatible with personal security or the rights of property; and have in general been as short in their lives as they have been violent in their deaths." The goal was to rein in democratic passions by subdividing the polity so that while "factious leaders may kindle a flame within their particular States, ... [they] will be unable to spread a general conflagration through the other States." (Hamilton et al., 1961: 81, 84) Or as Madison put it in a letter to Thomas Jefferson in late 1787: "*Divide et impera,* the reprobate axiom of tyranny, is under certain conditions, the only policy, by which a republic can be administered on just principles." (Kramnick, 1990: 263) The *demos* was to conquer itself by breaking itself up into ever smaller pieces. Stability was to be achieved through self-fragmentation. Madison was so worried about the problem of irresponsibility majorities that he was willing to close the door to majority rule altogether.

From a late-twentieth-century, the problem with such thinking seems fairly obvious. By crippling the power of the democratic majority, Madison was preventing the emergence of any kind of sovereign force capable of taking charge of the republic as a whole. If the majority was not to rule in a people's republic, then no one was to rule. Instead, the machinery would continue forward under its own steam, with essentially no one at the helm. Over the years, various thinkers have tried to portray this driver-less quality as something of a virtue. As the editor, poet, and diplomat James Russell Lowell observed in the 1880s, the government that America had come up with was a kind of self-directing perpetual-motion machine:

"After our Constitution got fairly into working order it really seemed as if we had invented a machine that would go of itself, and this begot a faith in our luck which even the civil war itself but momentarily disturbed. Circumstances continued favorable, and our prosperity went on increasing. I admire the splendid complacency of my countrymen, and find something exhilarating and inspiring in it. We are a nation which *struck ile,* but we are also a nation that is sure the well will never run dry." (Kammen, 1986: 18)

But perpetual-motion machines are as unlikely in government as anywhere else. Any attempt to create one, no matter how clever or complex, founders on the fact that friction will invariably assert itself and cause the mechanism to begin winding down. A constitutional system designed to "go of itself," similarly, can't help but wind down as well as it comes more and more into conflict with the needs of a fast-changing society. The more resistant the system is to change, the more friction will pile up.

Which brings us to transportation policy. America embraced Henry Ford's revolution of 1908-14 chiefly because mass production of the automobile promised a quick and easy escape from political tensions that were rising to dangerous levels in cities like Chicago and New York. Mass motorization promised to bring about a new era of individualism, an end to class conflict, and a reinvigoration of small-town life - in other words, a return to Jeffersonian values that America's eighteenth-century constitution reflects, extols, and reinforces. It represented not so much political change as the avoidance of political change via a return to pre-existing political values. For that reason, there was virtually no debate as to costs and benefits, the practical advantages of a mixed transportation system built around rail, waterways, bicycles, walking, and motor vehicles versus one increasingly dominated by the automobile, etc. Although the United States prides itself on being the most business-like society on earth, the policy was anything but business-like. Rather, it was almost exclusively moralistic. The auto represented progress, individualism, and the triumph of American values. As a result, it transcended cost-benefit analysis. Anything that helped speed it on its way was good; anything that impeded it was bad.

To be fair, the benefits of the new technology did outweigh the costs, according to any objective reckoning, for several decades. But the balance began to shift in the 1950s and '60s when problems such as chronic traffic congestion, urban decay and suburban sprawl, and so on began piling up alarmingly. This should have been an occasion for renewed debate over transportation and development priorities in general. Yet America's balkanized political structure, in which power is divided not only among three branches of government at the federal level, but among fifty states and some 83,000 semi-autonomous local governments, tends to inhibit and scatter political debate. Since an absence of debate means an absence of any prospect of fundamental political change, Americans did the only thing they could under the circumstances, which was to rededicate themselves to the status quo. They built more highways, saw to it that motor vehicles became available to a broader portion of the population, and did everything in their power to hold down petrol prices as well. Such efforts were doomed to failure. Cheap fuel and an ever-expanding auto fleet meant that traffic growth would grow, continually outpacing the best efforts of highway builders to accommodate it. Ever-rising traffic levels meant ever-rising levels of congestion and hence mounting waste in the form of lost time, environmental degradation, and a declining quality of life. The more resources America poured into its increasingly mono-cultural transportation system, the more inefficient it would become. Yet each failure led to renewed effort, which led to renewed failure.

Qualitatively speaking, the problem is no different in the United States than it is in any other advanced industrial economy. The solution to growing auto dependency throughout the industrialized world is for society to gain a better understanding of the costs of motor transport so as to better weigh the benefits. This means a combination of administrative and economic measures designed to promote more rational use of the automobile by requiring motorists to assume responsibility for at least a portion of the costs they generate, if not the entire amount. The idea is not to eliminate the automobile, as some activists would have it. Rather, it is to promote its use it in such a way that is least costly and hence most profitable for society as whole.

This is the case whether we are discussing chronic highway congestion in California, Germany, or Great Britain. On the other hand, if the problem is qualitatively similar across the board, in quantitative terms it is not. Given that the United States has barely embarked on the great debate over motor-vehicle costs and benefits, it has by far the longest way to go of any First World nation. Super-low gasoline prices do not represent a victory for people's power, as certain American populists maintain. To the contrary, they are indicative of the backwards nature of American democracy, an example of how it is still mired in eighteenth-century shibboleths concerning the essentially unbridgeable gap between the people and their representatives in Washington. An advanced democracy assumes that the people are capable of assuming responsibility for their own actions and as a result are capable of rational self-government. There is no more need to disguise the truth concerning the mounting real cost of certain common activities any more than there would be a need to disguise the truth about certain excessive household expenses. A backwards democracy, by contrast, assumes that the people are incapable of assuming responsibility, that they can't handle the truth, and hence that they must protected from reality. Much as the former Soviet Union did with the price of bread or Peronist Argentina did with the price of beef, it strives to keep certain the prices of certain sensitive commodities at unrealistically low because it fears the consequences if it doesn't. It may recognize that such policies are wasteful and counter-productive. But it is so pessimistic concerning the prospects for fundamental democratic reform that it sees no practical alternative. It sees rising economic inefficiency as the price for maintaining political stability.

This in essence is the problem faced by the United States. Because it believes the people are incapable of responding in a mature fashion to the problem of mounting real driving costs – because it is incapable of even beginning to sort the real costs and benefits of the automotive transport itself – it prefers to let sleeping dogs lie. It prefers the devil it knows, i.e. rising levels of waste and inefficiency, to the devil it doesn't, i.e. fundamental democratic reform (see Lazare, 1998). Rather than moving forward politically, it prefers to remain mired in economic backwardness.

Once again, this is a difference only of degree from political problems that all OECD nations will face in the coming years as they struggle to adopt more sophisticated transportation and energy policies in the face of such growing problems as chronic traffic congestion, urban decay and suburban sprawl, pollution and global warming. Even at a dollar a liter, gasoline prices still do not reflect the full range of social and environmental costs, which is why auto dependency is increasingly problematic throughout the First World (not to mention the former Soviet bloc and the Third World as well). Even in the most advanced countries such as Denmark, citizens have only begun to address the manifold problems generated by decades of rising auto dependency. Difficult political adjustments are still in store. Yet as difficult as those adjustments will be in Europe and other regions of the OECD, they are minor compared to those in the United States. Here reformers must not only grapple with the enormous wastes generated by a transportation system unequalled in its dependency on the automobile, but with an archaic, unresponsive political system that cannot begin to understand the dimensions of the problem or how to turn it around.

References

Anonymus (1996): Gas Prices, Gas Politics. In: The New York Times, 1 May 1996, p. A18.

Federal Highway Administration (1995): Highway Statistics 1994. Washington, D.C.: U.S. Government Printing Office.

Hamilton, A./Madison, J./Jay, J. (1961): The Federalist Papers. New York: New American Library, 1961.

Ifill, G.(1994): "President Chooses Breyer, An Appeals Judge, for Blackmun's Court Seat. In: The New York Times, May 14 1994, p. A1.

International Energy Agency (1998): Oil Market Report, 7 Aug. 1998.

Kammen, M. (1986): A Machine That Would Go of Itself: The Constitution in American Culture. NewYork: Knopf, 1986.

Kenworthy, J./Laube, F./Newman, P./Barter, P. (1997): Indicators of Transport Efficiency in 37 Global Cities. New York: World Bank.

Kramnick, I. (1990): Republicanism and Bourgeois Radicalism: Political Ideology in Late Eighteenth-Century England and America.New York: Cornell Univ. Press, Ithaca.

Lazare, D. (1998): America the Undemocratic. In: New Left Review 232 (Nov.-Dec. 1998), pp. 3-40

McLennan, W. (1998): 1998 Year Book Australia. Canberra: Australian Bureau of Statistics.

OECD (Organization for Economic Co-operation and Development) (1991): The State of the Environment. Paris: OECD.

OECD (Organization for Economic Co-operation and Development) (1994): OECD in Figures. Paris: OECD.

U.S. Bureau of the Census (1997): Statistical Abstract of the United States: 1997. 117th ed. Washington, D.C.: Government Printing Office.

Strategic Niche Management for Sustainable Mobility

René Kemp

Maastricht Research Institute on Innovation and Technology (MERIT)
Maastricht University, P.O. Box 616, 6200 MD Maastricht
Netherlands

Bernhard Truffer

Swiss Federal Institute of Environmental Science and Technology (EAWAG)
CH-6047 Kastanienbaum
Switzerland

Sylvia Harms

EAWAG, Dept. of Human Ecology
Überlandstr. 133, CH-8600 Dübendorf
Switzerland

Abstract. The existing system of land-based transport based on the individual use of automobiles for passenger transport and trucks for freight transport is not sustainable. Problems of pollution and congestion are pressing public authorities to take action but this is far from easy. One reason why it so difficult for authorities to do something about transport-related problems is that there appear to be no attractive alternatives. Sustainable technologies that fulfil important user requirements in terms of performance and price are most often not available on the market. Ideas of what might be more sustainable technologies and systems exist, but the long development times, uncertainty about market demand and social gains, and the need for change at different levels - in organisation, technology, infrastructure and the wider social and institutional context - provide a great barrier. This paper offers a way to escape the gridlock by engaging in what we call "Strategic Niche Management" (SNM). SNM aims at taking the new technologies to the market place to try and use them in selected settings – niches - by real users. The niches consist of domains of application in which the technology (or new mobility system) is already attractive to use due to specific circumstances (a local problem or the availability of specific, low cost resources). Experiences in the niche are then used to inform decisions about technical improvement and support policies, aimed at expanding the original niche and making a transition towards a more sustainable transport system. The protected space, in which the technology is temporary protected from the full force of normal selection pressures, acts as a test bed and incubator for the new technology. It may pave the way for private and government support policies in a gradual, non-distortionary, and thus feasable way. The paper provides three examples of SNM in Europe: the large-scale experiment with light-weight electric vehicles in Mendrisio (CH), organised car sharing in Switzerland and Rolling Highway in Sweden.

1 The Non-Sustainability of Present Transport Technologies and Practices [1]

Passenger transport is not sustainable. Each year around 250,000 people get killed in road accidents while 10 million people get injured. Road transport accidents are rapidly becoming the world-wide killer number one, ahead of all transmissible diseases together, or all natural catastrophes. Fossil-fuel based transport is also a more slow killer through the release of toxic compounds (e.g. CO, lead, benzene and other VOCs,) and the release of fine particulate matter that endanger human health and impair ecosystems. Another major problem is congestion, which limits people's mobility and creates a high economic cost for society through time delays.[2] Other problems associated with road transport are noise[3], land use (especially in urban areas), energy dependence, and the undermining of communities (Whitelegg, 1993).

Trends in transport are likely to worsen the above problems. The OECD Environmentally Sustainable Transport study projects on the basis of business-as-usual trends for many OECD countries for 2030 an increase in car ownership and total distances travelled (up to 200% more) plus even higher increases for freight transport and especially aviation with projected increases of up to 600% over 1990 levels. These increases will lead to increased emissions levels for most transport pollutants in 2030 despite significant reductions of emissions per (ton)km. The highest increase in automobile emissions will be for CO_2, which is likely to double in 2030, given foreseeable policy action. The overall conclusion of this study

1 Research leading to this paper was financed by the Swiss Federal Office for Education and Science (grant no. 95.0450) in the context of the European research project on "Strategic Niche Management" (see http://www.jrc.es/snm/).

2 In the Netherlands, 1.4 millions of vehicle hours were lost in traffic jams in 1994.

3 In the EU almost 80 million people (20% of the population) are subjected to noise levels above what is considered to be acceptable by the World Health Organisation.

is that likely advances in technology will not be sufficient to overcome increased environmental impacts stemming from growing transport demand. Assuming current trend projections, transport in 2030 will be moving *away* rather than moving toward environmental sustainability. In the EU, CO_2 emissions from transport are estimated to increase with 39% between 1990 and 2010, in the pre-Kyoto scenario.[4]

2 The Problem of Making a Shift Towards Sustainable Transport

Transport is a sector in which any action to change the course of existing paths is difficult because of the long development times, the need of up-front investment in new infrastructure, production outlays and maintenance systems, the need to co-ordinate the policies and actions of interdependent actors, and finally the attachment of people to existing modes of transport. In transport, the problem-solving capabilities are dispersed, even though there are some powerful actors such as automobile manufacturers, oil companies and transport companies with a strong technical and organisational competence using time horizons of one decade or more in their strategic plans - far beyond the time horizons of most policy makers and households. One of the problems from a climate protection perspective is that the actors have an interest in maintaining the current trajectories of development. This does not only pertain to private actors but also to public actors who too are committed to the fossil-fuel based path of development in transport, both financially and politically: financially they are committed because of the tax revenues (accounting for 4-14% of government tax revenues, excl. VAT)[5] and politically through the powerful motor vehicle constituency, which includes car drivers that have gained a strong preference for individual car-based travel and have developed a set of requirements of what a car should do (in terms of range, speed, acceleration, maintenance, etc.).[6] The great value that people attach to cars is reflected in the uprise of car parties in several European countries (e.g. Switzerland). It is telling that for more than 70 years the internal combustion engine vehicle has been the dominant technology in transport. Attempts to introduce alternative drive systems have all foundered.

4 Climate change - Analysis of proposed EU emission reduction objectives for Kyoto, Commission Staff Working Paper, p. 3.

5 The tax revenues consists of petroleum taxes on non-aviation fuels, registration fees, and taxes on ownership or use (figures are based on Road Transport and the Environment – Energy and Fiscal Aspects, Statistics in Focus – Environment, 1996: 2).

6 The cultural aspects of what a car is and how it is embedded in the rule system of a technological regime are examined in Truffer and Kemp (1998).

This is not to say that nothing happens. Alternative vehicles that pollute less are in the focus of attention. In the US, Japan and Europe there are research programmes linked to regulatory policies to built less polluting cars. In the US the three main car producers are collaborating with 11 government agencies and the US council for Automotive Research in the Partnership for a New Generation of Vehicles. In Japan motor companies are very active to developing more fuel efficient, low-polluting cars, like gasoline direct injection vehicles and hybrid vehicles with a dual propulsion system, one being electric. The steel and aluminium industries are involved in a race to provide low-weight solutions for car bodies. In Europe the car manufacturers association ACEA has committed itself to the following standards for new cars: 140 g CO_2/km until 2008, 120 g/km by 2012. The CO_2 standards represent a reduction of 25% with regard to the emissions from 1995. Within the 5th framework programme there are many programmes dealing with (non climate) transport problems There has also been a huge investment in transport telematics research in previous programmes. Under the 8-year EU Prometheus programme 900 mio ECU has been spend to develop transport telematics systems that help to make road vehicles more safe and traffic flows more efficient.

All over the world car manufacturers are exploring more environmentally friendly vehicles. They are taking strategic positions to build the 'environmentally benign car of the future', with Daimler-Benz working on the fuel cell vehicle, together with Ballard and Shell, a vehicle which emits water vapour. There is also the Californian initiative which sets standards for the sales of ultra low emission vehicles and zero emission vehicles. It is an example of forced commercialisation of alternative vehicles which by requiring car manufacturers to mass-produce zero-emission vehicles, helped to surpass a technological stalemate in which car manufacturers were reluctant to introduce electric vehicles for fears that consumers would not want to purchase alternative-fuel cars, whereas demand for electrically-powered vehicles could not develop since electric vehicles were not for sale. According to the Californian rules, zero-emissions cars must account for 10% of new-car production in the 2003, with strict standards pertaining towards hydrocarbon and nitrogen oxide emissions.

Most of the policies are car-centered: they do little to change the individual use of cars for the entire trip. What is needed are policies that encourage people to engage in the collective use of transport means, either a car, bus, tram or train, for at least part of their trip, or to encourage people to travel less by reducing the need for travel. This raises the question how a shift to more sustainable mobility systems and travel behaviour may be promoted in a way that is acceptable for the people involved. In the remainder of the paper we will describe a method for making a regime shift to alternative mobility: strategic niche management.

3 Strategic Niche Management for Sustainable Mobility

There are many barriers to more environmentally sustainable mobility systems. Three important barriers are the high up-front costs for providers, the preference of travellers for the individual use of cars, given present ownership structures in which every family owns a car, the sense of privacy (a person's car being a person's home), and the availability of an extended road infrastructure. A fourth barrier is unawareness and negative perceptions (right or wrong) on the part of potential users about alternative, more sustainable modes of transport. These four factors reinforce each other, creating a gridlock situation in which a new system will not readily develop.

This raises the question: how to escape this gridlock? Below we will describe a method for escaping the gridlock and moving towards sustainable mobility. This method is called "Strategic Niche Management" (SNM), and has been investigated in a social research project "SNM as a Tool for Transition to a Sustainable Transportation System" for the Environment and Climate programme of the EU (DG XII). SNM is a method for introducing new technologies in society, which relies on the real use of new technologies in selected settings (niches). The niches consist of selected domains of application in which the technology (or new mobility system) is already attractive to use due to specific circumstances (a local problem or the availability of specific, low cost resources). Experiences in the niche are then used to inform decisions about technical improvement and support policies, aimed at expanding the original niche and making a transition towards a more sustainable transport system.

Strategic niche management is thus a concentrated effort to develop protected spaces for certain applications of a new technology. Specifically, SNM is

> the creation and management of protected spaces (niches) for promising technologies by means of experimentation with the aim of learning about the performance, effects, economic viability and social desirability of the technology and to use this knowledge to inform private and public (support and control) policies that are needed for the further development and rate of application of new technologies and technology systems.

The protection may be offered by private and public decisions: by suppliers, development and regulatory agencies, local authorities and/or users.

SNM may be used for all innovations, but is especially suited for sustainable technologies and mobility systems offering environmental and social benefits which are undervalued in the market place.

The idea of SNM for new technologies comes from the literature on sequential decision making to deal with complexity (Simon), trial-and-error modes of learning, evolutionary theories of technical change (Nelson and Winter, 1982; Ayres;

Rip and Kemp, 1998), and studies on the critical role of users in innovation (von Hippel, 1988).

Arguments in favour of technology experiments involving real users:

1. The under-utilisation of technological possibilities: many ideas and prototypes never reach the stage of market introduction, which means that their potential and viability is not adequately investigated and abundantly tested. This pertains especially to radical, systemic technologies and technologies offering societal benefits as opposed to benefits for individual users;
2. Some things you can only learn through the real use of new technologies, such as market acceptance, the performance of a technology in real use situations, the best design configuration for different groups of users, etc;
3. Users are an important source of knowledge; involvement of users helps to better deal with their needs, whereas experiences with new technologies help users to develop a better understanding of new technologies and subject them to learning processes with respect to their own behaviour and mobility needs;
4. Experiments help to set into motion or facilitate processes of institutional embedding, and by doing so they act as a stepping stone/engine for change.

The strategic niche management approach differs from the "technology-push" approach that underlies most of today's technology promotion policies, by bringing in knowledge and expertise of users and other actors into the technology development process and to generate interactive learning processes and institutional adaptation.[7] Learning is an important aspect of strategic niche management. But SNM is more than a learning strategy through user experiments. It is also aimed at creating a platform for interaction and at building a product constituency of private and public decision makers. The latter is very important for escaping the gridlock of dominant practices and vested interests and beliefs. SNM thus helps not only to deal with problems of uncertainty and fragmented and dispersed knowledge and organisational resources - being common obstacles to change - but also helps to deal with opposition from vested interests and to deal with the conservatism of established views and beliefs that the innovation is not economically or technologically viable, or inferior to alternative solutions that reside within the existing technological regime. Apart from facilitating learning, SNM helps set into motion a processes *institutional embedding*, that are necessary for the develop-

7 We specifically include the adjective 'strategic' in the label of the approach, to stress the importance of anticipation. In running an experiment, the actors should adopt a forward-looking perspective, by anticipating emerging opportunities and possible threats that create, widen or close windows of opportunity. Strategic niche management as a process management approach has nothing to do with strategic planning: it differs from the strategic planning paradigm through its focus on interactive learning and adjustment.

ment and wider use of a new technology. Institutional embedding involves network formation, co-ordination of policies of private and public actors, the making of capital investments, establishment of production and use practices, standardisation of a technology, and the development of shared belief systems, roles and expectations.

After having talked about the "what" we now turn to the "how" question. How to do SNM? What does strategic niche management imply in practical terms? In the framework of the SNM project earlier enunciated we developed a five step plan, delineating key elements of SNM. The five step plan is described in Kemp *et al.* (1998). The five steps are: 1) the selection of a technology, 2) the selection of an experiment, 3) set up of the experiment, 4) scaling up of the experiment, 5) and break down of protection. Whilst the choice of a step plan may look like a deterministic exercise, obfuscating the feedback loops and reflexive nature of SNM, it does bring out the key features. The steps are:

The selection of a technology

There are usually different types of solutions for a problem, with different costs and benefits. A choice must be made which technology will be supported: a technology offering local benefits or wider benefits in the long term. Although there is a need to experiment with all kind of solutions, there is a special need to support technologies that are outside the existing regime or paradigm. Of course, it is exactly these kind of solutions that are often unattractive to use from a user point of view. On the other hand there may be niches in which the costs do not count high. If such niches exist, we may use strategic niche management. Technologies that are suited for strategic niche management are thus technologies that:

- have sufficient development potential and a synergy with ongoing developments (like the evolution of user preferences and societal values, policy developments, areas of rapid technical advances);
- be attractive to use for certain applications in which the disadvantages of the new technology count less and the advantages are valued high.

The selection of the technology can be done in a consultative and co-operative mode together with stakeholders or in a more competitive mode through the use of tenders in which people (consortia) are asked to come up with proposals.

The selection of an experiment or niche

After choosing a technology eligible for support, an appropriate setting for the new technology needs to be chosen. This should be a setting or space in which the advantages of the technology are valued high (because of specific problems like local pollution) and the disadvantages (in terms of costs of discomfort) count less. The space may be a certain application (for example, the use of solar cells for pleasure boats), a geographical area (a region or a city), or a jurisdictional unit.

The heterogeneity of the selection environment means that there are almost always areas and types of application for which the new technology is attractive, in which the disadvantages count less and the advantages are valued higher. Electric vehicles that do not emit pollutants at the point of use are attractive for use in cities with high levels of pollution. Their small size makes them suited in tourist resorts with narrow roads. They are also attractive to use in fleets because of the low operating costs. These are just three applications for EVs.

The set-up of the experiment

This is perhaps the most difficult step, because a balance must be struck between protection and selection pressure. Finding a balance between protection and selection pressure is a continuing task for niche managers. As a rule, protection should be not too generous: technology developers must be forced to take care of user requirements and impelled to eliminate negative side effects connected with the widespread application of a new technology; on the other hand the selection pressures should not be so strong, putting development work under time pressures making companies opt for conventional solutions that offer short term benefits at the expense of long term benefits. Too much protection may in the end lead to 'white elephants', and too little protection may forestall different paths of development.

The choice of niche policies needs to be based on the barriers to the use and diffusion of the new technology. These barriers may be economic, when the new technology is unable to compete with conventional technologies, given the prevailing cost structure. They may be technical, such as the lack of complementary technologies, needed new infrastructure or appropriate skills. And they may be social and institutional barriers, such as existing laws, practices, perceptions, norms or habits. An integrated and co-ordinated policy is required to deal successfully with these barriers. Possible elements of such a policy are: the formulation of long-term goals, the creation of an actor network, co-ordination of actions and strategies, and, where needed, the use of taxes, subsidies, public procurement and standards.

Scaling up the experiment or niche

The next step concerns scaling up the experiment or niche by making a product or service widely available and the introduction of promotion measures. The first will be the task for private companies, the second for both private and public decision makers. Even a highly successful experiment may require some kind of support from public policy makers in the form of preferential treatment vis-à-vis less environmentally benign technologies. Again this raises the question how far governments should go in the support of a particular technology. Overly generous support in the form of subsidies will give rise to windfall profits for the recipients, whereas too scarce support may prevent the new technology system in acquiring a 'critical mass' which is necessary for the wider diffusion. Apart from promoting a technology offering social benefits there is also a need to limit the side effects.

The break down of protection

The final step is the phased break down of protection. Support for the new technology may no longer be necessary or it may no longer be desirable, when the results are disappointing and prospects are dim. On the other hand, the continuation of protection may be warranted for setting a level playing field with technologies of which the external costs are not fully internalised. The break down should be done in a phased way in order not to create adjustment problems for the companies involved.

It should be stressed that strategic niche management is more than the execution of the above five steps. If the execution of the steps would be done too mechanically, the reflexive side of strategic niche management is degraded. The primary aim of SNM is not to push a technology but to stimulate learning about problems, user needs and technological solutions to a problem, to assist in the building of sociotechnical constituencies for a product, to align different interests to a set of goals, and foster institutional adaptation; the steps should be viewed as ways to achieve this.

So far we haven't talked about *who* should do strategic niche management, whether this should be done by a government agency, a private company or (policy) entrepreneur. In practice, different actors may be the niche manager: a private company, a local authority, state policy maker, a regulatory agency, a development agency, an NGO, citizen group, a consortium consisting of a private and public actors, or an independent individual possessed with managerial capabilities, depending on who is best qualified to take on this task, which will differ from case to case and will possibly change in the course of time.

It is worth stressing that strategic niche management is not just something for governments. The role of government is limited. For example, industry and NGOs are better suited to initiate and run niche projects. As a rule, government should take on those roles that they can do better than others; they should not take on the responsibility for running the experiment, as this is probably best done by professionals with their own social networks. As noted, governments have a special role as an enabler or facilitator to make sure that something happens, and that the project yields satisfactory results (which requires monitoring, evaluation of outcomes and policies, and in the case of undesirable outcomes, the judicious exertion of pressures and correction of adverse actions and policies). As to the role of different levels of government. Local governments are best placed to engage in local affairs such as network management. Regional and state governments may act as co-sponsor for projects that may be used on a larger scale. They could also help in the up-scaling of successful experiments, through sponsorship or macro-policies (like changes in the regulatory framework and the use of fiscal incentives). National and regional governments also have a special responsibility for making sure that there is a broad social learning process. This could be done by supporting a portfolio of niche projects, institute technology appraisals and social discourses (in which the technologies are evaluated along a wide range of dimensions), and disseminating the knowledge that is gathered in the projects. A good example of SNM is the Danish policy towards wind power in which the government provided *leverage* to WP developments in a timely, not over-supportive, manner, adapted to the changing political and economic circumstances. The development was not staged by Danish policy makers but was carried originally by WP pioneers, and later on by wind turbine manufacturers and energy utilities (See Kemp *et al.*, 1998).

4 Three Examples of SNM in Transport

We will now describe three examples of SNM in passenger transport, which were studied in the EU project "Strategic Niche Management as a Tool of Transition in the Transportation Sector". The examples are: the large scale experiment with light-weight electric vehicles in Mendrisio (CH), organised car sharing in Switzerland, and the Rolling Highway in Sweden. The experiments demonstrate in their own unique way positive features of SNM such as the combination of protection *and* selection pressure (with neither being too strong), the importance of users as a source of information and protector of a new technology, and the benefits of adaptive planning informed by assessments of technologies, user experiences and policy measures.

Example 1. The use of light-weight electric vehicles in Mendrisio

In the Swiss town of Mendrisio (10,000 inhabitants), a large scale experiment is being conducted with light-weight electric vehicles (LEVs).[8] Its main goal is to substitute a proportion of 8% (i.e. about 350) of all vehicles by electric vehicles. This substitution shall be achieved by a whole series of promotional measures.

First, a set of different political support measures is tested to see which of them are most effective in order to promote a wider market diffusion of LEVs. These measures include, among many others, vehicle subsidies, reduced vehicle taxes, reduced fuel and parking costs and access to charging infrastructure. Second, marketing and market introduction strategies are being evaluated regarding their respective importance. Third, the usefulness of LEVs in everyday use shall be demonstrated. Finally, it will be tested if (and how) LEVs contribute to more sustainable mobility forms. Therefore, the energy use of LEVs is being determined in everyday conditions, additional mobility services are being offered to LEV-users (e.g. advantageous conditions in car sharing, car rental, taxi use and

8 A more detailed description of the Mendrisio experiment is given in Harms and Truffer (1998b).

public transport), and the overall traffic evolution through the introduction of LEVs shall be analysed. The relative effectiveness of these measures will indicate how a politically supported diffusion process could be generalised at a national level, aiming at a nation-wide substitution of 8% of all vehicles by LEVs.

Despite of the experiment's main goal of substituting conventional cars by LEVs, it follows a much more far-reaching approach. By introducing an extensive vehicle monitoring that assesses the LEV's actual (as opposed to bench-test) road performance, data are collected that are used to calculate the environmental impact of LEV use. Many different vehicle types can be compared here, since the experiment is open to different models as long as they do not surpass a certain level of energy use. Vehicles that are being driven within the experiment use a wide range of battery-, recharging- and drive-train systems. By this, the risk of getting "locked into" a particular LEV technology is avoided. Several technologies are tested in parallel.

The Mendrisio experiment was initiated as part of a federal promotion program for LEVs in 1995 in order to simulate the market diffusion of the technology. This approach was motivated by the belief that the main problem of the current LEV-technology was less the technological weakness of the vehicles but rather the reaping of economies of scale at the level of manufacturing, infrastructure and the market. Up to the beginning of the experiment, about 2,000 LEVs had been sold in Switzerland. By this time, Switzerland held 20% of the world market of electric vehicles. In the first years, the market experienced exponential growth rates. In 1992, however, sales numbers began to fall and reached a constant level of about one to two hundred vehicles per year. Therefore, the experiment can also be seen as a means to actively support the market niche of LEVs. The project will be carried out within six years time. It is divided into three project phases of a duration of two years each. After each phase an evaluation is made, and it is decided if and how to continue. Thus, there is a guarantee for flexibility in the project structure plus a safeguard that the project can be stopped at an earlier point in time if lacks success.

Though initiated in a top-down manner by policy makers, the experiment already has a long history and can be considered as based on a user-led bottom-up movement. Starting in the 1980s, a number of small and medium-sized enterprises, university institutes, interested individuals and spin-off firms built up a support and innovation network for the development and diffusion of LEVs. By these initiatives some of the most pressing technological problems regarding lightweight construction for vehicles and electric propulsion were tackled at that time. One of the most important events for an exchange on the technology development and for mutual learning was the Tour de Sol-race. It was organised from 1985 to 1992 and consisted of a one week race for prototypes and commercially available LEVs, and crossed the whole national territory of Switzerland. Due to this race, a market for LEVs slowly began to establish itself. Technologically interested persons invented solar cars or electric vehicles and tested them in the race. Some of the developers also used their racing cars in everyday life. Later, mere selling and "converting" firms were founded, and users with other than technological motivations appeared. In the early times, developers resp. converters and users were in direct contact with each other. As soon as technological problems occurred, they could be passed on to the developers and solved by them. By this, the developers learnt about the quality of their vehicles in every day use. With a growing market, this direct contact broke down, and a top-down structure was needed for enabling ongoing learning, not only with respect to technical aspects, but mainly with respect to consumer acceptance and market diffusion.

The project runs for more than two years, now. Up to June 1997 (the end of the first project phase), 82 vehicles were sold in Mendrisio, 32 of them to private users. 14 out of those 32 vehicles counted as cars. The rest is categorised as bicycles or motorcycles (Studienreihe Grossversuch Nr. 18, 1997). More than half of the LEV-users (cars, motorcycles and bicycles taken together) substituted another vehicle with the purchase of their LEV, the other half bought a LEV as an additional vehicle (Pulfer 1997). In general, the first project phase is perceived a success, although the number of vehicles sold somewhat lags expectations of the organisers. Like mentioned above, success is not only measured by the number of cars sold, but also by being able to demonstrate the usefulness of LEVs in everyday use. Furthermore, first hints on the success of different political support measures in order to promote market diffusion of LEVs can be given.

The Mendrisio experiment clearly demonstrates the potential usefulness of the SNM approach for sustainable mobility. Although the experiment is carried out with no explicit innovation-theoretical background, the above mentioned processes of learning and societal embedding were considered by the managers of the experiment. The project involves learning that goes much further than the conventional technical testing of vehicles and market assessment of potential sales. There was an assessment of promotion measures and lessons are sought for how to scale-up the use of LEVs in Switzerland and beyond.

There was also an assessment of peoples' mobility patterns, including the question whether LEVs can constitute an element of new, integrated forms of individual mobility. While the data base in Mendrisio is still too small to give an answer here, analyses of the mobility patterns of LEV-users in the rest of Switzerland as well as in other European countries show that LEVs have a potential for leading to a more sustainable individual transport system (Knie et al 1997). Though the total number of kilometres made by an individual means of transportation (gasoline car and LEV taken together) is not reduced (but not enhanced neither), LEV-users undergo a number of qualitative learning processes. Their modal split changes (the LEV becomes the most frequently and preferringly used vehicle), they drive more cautiously and become more conscious about energy use in transportation.

Taken together, the experiment has, up to date, been very successful in terms of learning and institutional embedding; it has been less successful in terms of the size of the market. In Switzerland, LEVs are a widely accepted technology today, and they form part of the portfolio of choice.

Example 2. The development of organised car sharing in Switzerland

A second example of strategic niche management is the development of organised car sharing in Switzerland.[9] Organised car sharing consists of the common use of vehicles by members of an organisation (be it a professional firm or a co-operative) in succession and independently of each other. The duration and target of individual car trips is self-determined by the respective car users. The individual right of disposal is substituted by a collective one (Baum & Pesch 1994).

Organised car sharing was pioneered in Switzerland by two co-operatives, both founded (independently of each other) in 1987. The first one *ShareCom,* had its focus in and around the city of Zurich, and the second one *ATG ("AutoTeilet Genossenschaft")* had its beginnings in the region of Lucerne. The emergence of a market for car sharing can thus be considered as a user-led bottom-up experiment. Only later was it taken up and supported by federal agencies. Both car-sharing co-operatives started out of groups of a dozen households who practised some form of private car sharing. Providers and users of the system were identical in those times. They were convinced of the economic and environmental virtues of their system and they wanted to facilitate the foundation of new car sharing locations in other places. Every member purchased a share of the co-operative and thus brought in the needed starting capital. He/she took over specific tasks, identified with the system and was a potential multiplier of the system. Besides high identification, all members profited from this task-sharing as it guaranteed low costs for car-use. However, the motivation to contribute on a non-paid basis was only possible as long as the user-group stayed small. With an increasing number of users the need for centralisation and bundling of activities rose. Nevertheless, in both organisations a direct coupling between the users and the management resp. persons taking over administrative and technical tasks always proved to be a key element.

Though following different organisational philosophies, both organisations were continuously showing equal growth rates. Besides the input of the co-operative members, the support of different societal actors was essential in order to reach a broader market. Traffic clubs, environmental organisations, the media and many others helped the car-sharing system on its way to success. From 1992-95, the Swiss Department of Energy financially supported both car-sharing organisations in the framework of a national energy saving program. This support accelerated the car- sharing development, and besides it legitimised the organisations' actions, so that contacts to other central players in the field of mobility were facilitated.

---

9 A more detailed description of the car sharing experiment is given in Harms and Truffer (1998b).

E.g., a number of local co-operations with public transport providers were created (in the form of so-called "driving passes" that allowed for a cheaper use of public transport, car sharing and the local taxi enterprises). Finally, in 1997, under the pressure of the Swiss government, the two organisations joined forces in a national co-operative called *Mobility CarSharing Switzerland*. Mid 1998, 22.000 members shared 1000 vehicles at 700 locations in 300 communities spread over the whole national territory. In autumn 1998, a co-operation with the federal railway was started, enabling users to develop new, integrated mobility forms (taking the train for long trips and using a car-sharing car from the station to the final destination). By this co-operation, Mobility hopes to win another 20.000 car-sharing customers within 1999 (Muheim 1998).

Car-sharing can be considered as a service innovation. Individual mobility is covered by conventional 'middle class' automobiles, and the main innovation consists of the organisation of shared car use. However, in order to be successful, a number of technological innovations had to be introduced as well. A reservation and accounting system as well as means for access control had to be invented (e.g. by installing on-board computers in the cars). The huge success of car sharing was thus dependent on the existence, diffusion and maturity of new information and telecommunication technologies.

Users were important to the development of the system by

- providing "cheap money" for the expansion of the system. The co-operative got money from its members at an interest rate which was very low or even zero.
- doing most of the billing, cleaning, repairing, information spreading etc. on a private basis. Administrative costs could thus be held extremely low. Despite of not having a professionalised service standard, cars were nevertheless clean and in a good technical state. Furthermore, small accidents and repairs were reported back to the central office or were solved on an individual basis. Small problems and not too tidy cars were largely accepted by the members. No expectations of a fully professionalised service existed due to the organisations' co-operative structure.
- spreading the virtues of the system by words of mouth, thereby keeping the costs of expansion low. They were also instrumental in obtaining preferential conditions for the system in their local communities (e.g. cheaper parking lots). Furthermore, they lowered the uncertainties of new members since they were "neighbours" on which new members of the system could rely. Car sharing was thus provided with a "familiar face" and the impression of a small scale system, despite of an exponentially growing number of locations. This lead to a gradual and geographically decentralised growth pattern which was associated with lower risks on the cost side.

- enabling the central offices and the managers to engage in a gradual learning process that would not have been possible if the whole system had been run in a top-down manner.

The users thus created a favourable environment for the technology to prosper, and for the promoters to learn how to deal with an ever expanding market. Given these protections from the early users, it seems highly unlikely that organised car sharing could have been built up by a professional provider. Up-front investments for achieving an attractive density of the location network would have been extremely high, and the users' requirements for well-performing system would have been much higher. By relying on bottom-up initiatives, a product profile could gradually shape, and the organisations could slowly professionalise. Today they have reached a standard that also allows users with high quality demands to join the system.

Switzerland is not the only country in which organised forms of car sharing were introduced. From 1988 onwards (and independently of the ongoing developments in Switzerland) a number of car-sharing organisations were founded in other European countries as well, especially in Germany, the Netherlands and Austria. However, in these countries the car-sharing market was much more diversified right from the beginning, both with respect to its providers as well as to its organisational form (for a detailed discussion, see Harms and Truffer, 1998). Mid 1997, about 70,000 people were members of a car-sharing organisation in those four countries, not to count those who privately share cars with friends, neighbours or family members. Annual growth rates are relatively high in all countries (e.g. in Switzerland initially over 100%, and later 50-75%).

Although based on the individual use of cars, car sharing opens ways to a more sustainable transport system. Former car owners substitute two thirds of their car kilometres by public transport, bicycle or walking after having joined a car-sharing organisation. The rest is substituted by a car-sharing car. For former non-car owners the amount of car driving remains constant (Harms and Truffer 1998, Meijkamp 1998, Muheim 1998). Those learning processes seem to be system-inherent: the reservation system and cost structure of car sharing organisations hinder consumers from making use of the car in a habitual way, i.e. they limit the instant-use of cars. Organised car sharing offers a pathway to lower automobility lifestyles, in which people replace part of their automobile-based travel with collective forms of travel and a reduction in travel.

Example 3. "Rolling highway" projects in Sweden

The third example concerns two "rolling highway" experiments in Sweden, one in the North and one at the West Coast.[10] Rolling highway is a transportation mode

---

10 This section is based on Schwartz and Maruo (1998) and the writings of Ben Lane in the SNM workbook (Weber *et al.*, 1998).

where complete trucks or trailers are transported by train on special wagons. This is already an established transport option in Switzerland and Austria (transalpine freight transport) and Germany. The Rolling Highway helps to combine advantages of two technologies: the trucks' flexibility when freight is distributed locally and the train's environmental advantage.

The first experiment was carried out in the North of Sweden and involved the regional distribution of freight by the food retailer ICA. In this project SJ (the Swedish railway company) organised a rail transportation service for trucks of ICA using wagons which were leased from Germany. The experience proved highly successful because the service (planning of schedule etc.) was customised to ICA's requirements thanks to good co-operation between the two companies.

In a second project, SJ wished to set up a second rolling highway system to decrease the heavy road traffic and related pollution problems caused by Norwegian-bound trucks on transit through Sweden to the continent of Europe. The project was part funded by the EU and the county who provided 100,000 ECU of the total costs of 600-900,000 ECU. Unlike the Northern experiment, the experiment on the West Coast was far from successful even though the technology employed was the same. Several factors were responsible for this. Two important factors were the presence of strong competition from ferries and road trucks and unprofessional project management. In particular, SJ did not involve their own employees with experience from the project with ICA; persons who may have been able to foresee problems on the West Coast experiment. Another important reason why the West Coast project failed was the failure of SJ to involve the road carriers or the forwarding and shipping agents in the planning process. As it turned out, the timetable did not fit the road carriers' requirements.

The lesson here is that the railroad company's departments did not learn from each other's experiences. There was no mechanism for dissemination of learning in place within SJ, so that the positive experience from the Northern experiment, especially with regard to the contacts with the clients was not transferred to the West Coast experiment. Perhaps surprisingly, the West Coast experiment did demonstrate the potential viability of the rolling highway at the Swedish West Coast. It was stated by several road carriers that they are still very interested to use the service in the future if the railroad company can solve the remaining problems (i.e. improve the time table). This buttresses in our view the need to do user experiments, accepting that sometimes lessons are learned the 'hard way'. Mistakes are inevitable in experiments. You cannot design optimal system modalities beforehand, especially not in transport where the sheer complexity and many uncertainties about technical choices and service modalities to be offered to a heterogeneous population of users simply defy such an optimalisation endeavour in one go. The task for niche managers is to start out with something, to learn from the mistakes and correct them, for example by changing the functionalities of the system and/or the economic conditions of their use. An overview of the three examples is given in Table 1.

Table 1: Examples of user experiments with sustainable transport technologies

Project	Technology	Partners	Period and costs	Learning	Institutional embedding
Large-scale experiment with light-weight electric vehicles (EVs) in Mendrisio, Switzerland	Electric vehicles (passenger cars; 350 planned), recharging stations (normal and fast charge)	Federal Energy Agency (funding), municipality (host), research institutes (evaluation), car importers, electric utility (recharging), canton, partner communities. Project manager is Info-VEL centre in Mendrisio	Start June '95; 6 years duration; costs 23.5 mln. ECU (33% federal government, 43% users buying EVs, 10% car importers, plus sponsors, cantons and municipality); no follow-up planned	Learning about user willingness to buy LEV, promotion policies and mobility behaviour; learning about environment friendly driving styles	Dissemination of knowledge about LEVs throughout Switzerland, establishment of constituency for LEVs, positive image of LEVs, internalisation of environmental values by LEV users; interest from other countries in LEVs
Organised car sharing in Switzerland	Shared (conventional) cars and vans, reservation and accounting software	ATG and Sharecom, later merged into Mobility Carsharing Switzerland (MCS), Swiss Federal Energy Agency	Start '87 with 2 dozen vehicles; in Oct '98: 1000 cars, 22,000 users, 700 locations	Learning about professionalisation, upscaling, new service modalities	Expansion of network of ocs, establishment of MCS, links with public transport companies to promote intermodal travel
'Rolling Highway' projects in Sweden	Trucks on railroad waggons (waggons leased from German railroads company).	*Westcoast:* Swedish railroads company SJ, forwarding and shipping agents, road carriers, county council *The North*: freight division of SJ, food retailer ICA	*Westcoast:* June - Nov. '96; estim. costs 0.6-0.9 mln. ECU, incl. 0.1 mln. ECU subsidies (50% EU, 50% county) *The North:* start '94; costs equal to transport by road trucks	Learning about technical operation and economic viability of scheme, identification of user requirements and needs and ways to satisfy these through customised services and the use of alt. waggons	Roll. Highway project on westcoast by SJ and Norwegian Railroads since Jan '97; other rail transport projects of SJ Freight with food/ wholesale retailers (including ICA)

Adapted from Table1.1 of Integrative Summary Report of SNM project (Hoogma *et al.*, 1998)

5 Conclusion

In this paper, we described a method for introducing sustainable transport innovations in society, which relies on the creation and management of protected spaces (niches) in which the technology is used by real users. This method is called Strategic Niche Management (SNM). SNM is an attempt to make the co-production of technological options, use, policy measures and sustainable development visible and productive; it highlights choices and options and will make the introduction process transparent and doable for all parties involved including producers, users and policy-makers (Weber *et al.*, 1998).

It should be stressed that SNM is not about pushing possible winners but about *testing* and *selecting* prospective winners. The pushing is done after a period of testing, and there is also an element of control, of limiting side effects. SNM thus combines elements of push and control.

SNM is process-based, involving sequential decision-making and learning-by-doing. It is not aimed at achieving pre-specified outcomes, as in a management-by-objectives approach, but an attempt to explore the potential of new technology in selected settings. By carefully choosing the domain of application, the limitations of a new technology for users may be identified and adequately addressed through a concerted action by public and private decision makers.

SNM is especially suited for promoting sustainable transport where the overriding need to respect established user requirements creates a barrier for the development of solutions offering social benefits. In doing SNM ones needs to find a balance between protection and selection pressure. In general, some kind of protection is needed for new technologies offering societal benefits rather than user benefits. It is not the task for the government alone to provide protection. Other parties should do the same. Users should carry a substantial part of the costs, as should be suppliers and other private actors having an interest in the new technology, to prevent the occurrence of 'white elephants'.

In the paper we described three experiments with the use of transport technologies that may form a part of a more sustainable transport system, two from passenger transport and one from freight transport. The three experiments illustrate in different ways the usefulness of doing user experiments and engage in SNM. The experiments set into motion learning processes both at the supply and user side. These included, at the supply side: a better idea of user needs and requirements, the identification of imperfections in the functioning of the technology, the economic conditions of its use, and ways to promote the new product; and at the user side a better understanding of a new technology and how it may be used beneficially. The experiments also contributed to processes of institutional embedding through the building of constituencies, user acceptance, the formation of product conceptual systems, and the establishing of more sustainable travel habits, like cautious driving and less driving using a more environmentally benign mode of transport. In general, experiments may pave the way for sustainable transport policies (like road and congestion pricing and restrictions on the use of cars in cities). As noted, one of the great obstacles for such policies is that there appear to be no attractive alternatives to car-based modes of travel.

The use of SNM is not limited to transport or energy, two areas in which there are great barriers to sustainable technologies. SNM may also be used for normal market innovations by private decision makers who want to use niche markets as a stepping stone for creating mass markets for radical products.[11]

So far policy support for technology experiments has been *ad hoc* and uninformed by theory. The approach of SNM offers a conceptual model for the use of user experiments with sustainable technologies and legitimitises government support for technology experiments with real users. It also offers a practical tool for doing social experiments with new technologies, through the 5 step plan and the practical lessons described in the workbook

References

Baum, H./Pesch, S. (1994): Untersuchung der Eignung von CarSharing im Hinblick auf Reduzierung von Stadtverkehrsproblemen. Schlussbericht. Research report No. 70421/93 on behalf of the Bundesminister für Verkehr. Köln

ECMT (1993): Transport Growth in Question, Paris: OECD.

Elzen, B./Hoogma, R./Schot, J. (1996): Mobiliteit met Toekomst - Naar een vraaggericht technologiebeleid, report to the Ministry of Traffic and Transport (in Dutch).

EPRI (1996): 'Pricing for success: using auto industry models to review electric vehicle costing and pricing'

Harms, S./Truffer, B. (1998a): The Emergence and Professionalisation of two Carsharing Co-operatives in Switzerland, final report for SNM project.

Harms, S./Truffer, B. (1998b): The Swiss large scale experiment with lightweight electric vehicles in Mendrisio, final report for SNM project.

Hippel, E. von (1988): The Sources of Innovation, Oxford, NY: Oxford University Press.

Hodge, D. (1995): Intelligent Transportation systems, Land Use, and Sustainable Transportation, paper presented at the ITS America Alternative Futures Symposium on Transportation, Technology and Society, March 13, 1995.

Hoogma, R./Schot, J./Kemp, R./Truffer, B. (1998): Integrative Summary Report of the project "Strategic Niche Management as a Tool for Transition to a Sustainable

11 Examples of companies who successfully adopted a SNM approach for their innovations are described in Lynn et al.

Transport System" for RTD programme "Environment and Climate" (EU DG XII) in the area of Human Dimension of Environmental Change.

IPTS (1996): The Car of the Future, the Future of the Car, Report EUR 17277 EN, Seville: IPTS-IPTS (1997), Special report on Urban Mobility, Seville: IPTS-JRC, Febr 1997.

Kemp, R./Soete, L. (1992): 'The Greening of Technological Progress: An Evolutionary Perspective', Futures 24(5), 437-457.

Kemp, R./Miles, I./Smith, K. et al. (1994b), Technology and the Transition to Environmental Stability. Continuity and Change in Complex Technology Systems, final report of the project Technological Paradigms and Transition Paths: The Case of Energy Technologies for SEER research programme of the Commission of the European Communities (DG XII).

Kemp, R. (1994): 'Technology and the Transition to Environmental Sustainability. The Problem of Technological Regime Shifts', Futures 26(10), 1023-46.

Kemp, R. (1996): 'The Transition from Hydrocarbons. The Issues for Policy', in S. Faucheux, D. Pearce and J.L.R. Proops (eds.), Models of Sustainable Development, Cheltenham: Edward Elgar, 151-175.

Kemp, R. (1997): Environmental Policy and Technical Change. A Comparison of the Technological Impact of Policy Instruments, Cheltenham: Edward Elgar.

Kemp, R./Schot, J./Hoogma, R. (1998): 'Regime Shifts to Sustainability through Processes of Niche Formation. The Approach of Strategic Niche Management', Technology analysis and Strategic Management, 10(2):175-195.

Kemp, R./Rip, A./Schot, J. (1997): 'Constructing Transition Paths through the Management of Niches', paper for Copenhagen workshop on "Path Creation and Dependence", 19-21 Aug 1997.

Knie, A./Berthold, O./Hård, M./Buland, T./Gjøen, H./Quéré, M./Streicher, W./Truffer, B./Harms, S. (997) Consumer user patterns of electric vehicles. WZB, Wissenschaftszentrum für Sozialforschung Berlin, FS-II 97-105.

Lynn, G./Morone, J./Paulson, A.: 'Marketing and Discontinuous Innovation: The Probe and Learn Process', California Management Review 38(3).

Meijkamp, R. (1996): 'Car Sharing: Consumer Acceptance and Changes on Mobility Behaviour', paper for the 24th European Transport Forum, Brunel University, Uxbridge, London.

Meyer, E. (1997): Grossversuch mit Leicht-Elektromobilen (LEM) in Mendrisio: Fahrleistungen und Energieverbrauch. 5. meeting on "light weight electric vehicles in every day use".

Michaelis, L./Davidson, O. (1996): 'GHG mitigation in the transport sector', Energy Policy 24.

Muheim, P. (1998): Carsharing—der Schlüssel zur kombinierten Mobilität. Synthese. Bundesamt für Energie, Bern.

Muntwyler, U. (1997a): The marketing concept in the Swiss fleet test in Mendrisio as an example of introducing EVs into the marketplace. 5. meeting on "light weight electric vehicles in every day use".

Muntwyler, U. (1997b): Leichtelektromobile. Neuzulassungen Schweiz. LEM-News 19/20.

Muntwyler, U. (1997c): Zwei Jahre Grossversuch mit Leicht-Elektromobilen in Mendrisio: Weltweit grösster Versuch mit Leicht-Elektromobilen erfolgreich. 5. meeting on "light weight electric vehicles in every day use".

Nelson, R./Winter, S. (1982): An Evolutionary Theory of Economic Change, Cambridge (Mass.): Bellknap Press.

OECD (1996): 'Prévention et contrôle de la pollution - Critères environnementaux pour des transports durables', Paris.

Pulfer, M. (1997): Zwischenstand und Auswertung der Fahrzeugzulassungen in Mendrisio und den Partnergemeinden. 5. meeting on "light weight electric vehicles in every day use".

Rip, A./Kemp, R. (1998): 'Technological Change', in Steve Rayner and Liz Malone (eds.), Human Choice and Climate Change, Batelle Press, Washington D.C.

Rip, A./Misa, T./Schot, J. (eds.) (1995): Managing Technology in Society. New Forms for the Control of Technology, London: Pinter Publishers.

Rosenberg, N. (1995): 'Uncertainty and Technological Change', in Ralph Landau et al. (eds.), Mosaic of Economic Growth, 334-53.

Schot, J.W. (1992): 'Constructive Technology Assessment and Technology Dynamics. The Case of Clean Technologies', Science, Technology and Human Values 17(1), 36-57.

Schot, J./Elzen, B./Hoogma, R. (1994): 'Strategies for Shifting Technological Systems. The Case of the Automobile System', Futures 26(10), 1060-76.

Schwartz, B./Maruo, K. (1998): Trucks on Trains. A Comparison of Two "Rolling Highway" projects in Sweden, final report for SNM project.

Simon, B. (1997), 'Industrial and institutional barriers to the diffusion of electric vehicles', Stockholm workshop on EV.

Truffer, B./Kemp, R. (1998): The Social Construction of a New Mobility Form—Experiments with Organized Car Sharing, paper for EASST conference, Lisbon, 30.9-3.10.1998

Volkskrant, 'Een auto van gemengde komaf', May 3, 1997.

Volkskrant, 'Stimuleren van autodelen doet autodichtheid dalen', June 18, 1997.

Weber, M./Hoogma, R./Lane,B./Schot, J. (1998): Expanding Technological Niches... How to Manage Experiments with Sustainable Transport Technologies, workbook of the project "Strategic Niche Management as a Tool for Transition to a Sustainable Transport System" for RTD programme "Environment and Climate" (EU DG XII) in the area of Human Dimension of Environmental Change, Sevilla/Enschede.

Whitelegg, J. (1993): Transport for Sustainable Future: The Case for Europe, Wiley.

Instruments for Attaining Urban Sustainability The Case for Tradable Vehicle Use Permits

Haynes Carson Goddard

Department of Economics, University of Cincinnati
Cincinnati, Ohio 45221
USA

Keywords. *Urban sustainability, sustainable transport, air pollution, tradable permits, supplementary licences, land use, growth boundaries*

1 Introduction: The Problem of Social Costing in Transport

What is now a litany among environmentalists and urban planners, the list of ills to be attributed to the unbridled use of the private vehicle is long, and getting longer: huge economic losses due to congestion on roads and highways, air, water and land pollution, loss of habitat due to road building and development, loss of farmland, destruction of social cohesiveness and now global climate change. In the U.S., perhaps the world's best (worst?) example of the overuse of the private automobile, a full 31% of its carbon dioxide emissions are generated in the transport sector.

While it used to be just Los Angeles in the news over its chronic vehicle generated air quality problems, in the last two decades added to the list are Atlanta, Paris, Mexico City, Hong Kong, Bangkok, São Paulo, Athens, Rome, and Santiago, Chile, and the list grows. It would seem that the answer to the problems generated by the over use of vehicles is simple, and in fact, if you ask nearly any economist, the reflexive response nearly always is to raise the price of gasoline, setting it at the level of the damages generated - that is, "getting the prices right" will solve the problem. But, perhaps as is usual, such quick answers are too simple, at a minimum because such damages are not easily measured in a comprehensive sense.

The problems that confront metropolitan communities over the environmental costs of unlimited vehicle use are 1) the awareness of the full social costs of unrestricted use of the private automobile is only now beginning to approach the level at which the public may accept controls, and 2) public managers have not felt that they have many good options and policy instruments, outside of more technological controls on vehicles, for stemming these costs. Significantly raising regional gas prices would be perverse in a spatial sense, because creating major spatial price differentials will induce metropolitan areas to become larger as economic activity would move beyond the price frontier to escape the higher charges. Further, gasoline surcharges cannot be varied to deal with the variability of congestion and air quality outcomes. As a result, gasoline surcharges are too blunt an instrument to be very useful in a regional context, except as a method to raise revenue for subsidizing other sustainability promoting activities, such as mass transit. In sum, there is a serious question of what traditional economic instruments can achieve to move the world's vehicle use practices to sustainable levels.

What are the dimensions to be controlled? There are emissions, congestion, water impacts and land use to mention the most prominent. The water impacts come mainly from the run-off of supporting infrastructural improvements such as highways and parking lots. The principal instruments that have been used to ameliorate vehicle use impacts are on-board technologies, land use controls and more recently, congestion charges.

2 Can We "Get the Prices Right" for Urban Transportation?

"Getting the prices right" has long been a justifiable argument for promoting resource conservation, and although economists typically refer to "resource allocation" instead of "resource conservation", the two terms are largely synonymous. After decades of advocacy of road pricing, but with little implementation, there is now much research and experimental activity in urban road pricing (Gomez-Ibanez 1994).

Road pricing began to attract serious research attention in the U.S. in the 1950's and 1960's with the writings of William Vickery and Herbert Mohring. At the time, congestion was viewed as the most serious externality associated with vehicles, although serious air pollution had already appeared in major metropolitan areas. As vehicles had virtually no on-board emissions controls at the time, it was reasonable to presume that the most cost-effective first steps for emissions control would be technological in nature. Pricing road capacity, however, never really attracted serious attention, in large part because the highway engineering community promised alleviation of congestion through added road capacity, preferring to ignore the clear warnings of economists, notably Anthony Downs who said that this would only increase congestion, not reduce it. Only now is Down's work being incorporated in congestion management, more than 30 years after publication.

Road pricing policies are basically conceived as congestion management policies, usually taking one of two forms: 1) "cordon" pricing such as in Singapore and

Tronheim, Norway, whereby access from outlying areas to a central region or core is priced, and 2) tolling access to a restricted access road or lane. Each of these can be applied through electronic tolling methods using smart cards and sensors embedded in the roadway to charge for use of a facility. The question examined here is whether such methods can be used to achieve *sustainable* use of the private automobile in large metropolitan areas.

Before we define what sustainable vehicle use would mean in practice, we first note that however defined, policies to implement it would have to been applied to entire economic regions in order not to induce perverse substitution, such the above mentioned inducement to expand the size of the region to avoid the control. For the case of road pricing, we need first to analyze possibility of having *generalized* road pricing in metropolitan areas, as opposed to simply pricing access to a region's high volume highways and to nearby corridors. Generalized road pricing is necessary so that there are no unpriced close substitutes to the priced facilities, or traffic and congestion will be simply diverted away from the tolled facility.

There is a serious reason to believe that generalized road pricing will be not feasible, and therefore not available as an instrument to promote sustainable vehicle use. Generalized road pricing requires that, in addition to limited access road, arterial roads also be priced. This, however, would immediately lead to a political difficulty that because residences are located on arterial roads, those residents would have to pay even to conduct personal business in their neighborhoods. It is perhaps partly for this reason that Tronheim and Singapore have opted for the cordon pricing approach, a policy which charges access to the cordoned area to those who travel to it from points outside the cordon. However, this approach still does not represent a generalized pricing regime for a region, as travel outside of the cordoned area is unaffected.

Further, the cordon creates a spatial price disequilibrium, whereby travel to and from points wholly outside of the cordoned area is unpriced. This therefore creates an incentive to locate economic activity outside the cordoned area, leading to greater dispersion and reduced density of economic activity, and to greater reliance on the private vehicle, thereby exacerbating the vehicle induced externalities.

The difficulties are even greater, however. The economics literature makes clear that even if it were possible to apply efficient prices to all dimensions of the environment that exhibit scarcity, pricing would not necessarily guarantee sustainability in resource use because of the pervasive influence of discounting or time preference in individual decision making. This is made dramatically clear in growth models, in which species extinction, for example, can be "optimal". The implication for road pricing is that while road pricing may indeed improve the allocation of road capacity, and provide clearer signals for determining whether increased capacity is warranted, and would move vehicle use in the right direction, there is no inherent reason to conclude that road pricing will achieve sustainable vehicle use.

Rather, it can be argued that road pricing as contemplated is "too little and too late". Traffic congestion is a centuries old phenomenon; only the technology of transportation has changed over time. Since unrestricted vehicle use has been the norm virtually everywhere, at least since the beginning of the automobile age, today the externalities attributed to the automobile have grown more pervasive and serious. There are serious air quality problems in virtually all large cities that cannot or should not, because of the cost, be controlled with technology alone. One should not underestimate the ability of technological advances to reduce vehicle induced social ills, but we cannot expect promising technological fixes for emissions to be widely available for at least two decades (namely, fossil fuel/electric hybrid vehicles and fuel cells). Even then, commission of the same policy error of focusing controls on grams per kilometer alone, and not on vehicle *use* as measured by vehicle kilometers traveled, will cause the problem to remain unsolved. In sum, even for the air quality dimension, we cannot expect technological fixes to lead to sustainable uses of regional air sheds.

But there are other serious externalities associated with unrestricted vehicle use. There is water pollution from urban runoff, virtually all from street and parking lots. There is a serious problem with urban noise, virtually all from vehicles, there is the impetus to sprawl from the artificially induced and subsidized movement out from city centers. And there is the problem of carbon emissions; it is estimated that a full 25% of global carbon emissions emanate from the world's vehicle fleets (IEA/OECD 1993).

It is possible to conceive of pricing policies for all of these dimensions and subsidized mass transit coupled with other quantitative controls, such as land use controls, that could point vehicle use in the direction of sustainability. But the political economy of such an array of interventions makes the prognosis for adoption of a full range of measures very problematical indeed. In this context, road pricing seems to attack only part of the problem, and this is "too little, too late".

3 How to Define Urban Sustainability?

These comments, of course, beg the question of how we should define *sustainable* vehicle use. Widely understood is the standard economic definition of sustainability, to wit, maximize the current generation's level of welfare subject to the constraint that future generation's welfare not be reduced–this follows from the standard formulation of the problem of efficient intertemporal resource allocation, expressed as a intertemporal net benefits problem in practice. Since future welfare (net benefits) cannot be measured over the essentially infinite time horizon congruent with the concept of sustainability, an operational definition of sustainability in any practical application is to express in physical terms the environmental medium or dimension subject to overuse and to be constrained: air shed capacity to disperse pollutants, water shed capacity to receive residuals, forested land area, species population, urban growth boundary and so on. This would mean in practice that the rate of use or access is to be controlled. In the present context we would define the constraint as an upper limit on the number of vehicles that can be in service during a given time period.

On what basis could such a constraint be defined? That would depend on the relevant ecological capacity or other capacity that is considered to be limiting in an urban area. The case study that motivated the line of thinking explored here is Mexico City, whose air quality problem is principally a problem caused by too many vehicles discharging emissions into the capacity constrained air shed. Mexico City decided to limit access to the air shed by establishing a program to restrict daily vehicle use ("Hoy no circula"–this one doesn't circulate today). The program has failed because of faulty implementation, but quite likely would have succeeded had the authorities recognized the economic nature of the problem in which access to the streets would have been rationed with a tradable permit program, rather than the command and control approach used (Goddard 1997).

4 A Sustainability Policy for Urban Vehicle Use

The design and operation of a program to restrict access to a local or regional air shed based on air shed capacity presents some measurement challenges in relating fleet emissions to air shed concentrations in a fashion precise enough to be used as a management tool, but it seems completely feasible. Given that many of the world's large cities have precisely this problem of exceeding the capacity of the regional air shed to disperse vehicular emissions, for this dimension, sustainable vehicle use simply means computing the dispersive capacity of the air shed, and using current emissions characteristics of the fleet, working back to the number of vehicles that can be circulating at any one time without violating the air quality constraint more than an exogenously chosen percent of the time. For example, the authorities could choose a constraint and program to restrict vehicle use so that the constraint (the air quality index in practice) is not violated more than 10% of the days in a year, or during the air pollution season.

The program would be implemented by distributing vehicle use permits to the driving public, but limiting the total number of permits in the driving public's possession consistent with the air quality objectives. A flexible program would envision three types of permits: 1) a permanent "base" permit, 2) an interruptible permit and 3) a temporary permit. The first two would be perpetual permits, and the initial free distribution would be conducted only once, never to be repeated. The base and interruptible permits would be distributed at the start of the program and be tradable in markets. The temporary permits would be sold as a price based instrument, through retail outlets at widely dispersed locations, such as gasoline stations, banks, groceries and brokers, and at entrances to the controlled region. Monitoring and enforcement would not be costly.

This program design carries great flexibility for the authorities to be able to control the base load of vehicular emissions as well as to adjust to daily and seasonal variations in air shed capacity, as the use of interruptible and price based temporary permits will provide the authorities with sufficient flexibility to deal with the stochastic nature of air quality outcomes. At the same time, vehicle users have complete flexibility to use their vehicles whenever, wherever and how much ever they wish, but now there would be an explicit opportunity cost associated with their vehicle use. Since the objective of the limiting the original endowment of permits is to restrict vehicle use, the endowment would not ratify the previous uncontrolled level of use, and vehicle users would now have to take into account the value of their permits in a market, as they could be rented, leased, bought and sold. And if they desire to use their vehicles more than their original free endowment allows, they will have to purchase long term vehicle use rights in the market place, or purchase temporary (dated) permits.

It can be seen that this is simply a supplementary licence scheme, but one which the licences would be tradable in a market for vehicle use rights.

5 Effects of a Vehicle Use Permit Program

This policy would influence a number of sustainability margins favorably. It would be a flexible and cost-effective mechanism by which to meet air quality targets. It would increase demand for mass transit. It would diminish the overall size of the vehicle fleet. It would reduce congestion. It would raise the demand for central locations, i.e., city centers, and reduce it for dispersed locations, raising the spatial density of economic activity. It would reduce urban runoff. It would preserve farm land at the boundary of the urbanized area. It would reduce migration to the world's megapoli. All of these margins are related to the concept of urban sustainability, and all would be served beneficially.

There is a very important political and administrative advantage to this instrument. This is conceived as a *regional* vehicle control instrument, and so implementation of the policy requires that a control boundary must be established. In Mexico City, this is conceived essentially as the regional air shed, which is largely coterminous with the regional economic area. This in effect would a *soft* growth boundary that preserves choice, in contrast to the usually suggested *hard* boundary, such as in Portland, Oregon, USA. A hard boundary means that no urban growth can take place outside of the boundary. In Portland's case, the boundary was established two decades ago before explosive metropolitan growth had occurred. The approach has basically been successful, but the likelihood that it can be transferred to older and more sprawled regions seems low. In effect, in those regions the horse is already out of the barn.

Hard boundaries are what economists refer to as command and control policies, for they mandate behavior, but do not supply *economic* incentive instruments that would cause the boundary or margin to be chosen and sustained as an equilibrium by the regulated entity. Instead legal inducements and administrative measures (e.g., building permits) are employed to regulate the supply of land for particular uses. For the urban context, hard growth boundaries do nothing to alter the relative spatial *demand* for locations. Because there are no explicit market prices that reflect the social costs of dispersed locations confront the demanders of residential, commercial and industrial locations, the demand for dispersed locations continues high, driven by the low costs and convenience of private vehicle transport and rising incomes. And, with the exception of Portland, authorities nearly always ratify what the improperly priced land market desires. In the U.S. context, variances to zoning are nearly always granted, and so land use policies are nearly always thwarted. In short, land use controls simply do not work, except when the land or the development rights are sold to the government or to special land preservation trusts.

In contrast, the soft boundary proposed here works on the demand side of the land market. Since transportation ease and cost is a major determinant of the demand for location in space, and the tradable vehicle use permit is exercised by individuals, not the suppliers of structures (the developers) the fact that the permit scarcity raises the opportunity cost of vehicle use causes the demand for central locations and mass transit to be higher than is now the case. This would cause land developers to change the locus of their attention from fringe areas to more central locations.

Finally, we note that because these permits would be given away free of charge, and because they have value due to their scarcity, the operation of the trading market could actually make the distribution of income more equal. This would result because the permit could become an income generating instrument, whether through sales, or through leasing and renting. As a result, this instrument could be a powerful complement to policies that promote urban revitalization and development, and be seen as an equitable and efficient mechanism by which to promote urban sustainability.

References

Downs, A. (1992): Stuck in Traffic: Coming with Peak-Hour Traffic Congestion. Washington.

Downs, A. (1962): The Law of Peak-Hour Expressway Congestion. in: Traffic Quarterly, vol. 16 (July 1962), pp. 393-409.

Emissions of Greenhouse Gases in the United States 1987-1994, DOE/EIA-0573(87-94): Energy Information Administration, U.S. Department of Energy, Government Printing Office, Washington, D.C. 1993.

Goddard, H. (1997): Using Tradeable Permits to Achieve Sustainability in the World's Large Cities: Policy Design Issues and Efficiency Conditions for Controlling Vehicle Emissions, Congestion and Urban Decentralization with an Application to Mexico City. in: Environmental and Resource Economics, Vol. 10, Num. 1, July, 1997.

Gomez-Ibanez, J./Small, K. (1994): Road Pricing for Congestion Management: A Survey of International Practice, Washington: Transportation Research Board, National Research Council, National Academy Press.

International Energy Agency/OECD (1993): Car and Global Climate Change. Paris

Mohring, H. (1965): Urban Highway Investments. in: Robert Dorfman, R. (ed.): Measuring Benefits of Government Investment. Washington, pp. 231-75.

Vickery, W. (1955): Some Implications of Marginal Cost Pricing for Public Utilities. in: American Economic Review, Papers and Proceedings, vol 45 (1955), pp. 605-20.

The *TransPrice* Project: Experiences with Transport Pricing in Eight European Cities

Manos Vougioukas

EuroTrans Consulting
Richmond Bridge House
419 Richmond Road, London Twickenham TW1 2EX
England

Keywords. *Urban Transport Pricing and Financing*

1 Introduction

1.1 Background

Several studies and previous research projects in various countries have considered urban transport pricing policies, actions and measures, towards changing modal split in favour of public transport, including road use charging options. However, there is still considerable reluctance by city authorities to implement integrated pricing policies due to a perceived lack of public acceptability, particularly related to road pricing. Previous studies on road pricing or congestion charging have concentrated on technology and operational issues, with the intermodality, financial, socio-economic, land use and environmental issues frequently not considered in detail. Demand management actions have focused on the implementation of physical, traffic control and public transport priority measures which, although having a positive effect, they have not produced the drastic modal split changes that are usually required.

A lot more could be done towards an integrated urban transport strategy for improving transport conditions, with sustainable mobility and accessibility, through the most effective pricing mechanism. Such an approach implies a *trans* modal, integrated *pricing* and financing regime for urban transport that is based on three fundamental principles, viz.:

- Clear policy objectives of optimising modal split: Optimum is defined as the modal split at which the total generalised costs of both public and private transport are minimised.

- Aiming towards pricing the environmental and other externalities of transport systems,
- Allowing for revenue allocation from road user charges to financing investment in public transport, non-motorised modes, road safety and environmental improvements.

It is important that the experience gained by several administrations and cities that have considered elements of such regimes is well understood, analysed, assessed, exchanged and disseminated towards recommendations on best practice and eventual implementation. The issue of political and public acceptability is crucial to the success of such implementation.

The European Commission Transport Policy White Paper published in 1993 makes reference to transport pricing as a means of optimising modal split in congested and other environmentally sensitive areas. Other initiatives in the European Union (EU) concerning integrated urban transport pricing towards modal split optimisation include the "Car Free Cities" Network and the European Conference on Sustainable Cities and Towns. The EU Transport Telematics Programme (DRIVE/ATT) has included substantial work on automatic debiting technology and integrated payment systems, including assessment of potential user response, travel behaviour and inter-operability issues (CARD-ME initiative). Other EU relevant initiatives have included assessment of the energy saving impacts of urban road pricing and of introduction of integrated payment systems (EY Programmes SAVE and THERMIE).

The European Commission Directorate-General for Transport (DG VII) together with researchers and authorities in eight European cities initiated and co-funded the ***TransPrice*** project which aims to address the issues of integrated *trans* modal transport *pricing,* towards achieving optimum modal split in urban areas, at pan-European level. The ***TransPrice*** project was launched in January 1996 with a 3-year work programme. The project start coincided with the publication by the European Commission Directorate General for Transport (DG VII) of the Green Paper "Towards Fair and Efficient Pricing in Transport: Policy Options for Internalising the External Costs of Transport in the European Union".

The Green Paper points out the current inconsistency between the actual costs of transport and the prices paid, particularly for road transport, and it explores policy options and ways of making transport pricing systems fairer and more efficient towards reducing congestion, accidents and environmental problems. The purpose of this policy is not to increase the overall costs of transport, but to reduce the negative side-effects of transport and the hidden costs they represent, towards decreasing the real costs of transport. In particular, the paper advocates road tolls in congested and/or sensitive areas and linking charges to infrastructure costs. Efficient infrastructure pricing, it is argued, would facilitate the introduction of public/private partnerships and relieve demands on tight public budgets. The combination of congestion charging and efficient infrastructure investment is seen as an essential precondition for a balanced transport system.

The above policy options and principles mentioned in the Green Paper are of direct relevance to ***TransPrice*** in terms of specification, demonstration and evaluation of integrated pricing measures towards changing modal split in urban areas.

1.2 Project Objectives and Approach

The objectives of the ***TransPrice*** project are as follows:

- Review and investigate technical and financial options for integrated *trans* modal *pricing*.
- Examine integrated *trans* modal *pricing* strategies, tariffs and generalised cost structures by mode of transport and their effects on modal split.
- Assess potential user response and operational, socio-economic, behavioural, financial, land use, environmental and energy impacts of demand management and mode choice-related *trans* modal *pricing* measures, including urban road pricing.
- Specify and demonstrate *trans* modal *pricing* and integrated payment systems in selected European cities and assess effects on modal split, public and political acceptability.
- Evaluate *trans* modal *pricing* and integrated payment scenarios and actions using a common and comprehensive framework.
- Investigate ways of exploiting traffic data likely to be generated from integrated payment systems and disseminate the overall project results, including cities in Central and Eastern Europe.

TransPrice is based on actions and analyses in eight European cities: **Athens, Madrid, Como, Leeds, York, Göteborg, Helsinki and Graz**, thus covering a wide range of urban areas. Demonstration of pricing measures by real life application and experimental initial limited field trials of systems and measures is included in **Athens, Como, Madrid, Leeds and York**.

Dissemination of the project findings to other European Union member states as well as to two Central and Eastern European sites in Budapest and Sofia is also included.

The integrated *trans* modal *pricing* measures examined in the ***TransPrice*** project comprise:

- Road use charging (cordon pricing, area licensing, expressway tolls)

- Integrated public transport fares and payment systems
- Parking charges (on-street, off-street, private non-residential)
- Intermodality (park & ride, bus/rail/metro/tram)
- Public transport system financing and revenue support
- smart card payment systems (travel and multi-purpose use)
- Combination with other measures (access control, urban traffic control, HOV lanes, regulatory traffic restrictions, public transport prioritisation, pedestrianisation/cycling facilities).

Various combinations of the above are considered in each project site. The actions and analyses in the eight project sites are illustrated in Figure 1.

2 Definitions and Methodology

2.1 Trans Modal

Integrated urban transport pricing measures and payment systems should be both **multimodal** and **intermodal**:

- **Multimodal,** as they may affect the characteristics of a number of competing modes (eg car vs. public transport vs. park & ride), thus ensuring user choice of travel mode
- **Intermodal,** as they may influence the use of a number of modes for different legs of a single journey (eg. feeder bus and metro, or park & ride) with appropriate interchange, thus facilitating "seamless" service and enhancing intermodality.

In the ***TransPrice*** project, *trans* modal *pricing* is defined as combination and integration of multimodality (choice of mode) and intermodality (seamless service).

Figure 1: Specific actions and analyses in *TransPrice* sites

ACTIONS	Athens	Como	Madrid	Leeds	York	Göteborg	Helsinki	Graz
Cordon Pricing	□						◆	◆
Area Pricing	□	◆		□		◆		
Parking Pricing		◆		◆	◆	□		□
HOV Lane Pricing Options			◆					
Public Transport Integrated Fares & Financing	◆		◆			◆		
Smart Card Payment System	◆	◆		◆	◆	◆	□	◆
Automatic Access Control		◆						
Park and Ride & Intermodality	◆		◆		◆			

ANALYSES	Athens	Como	Madrid	Leeds	York	Göteborg	Helsinki	Graz
Mode Choice Analysis	◆	□	◆	□	◆	□	□	◆
Attitudes and Public Acceptability	◆	◆	□	◆	◆	□	◆	□
Congestion Costs	◆		◆	□				
Tolling Effects	◆					□	◆	◆
Decision Making Process						◆		
Environmental Analysis	◆		□				□	
Dissemination Activities	□	□	□	□	□	□	□	□

◆ primary □ secondary

2.2 Integrated Transport Pricing

The objectives of "integrated transport pricing" are:

- Improving intermodality
- Optimising modal split
- Alleviating congestion
- Internalising external costs of transport
- Facilitating infrastructure cost recovery
- Enabling environmental improvements.

The means or "elements" of a integrated transport pricing approach are:

- multimodal and intermodal approach
- Road use charges (including tolls)
- Public transport fares structures, ticketing methods and revenue support
- Parking charges
- Revenue allocation between modes
- SmartCard-based automatic debiting and multi-purpose payment systems.

Regarding the latter (Integrated Payment Systems), their role in the integrated transport pricing approach is due to their advantages, viz.:

- convenience for users
- Improved accounting for operators
- Reduced fraud
- Information on usage
- Trading between modes of transport
- Differential pricing
- Discounts and incentives.

2.3 Pricing Measures and Actions

The specified measures in each test-site are as follows (**demonstrations** are shown in **bold**):

- **Athens:** **road use pricing with park & ride and integrated payment** (main), and **(re)introduction of monthly pass for all public transport modes** (secondary), road use pricing options (modelling tests)
- **Como:** **automatic access control for residents and time-based parking pricing for visitors in a tourist area**, parking pricing policy, road use pricing options (modelling tests)
- **Madrid:** **park & ride with integrated ticketing, tariff integration by monthly pass for all public transport modes** (10 years ex-post assessment), congestion costs and public transport subsidies, and HOV lane pricing option (modelling test)
- **Leeds:** **multi-service smartcard pilot application for parking and public transport,** attitudinal research into potential for modal change through changes to parking, park & ride and public transport prices, potential for cordon parking charges and charging for private spaces (modelling test)
- **York:** **changes to central car park and park & ride tariffs, introduction of multi-use smartcards, and generalised cost changes through bus priorities** (supporting measure), road pricing options (modelling tests)
- **Göteborg:** cordon pricing with alternative fee structures, area pricing
- Helsinki: cordon pricing with alternative rings
- Graz: cordon pricing with public transport bonus and shopping traffic bonus.

The cities involved have been classified into three groups: large/capital cities (Athens, Madrid, Helsinki), medium cities (Leeds, Göteborg, Graz) and small cities (Como, York). The measures have been grouped into three categories: main pricing, regulation (access control, intermodality) and complementary (smartcard integrated payment systems). All of the important interactions of city type and measures category are covered in the specification, so that the project results can have a potential pan-European transferability.

2.4 Travel Behaviour Research

The potential changes in travel behaviour from pricing measures was at first assessed by means of a Stated Preference (SP) Survey in all 8 sites with a Common Experimental Design involving:

- Mode choice: car vs. public transport vs. park & ride

- Car costs: +50 and +100% from present operating and parking costs
- Car and public transport times: -20% and +20% form present times
- Public transport costs: -20% and +20% from present costs
- 2155 total sample (existing car users)
- Analysis by ALOGIT resulted in value of time estimates and willingness to pay

The SP survey was addressed to current car users mainly for commuting trip purpose that would consider changing mode to public transport or Park and Ride through increases of car costs and/or time and cost improvements to the alternative modes of travel. This was the first time that such a survey was applied to several urban areas with a common experimental design.

The SP survey gave estimates of Value of Time (VoT) and mode-specific constants. The SP survey data were analysed by the Helsinki University of Technology.

2.5 Evaluation Methodology

The evaluation of the measures examined in the ***TransPrice*** project was based on a multi-criteria evaluation framework, involving the following evaluation criteria:

- Operational: functional analysis of impacts
- Socio-economic: costs, time savings and accident savings
- Financial: revenue generation/allocation, profitability and cost recovery
- Land use and accessibility impacts
- Environmental impact
- Energy: efficiency and saving
- Social equity and public acceptability.

A common evaluation framework was developed for all eight participating cities, in order to bring together the results from travel behaviour research and modelling tests with the results from the demonstrations, towards developing general guidelines on a pan-European level. The evaluation was undertaken by University Polytechnic of Madrid.

3 Modelling Results

The pricing measures modelled and the main conclusions for each site, are given below.

3.1 Athens

In Athens the main interest was to evaluate the impacts and potential benefits from alternative road pricing schemes in the area. Seven different scenarios have been considered, depending on the extent and type of road pricing scheme and as to whether Park and Ride is included as a complementary measure. The modelling results show that distance based charging with Park and Ride achieve substantial reduction in total distance travelled and total travel time within the cordoned area, while providing significant revenues.

A scenario involving two co-centric cordons (outer and inner), with morning peak-hour toll levels of 1 and 2 ECU respectively, produced the most reductions in inner area road traffic levels with associated operational and environmental benefits as well as significant revenues.

3.2 Madrid

In Madrid the interest was to model congestion costs for assessing the benefits of subsidy in public transport and of introducing new infrastructure to alleviate congestion problems, and pricing the use of a High Occupancy Vehicle (HOV) lane by solo and two-occupant cars. The main finding of this analysis was that total time delay due to congestion is some 37,482 hours per day. Most of this time is allocated during peak periods (morning 64%). Any subsidy to public transport and state investment in new infrastructure would need to be assessed against the benefits of reducing congestion.

Regarding the HOV lane pricing, it was found that strategies that charge only 2-occupants for the use of the HOV lane produce 7.5-12% trip time savings for car users (and 5-7% for bus users), but adversely affects the users of conventional lanes. The results are almost balanced at corridor level resulting in small trip time reduction (3% with a low toll for 2-occupants and no reduction for a high toll). Strategies that charge solo-drivers only to use the HOV lane, do not seem to produce much changes in average HOV lane trip time (0%-2%), nor do they in the conventional lanes (-2%). Again at corridor level total trip time spent remains almost constant (0% -1%). Strategies that charge both 2-occupants and solo-drivers (although with higher toll levels for solo-drivers) produce different effects. On the one hand, a scenario whereby 2 occupants are charged 0.10 ECU and solo-drivers 0.15 ECU for the use of the HOV lanes, produces a 2.7% increase in HOV lane trip time, a 2% decrease in conventional lanes, and a 2% increase at corridor level. On the other hand, a scenario whereby 2 occupants are charged 0.10 ECU and solo-drivers 0.25 ECU for the use of the HOV lanes, produces significant decreases in HOV lanes trip time (7%), and a slightly smaller trip time increases in conventional lanes (3%). At corridor level, a 3% decrease in average trip time spent is attained.

3.3 Como

In Como simulation evaluated the impact on mode choice, change of destination and revenues of introducing parking pricing and cordon-, time- and distance-based road use pricing. For parking pricing four scenarios related to four different pricing structures were evaluated (*base*, *higher*, *decreasing* with respect to duration of stay, and *constant* with respect to duration of stay). For cordon-based pricing, six scenarios, differing by the toll value and as to whether tolling is time specific or not, were evaluated. For time-based and distance-based pricing, 5 and 6 scenarios, differing by the toll value, were respectively evaluated.

The parking pricing results suggest that the scenario with the *higher* fare structure substantially reduces car usage in the pricing area (by approximately 40%), total car trips on the network (by approximately 6%), and congestion by 21%, when considering only the congested length of the network.

The cordon pricing results show that the scenario with a fixed toll throughout the day maximises revenues for the peak hour, while reducing car travel the most (4%). The scenario whereby tolling is only applied to the peak period, is more effective in reducing network congestion than the scenario with fixed toll throughout the day by spreading the peak period, while increasing the share of non-car travel modes. With time- and distance-based pricing, the results indicate that total distance travelled, total time, emissions and fuel consumption decrease as the toll increases. For a moderate toll of 0.45 ECU/hr with time-based, a reduction of about 14% in total travel time, and a similar reduction in fuel consumption are expected. With a distance-based toll of 0.09 ECU/km, a reduction of about 8% in total travel time, and a reduction of about 11% in fuel consumption are expected.

3.4 Leeds

In Leeds a 'parking cordon' around the city centre, which would charge all motorists accessing the central area as if they were spending time in a public car park or in a private non-residential car park, and four road-sue charging systems have been assessed. Simulation modelling has been utilised to assess the potential of the parking cordon on trip making.

Amongst four different scenarios tested, the scenario whereby current parking charges are all increased by 50% with free park and ride (assumed to be subsidised by parking revenue) has been found to achieve the most benefits in terms of total distance travelled, with a reduction of about 7% compared to the base scenario. Time spent in delay in the centre of Leeds is reduced by more than three quarters with this scenario, trip making by car into the centre of Leeds is reduced by 41%, and current unpaid 'private non-residential' parking by a notable 56%. In scenario 2 cordon-, distance- and time-based pricing systems were considered. With cordon-based, a reduction of about 10% is expected in total travel time in the whole of Leeds with a moderate charge of 0.63 ECU per crossing. Corresponding revenues is estimated to be 51 MECU. With distance-based, for a charge rate of 0.21 ECU/km the reduction in total travel time is over 10%, and revenues are about 52.5 MECU. With time-based, for a charge rate of 0.14 ECU/min, the reduction in total travel time is over 12%, and revenues are about 57 MECU.

3.5 York

In York the objective of simulation modelling is to evaluate the impact of increasing car parking charges in the city centre and Park and Ride fares on Park and Ride usage, and the impact of road use pricing on network efficiency and mode of travel. The results of car parking and park-and-ride tariff increases indicate that the mode split of P&R is likely to increase by 45% and revenues by 78% if current car parking charges were increased by 50% and tariffs by about 18%.

The results of road pricing are in line with current expectations that substantial reductions in total travel time and delays can be achieved by charging the road use. Three pricing systems were considered: time-, delay- and distance-based. With time- and delay-based significant reductions in total travel time, distance travelled, delays, and fuel consumption are attained network wide; that is within and outside the charging area. With distance-based benefits are achieved generally within the charging area. Distance-based pricing does not bring about reductions in network performance indicators in the whole of York.

3.6 Helsinki

In Helsinki, a series of toll points have been proposed, with a view to influencing travel choice in terms of mode and route, and trip distribution. Two options were considered in choosing the location of the toll points. The toll is the same in both options. The results show that high benefits in terms of network performance can be achieved; namely that total travel time can be reduced by nearly 8%, total distance travelled by about 9%, and car volume by 6%, whereby trips are made either by public transport, bike, or on foot.

3.7 Göteborg

In Göteborg model based evaluation focused on the overall impacts of introducing a road user cordon toll system surrounding the central area of the city, and area pricing, together with improvements in the road and public transport systems. With the cordon toll system, three different scenarios were investigated corresponding to three different toll charges (SEK 10, SEK 15 and SEK 20). With area pricing, two scenarios were considered, depending on whether the charging area is confined to the city centre or the whole of Göteborg. The main results indicate that implementing a cordon toll system in Göteborg would substantially reduce the traffic volume in the Central City Area. With a toll fee of SEK 10 a reduction of nearly 15% is expected. With a toll of SEK 20 a reduction of 22% is possible. Total revenues are estimated to be between 533 to 821 million SEK per year. With area pricing, a 15 SEK charge within the central area of Göteborg results in a 20% reduction in the traffic volume in the Central City Area, and levies about 607 million SEK per year.

3.8 Graz

In Graz modelling comprised investigating the influence of introducing a cordon toll surrounding the central part of Graz together with other complementary measures, such as provision of car parks just outside the toll cordon. For a test corresponding to a toll of ECU 1.1 during the off-peak period and twice that during the peak period, it has been found that the number of trips by car, in and out of the tolled area, is reduced by 17% as compared to the base scenario; the share of public transport increases by 35%.

3.9 Cross-Site Comparisons

Cross-site comparisons have been made towards identifying guidelines at pan-European level for the implementation of transport pricing measures. In terms of cordon pricing (based on analysis for Athens, Como, Helsinki, Göteborg and Graz), these show that reductions of 5-20% in total distance travelled by private car are possible for cordon toll levels of between 1 and 3 ECUs (after allowing for Purchase Power Parity differentials between EU member states). In terms of the number of private cars entering inner urban areas, reductions of between 5% (Helsinki) and 40-50% (Como, Athens) can be expected, depending on toll levels (around the 1-3 ECU range) and city characteristics. It is evident that the higher the present level of congestion, the more the scope for road pricing. Regarding parking pricing measures, reductions in distance travelled by private car of 8-48% can be expected for a parking charge of 5-10 ECU (based on analysis for Leeds and Como only).

4 Demonstration Results

The results from the demonstrations can be summarised as follows:

- In **Athens** the results of the road pricing trial suggest that up to 15% of car drivers would transfer to Park & Ride with a 5:1 pricing regime in favour of Park & Ride. The price elasticity for road use pricing was estimated at -0.2 from the limited sample of users that took part in the road pricing demonstration. Attitudinal research suggested that a vignette-based system of area pricing would be more acceptable to the public and politicians than electronic cordon charging. Demand for the all modes travel card has stabilised at about 10% of all public transport ticket sales.

- In **Como** the demonstration results suggest that the introduction of parking charges reduced the traffic entering the designated area and corresponding improvements on congestion levels. There has been a positive change in modal split from cars to motor bikes and bicycles.

- In **Madrid** the multimodal travel card has encouraged greater use of public transport amongst captive groups and encouraged some modal shift, particularly amongst commuters (PT trips increased by 35% following a decade of decline). Investigations into the effects of the Park and Ride and integrated ticketing showed that around 300 extra cars used the Park & Ride and that 2.7% of users had changed mode form car to Park & Ride.

- In **Leeds** the introduction of the multi use smart card was not seen as a prime reason for modal shift, but it was seen as an important element when used in conjunction wit tariff increases for parking and improved public transport services.

- In **York** the differential changes in tariffs for city centre parking and Park and Ride have resulted in increased Park & Ride patronage. City Centre Parking tariffs increased by 20% while P&R by 9%; this resulted in a 6% reduction in city centre parking demand and a 12% increase in P&R demand. The introduction of smart card with discounts for regular travellers resulted in about 5% of trips transferring to Park & Ride.

5 Evaluation Results

The results from the multi-criteria evaluation showed that:

- **HOV lane pricing** is effective for some indicators but acceptable social utility is only achieved when congestion level is very high.

- **Parking pricing** is always effective but it must not be an isolated measure; it is rather an accompanying measure.
- **Cordon pricing** is clearly effective when it is applied to congested central areas. To enlarge the cordon pricing scheme to a broader area or to a whole day does not provide much supplementary social benefits.
- **Other forms of road pricing** are very beneficial for most of the multicriteria indicators.

In a comparative way, the results from the multi-criteria evaluation show that the highest level of the value function is achieved through road pricing options. Parking pricing is less effective than road pricing by 20 percentage points when the maximum end of the range is considered; however, for the minimum end of the range the results show that parking pricing could achieve about the same level of effectiveness as road pricing options. The conclusion from this is that road pricing options should be implemented when parking pricing measures have been proven to have exhausted their effectiveness. HOV lane pricing options give the lowest range and therefore they are applicable in special cases.

6 Conclusions

The following general conclusions can be drawn from the experiences of urban transport within the ***TransPrice*** project:

- **Pricing measures offer several possibilities of changing modal split, particularly in a package of demand management measures**
- **Use of the revenues affects the acceptability of pricing measures**
- **If sustainable mobility is the target for the 21st century, somebody should pay the price: the user.**

"Paying the price" for sustainable mobility is used with all three possible meanings, ie:

- handing over the correct price (through appropriate payment systems)
- bearing the (real) cost of transport
- suffer or be punished (through congestion and environmental damage, if the real costs are not borne by the user).

Transport prices may be paid at present but not necessarily by the right actors and not at the correct level. "Paying the price" could be through proper, integrated and trans modal pricing measures and payment systems, as the ***TransPrice*** project suggests, or through more congestion and environmental damage (as the past trend has been). The choice of appropriate pricing measures exists, and it is a matter of adopting them into policies towards sustainability. It is hoped that the ***TransPrice*** project results will be further applied and exploited in wider, integrated demonstrations and policy development at local, national and pan-European levels.

Acknowledgements

The author wishes to thank:

- The European Commission Directorate-General for Transport (DG VII) for part-funding the work reported here in the ***TransPrice*** project, within the Transport RTD programme of the EU 4th Framework Programme for Research and Technological Development.
- The urban authorities of Athens, Madrid, Como, Leeds, York, Göteborg, Helsinki and Graz for their support of the project.
- The ***TransPrice*** project partners: EuroTrans Consulting Ltd (GB), Trinity College Dublin (IE), Consorzio Universitario MIP (IT), Comune di Como (IT), Universidad Politecnica de Madrid (ES), Consorcio de Transportes de Madrid (ES), Anysma (GR), Athens Area Urban Transport Organisation OASA (GR), Leeds City Council (GB), University of Leeds ITS (GB), Technical University of Graz (AT), Magistrat Graz (AT), Chalmers University of Technology (SE), Technical University of Dresden (DE), University of York (GB), City of York Council (GB), Viatek (FI), Helsinki University of Technology (FI).

References

Commission of the European Communities (1992). The future development of the common transport policy: A global approach to the construction of a Community framework for sustainable mobility. COM(92) 494 final. December 1992.

Commission of the European Communities (1995). Towards fair and efficient pricing in transport: Policy options for internalising the external costs of transport in the European Union. Green Paper presented by the Commission. COM(95)691 final, Dec. 1995.

European Commission (1996). Pricing and financing of Urban Transport. APAS Transport Research, Brussels, Luxembourg, 1996.

TransPrice Consortium (1997). Deliverable 1: Review of Issues and Options, London, March 1997

TransPrice Consortium (1997). Deliverable 3: Modelling Results, London, August 1997.

TransPrice Consortium (1997). Deliverable 4: Specification and Demonstration Design, London, November 1997.

TransPrice Consortium (1998). Deliverable 5: Demonstration Results, London, Oct. 1998.

TransPrice Consortium (1999). Deliverable 7: Evaluation Results, London, March 1999 (forthcoming).

GPSR Compliance

The European Union's (EU) General Product Safety Regulation (GPSR) is a set of rules that requires consumer products to be safe and our obligations to ensure this.

If you have any concerns about our products, you can contact us on ProductSafety@springernature.com

In case Publisher is established outside the EU, the EU authorized representative is:

Springer Nature Customer Service Center GmbH
Europaplatz 3
69115 Heidelberg, Germany

Batch number: 10725973

Printed by Printforce, the Netherlands